"*Teaching entrepreneurship, I have a high bar for wh[...] use to educate themselves and use as a reference. Th[...] resource in its rigor, accessibility and comprehensive[...] book readily accessible at all times for myself and highly recommend it to serious entrepreneurs everywhere.*"

Bill Aulet, Professor and Managing Director of the Martin Trust Center for MIT Entrepreneurship

"*Becoming an entrepreneur is a great way to make a difference in the world, and this book shows you how.*"

Anders Fogh Rasmussen, Founder and CEO of Rasmussen Global, Former Secretary General of NATO and Prime Minister of Denmark

"*Entrepreneurs are essential for our world, as they develop new solutions to key problems. This book tells you how to be successful as an entrepreneur.*"

Taavi Roivas, former Prime Minister of Estonia and youngest Prime Minister in the EU

"*To all the entrepreneurial minds out there: this book is a must read!*"

Oliver Samwer, Founder and CEO of Rocket Internet

"*Even though technology will keep changing the world, there is no certain recipe for success. All companies are unique and at the end of the day, it's the entrepreneurial people behind the companies, their approach and leadership that makes the difference. Lars and Mads make an absolute stunner of a team, giving hands-on and valuable advice allowing start-ups to leverage these into great opportunities.*"

Preben Damgaard, Member of the Danish Research and Development Ministry's Board, co-founder and former CEO of Damgaard Data, former VP of Microsoft.

"*Entrepreneur is a great practical guide on how to build a company and become inspired to make things happen, from guys who have done exactly that, many times over. You can learn to be an entrepreneur. You can have a go at making your dreams reality. You can learn a lot from this encouraging, fun and accessible book.*"

Hugo Burge, former CEO of Momondo Group

"*A great practical guide by entrepreneurs for entrepreneurs on the power of execution, stamina and how to unlock the full potential of your ideas.*"

Jimmy Maymann, Entrepreneur, Investor, former CEO of Huffington Post

"*It is surprising how much useful guidance and information Lars and Mads have managed to squeeze into this book. I would definitely recommend it strongly to any ambitious entrepreneur.*"

Christian M. Motzfeldt, CEO Danish Growth Fund

"*This is an excellent book with lots of great hands-on advice for ambitious entrepreneurs. Very practical and highly recommendable.*"

Brian Mikkelsen, Danish Minister of Industry, Business and Financial Affairs

"*Finally an entrepreneurship book that is based on first hand experiences! The reality of having a start-up is really captured here - from strategy to the 'street smarts' one accumulates along the way.*"

Sophie Trelles-Tvede, Entrepreneur, winner of Forbes 30 under 30 Europe and Nordic Business Forum 25 and Under in Northern Europe

"*The book provides a comprehensive scope of practical decision-making tools and philosophies to overcome all the unavoidable obstacles and challenges every start-up founder faces on the journey. A must read for any aspiring entrepreneur.*"

Mads Fibiger, CEO & Co-founder, Organic Basics

"*This book covers in depth how to build a company whether you are dreaming about starting one, have already started or are running a larger organization.*"

Peter Holten Muhlmann, Founder and CEO of Trustpilot

"*Mads and Lars explain all aspects and considerations of a business in thorough and precise detail. If you read this book and add your own naive persistence, you will succeed. Moreover, funny enough I never really saw myself as an entrepreneur, having read* Entrepreneur, *I now do, and I'm proud of it! - Thank you for that Mads & Lars!*"

Kaspar Basse, Founder and CEO of Joe and Juice

entrepreneur

lars tvede & mads faurholt

entrepreneur

building your business from start to success

WILEY

Library of Congress Cataloging-in-Publication Data

Names: Tvede, Lars, 1957- author. | Faurholt, Mads, author. | Faurholt, Mads.
   Iværksætter. English.
Title: Entrepreneur : building your business from start to success / Lars
   Tvede, Mads Faurholt.
Description: Chichester, West Sussex, United Kingdom : John Wiley & Sons,
   2018. | Includes bibliographical references and index. | Originally
   published in Denmark in 2017 by Gyldendal as: Iværksætter / Mads Faurholt
   Lars Tvede. |
Identifiers: LCCN 2018023716 (print) | LCCN 2018025759 (ebook) | ISBN
   9781119521280 (Adobe PDF) | ISBN 9781119521259 (ePub) | ISBN 9781119521235
   (pbk.)
Subjects: LCSH: New business enterprises. | Entrepreneurship.
Classification: LCC HD62.5 (ebook) | LCC HD62.5 .T94 2018 (print) | DDC
   658.1/1—dc23
LC record available at https://lccn.loc.gov/2018023716

10 9 8 7 6 5 4 3 2 1

CONTENTS

Part 5. About my exit and what comes after 358

Appendices

INTRODUCTION BY PETER WARNOE

'Peter, do you think we can . . .?'

I don't know how many times I have heard these words from Lars Tvede, co-author of this book – but it's many. For instance, once when we were three couples sailing his boat along the Italian coast, he suddenly asked:

'Peter, do you think we can drink beer under water?'

I guess I didn't, but Lars soon became quite insistent and before I knew it, we were three guys in scuba gear deep down drinking beer. (You hold it upside down, blow air in and swallow, as beer comes out. I have it on video.)

Another example: in 2017, Lars was invited as speaker for the Danish Growth Fund's annual meeting, a yearly flagship event in Danish venture business attended by government ministers, leading investors and entrepreneurs, etc. However, about half an hour before he went on stage, he pulled me aside in a hallway and asked with a smirky grin: 'Peter, do you think I can end my speech by saying "Fuck you"?'

I thought he was joking, so I laughed it off. OK, mistake, because when he later jumped on stage, he immediately pointed me out in front of the 1900 delegates and proclaimed that I didn't believe that he would end this speech by saying 'Fuck you'. 'Just watch me', he continued while staring at me from the stage. OMG!

Towards the end of his speech, he called me up on stage, put his arms around my shoulders and then pulled up a PowerPoint slide of a now famous email from Marc Andreessen to Ben Horowitz, which ended with the words 'Next time do the fucking interview yourself. Fuck you'. I am not sure I would have done this, but people actually laughed.

Two years before that, in April 2015, Lars called me and said, 'Peter, I met the craziest guy at a TEDx event. His name is Mads Faurholt'. He then rambled on and on about how clever Mads apparently was. Next thing I knew, Lars had invited Mads and his girlfriend to go sailing in Greece. That became the beginning of a great friendship leading, among many other things, to the production of this book.

Today, I know Mads very well privately and as a businessman. Personally, I don't think 'crazy' is the right word to describe Mads. 'Impressive' would come closer, but also 'efficient' and indeed 'very fast'. About the latter – as a student, Mads set a speed record by completing his Bachelor's degree at CBS (Copenhagen Business School) within one year and nine months against a norm of three years, and amazingly, he achieved this while having two demanding jobs on the side – one of them managing 50 sales people. He then went to MIT where he graduated with his Master's at age 23, after which he became one of the youngest associates ever in McKinsey & Co. This is what I mean by very fast.

Working at McKinsey sounds like a great job, but Mads soon – pretty fast again – moved on to Rocket Internet, where he quickly became CEO of 3500 employees in Asia at Groupon. This was when he was still only 26 years of age. While living in Asia, he also co-founded numerous web companies, including Zalora, Lazada, Zanui, The Iconic, Airizu, GlassesOnline, HelloFresh and Foodpanda. In 2017 he raised $50 million for his company CompareAsiaGroup. As I write this, his other businesses include CompareEuropeGroup, CompareLatAmGroup, Startech Asia, Private Equity Insights and others.

Like Mads, Lars is also fast, even though this might not be the first impression you get of him. In fact, he typically appears calm, if not even slightly absent and perhaps nerdy. But then take a look at his career: after dropping out of college for a year to travel in South America, he returned to Copenhagen to graduate and then completed a Graduate Diploma in Business Administration at CBS within three years – it normally takes four – while *in parallel* taking a Master's degree in engineering. Oh, and while also *in parallel* co-founding several companies. Aged 19, he and a friend bought a summer house in Spain with money they had earned in their spare time during their studies.

Then he had a hectic career in marketing and finance while also being part-time professor and censor at a university and writing the first few of his by now 15 books. Eventually, he ended up as chief corporate dealer trading bonds, forex and futures for what is now the dairy giant Arla Food, after which he became a serial entrepreneur within tech, lifestyle, property and finance.

One of my personal observations about Lars is an amazing tendency to get things done and deliver on his plans, even though he does the latter partly by often having, say, 10 alternative plans, out of which one (almost) always works.

It appears to me that Lars sees business partly as a sport. For instance, some years ago, he had a portfolio of investments in global top quartile hedge funds. However, as they failed to deliver his expected 15% annual return, he set up his own investment company to see whether he could beat them. During the following six years, he grew an initial investment of CHF 20 000 plus a private pledge into approximately CHF 50 million in cool cash, after which he rather abruptly stopped trading, cashed out most of the money and spent it on charity, a villa in Mallorca, a Learjet, a collection of sports cars and his ever-since beloved boat.

Lars is convinced that he cannot sell, and as he also doesn't like to manage people, he typically starts his companies with one or several partners for those challenges. However, apart from that, he is very flexible in the challenges he takes on. For instance, he has built up businesses dealing within anything from satellite communication to mobile information services, property development, financial trading, wholesale food trading, IT supplies and more.

His latest and probably last and thus lasting adventure is within venture capital, which of course is an ideal way to combine his two favourite playgrounds: serial entrepreneurship and finance. To be more specific, he co-founded Nordic Eye Venture Capital with me in 2016.

Being who he is, he subsequently virtually disappeared for four months, ploughing through mountains of literature about venture business, after which he reappeared and declared that the venture sector had been lousy in Europe for decades but that there were several ways to do much better, out of which the most important, funny enough, was helping portfolio companies very actively with the one and only discipline he believes himself to be incapable of – sales.

Fortunately, this is *my* home ground, and together with our great team, we proceeded to produce 203% return (IRR) within our first full year, where we also returned more than the entire investor commitments in the fund in the form of a single distribution (dividend).

As I read the manuscript for this book, it struck me that there is nothing in it that at least one of the two authors hasn't done hands-on, and for the most part, they both master what they write about here to near-perfection.

Take, for instance, raising money for start-ups. Mads has done this from numerous investors, including Summit Partners, JPMorgan, Kinnevik, Goldman Sachs, The World Bank, Alibaba and SoftBank, and Lars has raised capital from various venture funds plus Intel, Deutsche Telekom, Reuters, Loral, BT, Telecom Italia, Lucent, Kirch Group and Singapore Press Holdings.

Another example: the book describes media activities and marketing via social media. This is also home ground for the authors – between them, Mads and Lars have probably done more than 1000 interviews and public speeches. Moreover, Mads was a radio host as an 11-year-old child and again in a TV series about start-ups when he was 31. Lars has been a guest host on Danish radio and TV plus CNBC. Furthermore, between them, Mads and Lars now have more than 50 000 friends and followers on social media.

In other words: these guys are rather experienced, including from the famous School of Hard Knocks, and both have closed down failing operations, hired the wrong people, failed to close vital contracts and messed up stuff like the rest of us. However, they have also created spectacular successes and made profitable exits, ranging from trade sales to asset sales and public listing. Furthermore, Lars has won numerous international awards for entrepreneurship and technology, including the Wall Street Journal Europe Innovation Award, the Red Herring Global 100 Award, the Bulli

Award (twice) and the IMD Swiss Start-up Award. In *The Guru Guide to Marketing*, he is listed as one of the world's leading thinkers in marketing strategy.

I guess what I mean to say is that they really do know what they are talking about. And I should add that even though I personally have been an entrepreneur since I was 23, there was much in this book that I actually didn't know.

I hope and trust that any reader will enjoy this manuscript as much as I did.

Peter Warnoe
CEO, Nordic Eye Venture Capital

entrepreneur

PART 1.

ABOUT ME AS AN ENTREPRENEUR

Do you want to own your own business? Become an entrepreneur? In this section, we describe the many alternative roles as self-employed and/or entrepreneur: why and how to learn from practice before possibly taking on the harder and more ambitious tasks.

We also look at how entrepreneurs can tackle the huge workload and a high risk of stress and health problems. It is all about efficiency — 'work smart, not hard', as one might say. Or at least smart if hard.

But how do you do that?

In the third chapter, we move on to study aspects of your ability to make a personal impact and break through when it really matters. People who work in large, well-renowned companies do not always have a big personal impact — they work well within the shelter of a powerful and well-known organization which can sometimes make the impact for them. But in start-ups you often need to get noticed and force your will through, even though your business is small and per-haps rather rickety. So how do you make an impact in everything from sales meetings and negotiations to public speeches, media interviews, on social media and more? We share some practical tips that can help you with this.

1.
MY ENTREPRE-
NEURIAL ROLE

Being an entrepreneur is about creating something new, moving into the unknown and maybe starting on projects where you can really foresee neither the outcome nor the financing. Many 'self-employed' people are 'entrepreneurs', but you may be one without being the other. For instance, a self-employed dentist is probably not an entrepreneur, and someone running a wild new project within Google might work as an entrepreneur but not be self-employed.

We believe it is important for anyone who has a dream of becoming an entrepreneur to understand which entrepreneurial roles exist and what they entail. In this chapter, we study various entrepreneurial roles and personal traits that increase the likelihood of success with start-up projects. We also consider the risks and benefits that are likely to occur when selecting the entrepreneurial life.

'I want to become an entrepreneur.' That's what both of us would say often when we were young students.

But what does that mean? When we were 15 or 18, we thought it meant only one thing: getting a brilliant idea and starting a company to pursue it. However, life has since taught us that there are many other ways to be an entrepreneur. And while there are many 'hows', there are also many 'whys', so let's start with those.

Why do people become entrepreneurs?

Statistics show that most entrepreneurs are highly motivated by:

- *money*: hoping to achieve financial freedom
- *freedom*: hoping to gain control over their lives and work.[1]

But there may be many other motives. For instance, quite a few people start their business as a result of frustration in their former job. Perhaps they were irritated by stupid bosses or unambitious co-workers. Possibly they felt that they didn't fit into the 'system' and were fired for exactly that reason.

For some entrepreneurs, the decision to start their company was a matter of self-image. Where their parents perhaps dreamed of owning a house, the next generation can dream of getting their feet underneath their own table.

Others may be primarily driven by a passion for motivating co-workers, or for delivering excellent products to the clients, working with cutting-edge technologies or trendy new styles.

There may also be more professional motives. Entrepreneurial work is very all-round and therefore offers a high degree of responsibility and a palette of different challenges that is almost impossible to find in normal jobs. An entrepreneur in the early stages can thus be sales, marketing, product and HR manager at once. Some will find this extremely stressful, but others – great entrepreneurs – will find it extremely fun. Some would also like to sit at the top of the pyramid and feel that the way to the top seat is shorter if they create the company themselves.

Some are attracted to the challenge and hardship – they almost regard entrepreneurship as a sport, if not a test of manhood (this includes women). These are the people who love to test themselves and find out where their limit is. 'How far can I go?' they might think. Let's face it: there are probably some adrenaline junkies among entrepreneurs, though others might rather end up as hobbits on their reluctant way to Mordor.

What kind of entrepreneur?

If you recognize yourself in any of these roles, the next question is: what kind of entrepreneur do you want to be?

In many people's imagination – and in our own, too, when we were younger – it is probably quite simple. You get a brilliant idea in the shower one morning. 'Bingo!' There it was! Then you persuade a bank to lend you a few million. A few years and a lot of work later you sell the company. And then . . . off south to the beaches!

Now we have become older, but none of us has seen such a course of events. Why not? First, brilliant ideas rarely arise out of the blue and in an instant. They evolve over time, in fits and starts. Second, a bank will not lend you money to implement your idea unless you pledge full collateral for it. Because why should they? To potentially earn 5% interest but risking a 100% loss if the company goes down, as it very well might? And third, we have never known entrepreneurs that settled themselves on a beach after they sold their first company. Maybe it happens every now and then, but as far as we can see, the typical successful entrepreneur loves work and immediately starts the next project as soon as there is time available.

It has become easier!

For sure, being an entrepreneur is typically very hard, but in our opinion, conditions for entrepreneurs have improved in important ways in recent decades. It has become a lot cheaper and technically easier to start new companies. Certainly, the amount of red tape may have increased, but overall costs of setting up a basic operation have dropped massively. For instance, software and hardware have become significantly cheaper, as have flights, and you can now use video conferencing free of cost. Furthermore, there is access to plug-and-play tools, cloud computing, crowdsourcing, focused and thus inexpensive advertising opportunities, global payment systems, effective logistics services, smartphones, tablets, etc., all of which are easy and inexpensive to use. Therefore, a lot that was previously expensive and cumbersome can now be dealt with cheap or for free. Overall, we believe that with the exception of salaries, running costs for many types of start-up have declined by as much as 90% over the past two decades.

Moreover, network effects sometimes can help start-ups to create huge value very quickly. In the entrepreneurial environment, the word 'unicorn' is used to describe companies which achieve a market value of more than $1 billion. In the 1990s and earlier, it took typically at least 20 years for the greatest winners to get there, but since then it has gone ever faster – Airbnb, for example, did it in less than five years, Snapchat within a year and a half and Slack within just nine months.

IT HAS THUS BECOME A LOT CHEAPER AND TECHNICALLY EASIER TO START COMPANIES.

Another advantage for modern-day entrepreneurs: today there exist several great online networks for entrepreneurs in all developed nations, such as Young Upstarts, Sandbox, Fast Company and YourStory. Here you can regularly seek advice and inspiration as well as find useful contacts. Appendix D contains a list of 76 of the best in the English language.

In addition, many new businesses manage to create large companies without having to invest much in equipment or production. As often pointed out, the world's largest property landlord, Airbnb, owns no hotels. Facebook, which is the world's largest media company by far, has no production of media content, and Uber, the world's largest taxi company, owns no cars. Therefore, they have been able to expand incredibly quickly.

So yes, in many ways it has become cheaper and easier to be an entrepreneur, even if taxation and legal tangle might have pulled the other way.

All of this, plus a new set of management tools called 'lean start-up', has contributed to a significant change in the entrepreneurial landscape. We see ever more 'micro-multinationals', which are global companies with limited staff and investment needs. And the fact that you can now start a company for less money means that investors such as venture capitalists (VCs) can spread their investments across multiple projects – some of them leaning towards the 'spray and pray' principle in which they invest small amounts in many start-ups. Finally, even on the funding and exit side, there is significant innovation, where the recent development of ICOs (initial coin offerings) is a prominent, if at times problematic, example.

Lifestyle or growth entrepreneur?

You can divide entrepreneurs into two main types. The first are lifestyle entrepreneurs. They are the ones who found and run, for example, a restaurant, a paint shop or a dental clinic. For sure, being a lifestyle entrepreneur requires some risk taking and typically a lot of work and determination, but it does not necessarily require great creativity (nor does it exclude it either, of course). But it is characterized by a limited growth ambition.

VCs typically don't invest in lifestyle entrepreneurships, since the profit potential is often quite limited and the founders are rarely interested in selling the company and therefore are not able to provide a reasonable return to foreign investors either. Also, lifestyle entrepreneurships are often related to some single person's unique skill or talent, which adds to the risk for an investor.

The second category are growth entrepreneurs. They are the ones who get their project to multiply or 'scale', as people in the industry often call it. If your restaurant is the first of an international chain of restaurants, you have 'scaled' it. For instance, McDonald's was a burger business and the McDonald brothers had little scaling ambition. However, then they met Ray Kroc, who offered to start scaling it for them and eventually bought them out for $2.7 million (we can recommend the movie 'The Founder'). Similarly, James Oliver is a cook, but instead of working as an employee or lifestyle entrepreneur, he became a growth entrepreneur.

The McDonald brothers were innovative but not growth entrepreneurs, but most growth entrepreneurs need to be both very innovative in terms of new technologies, products or business practices and able to drive scaling.

Some entrepreneurs start only one company that they keep for life. Often, after some years they will continuously pull money out of their company and invest it in other things such as property or private equity funds, but without starting new companies. Others, meanwhile, become 'serial entrepreneurs' – they constantly see new opportunities which tempt them. An extreme example is Richard Branson, who has founded around 500 companies within lots of different sectors.

Perhaps the explanation of the difference between single-company founders and serial entrepreneurs is that those who keep the same company for life are most fascinated by people management, whereas serial entrepreneurs may be more fascinated with ideas.

How big is the risk?

Is it risky to be an entrepreneur? The literature is full of studies of what proportion of start-ups go belly up. You might find some that say that around 90% fail, or that 75% fail within three years. We have looked at the statistics, and they are . . . err . . . confusing.

But let us give some examples. Shikhar Ghosh from Harvard Business School found that 75% of all companies receiving VC investments do not give a profit to these investors.[2]

It can be worse. A major study covered 2462 Israeli technology start-ups over many years. Among these, 46% went out of business. Splash! Even more alarming was that about two-thirds of those that had received investment from venture capital firms failed. Two-thirds! And even worse: no less than 96.5% of the 531 of the companies that had received incubator investments failed.[3] (Incubators are facilities for young start-up companies offering special service functions – we describe them in more detail later.) Now it must be said that incubators invest in early stages where the risks are higher but so are the potential gains; nevertheless, these are not pretty numbers. Just think about it: nearly 97% failed!

An even larger study included close to 10 000 US start-ups that had received venture capital funds between 1975 and 2007.[4] It showed that 87% of start-ups led by first-time entrepreneurs did not (not!) succeed. Of those which were led by entrepreneurs that previously had tried and failed, 80% failed, and of those whose leaders had previously managed successful start-ups, 'only' 70% failed. Clearly, past performance is no guarantee of future results, as bank disclaimers often say.

NEARLY 97% FAILED!

Let's conclude that entrepreneurship is not easy. And then there are the statistics showing the proportion of start-ups in the United States that fail within a given period after founding:[5]

US business failure rate, year-over-year, % of business failed.

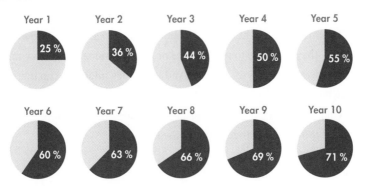

Another survey shows that among 4841 German internet and ecommerce start-ups up until 2004, 21% failed, but bizarrely a *higher* proportion, namely no less than 53% of the 895 of the companies that received VC funding, went out of business.[6] Oops!

There are numerous other studies, but comparing them is challenging. For instance, the data may involve growth entrepreneurs only, in one country, for a short time span, often within a limited sector, and typically only with companies that have received a certain kind of external funding, e.g. from the VC funds. In addition, there are widely divergent definitions of 'failure' and 'success'. To fail, for example, in some studies may be referred to as going bankrupt and in others not providing profit for a venture capital fund. (When we use the term 'fail' later in this book, we simply mean that one does not live up to their own expectations.)

But again, the studies make one thing quite clear: it's hard. The typical impression people in the venture capital industry express is this:

- Approximately 25% of lifestyle entrepreneurs fail within the first three years or so.
- Approximately 75% of growth entrepreneurs fail within the first three years or so.

Venture capital funds are therefore cautious. A typical VC fund receives around 500–1000 investment proposals per year. They do a quick screening of them all and might then give a closer look at perhaps 100, where, for example, they meet the founders once or twice. Among these, they might perform deeper studies of 20 or so. And then, they might end up investing in maybe two.

What happens with the two perhaps that they invest in out of, say, 700? A rule of thumb in the industry says the following:

- 30% go bankrupt.
- 30% survive but nevertheless provide a negative return of the fund's investment.
- 30% survive but provide a roughly break-even result for the fund.
- 10% go extremely well and may even give a 1000% return or more.

So, it is 10% of the two out of 700 that do really well, so now we are talking about the order of one company out of 23 500 that reaches the stars. Again: The number is very uncertain, so think of it only as an indicative range.

In any case, if anyone asks whether starting companies is risky, our best answer would be: 'Yes, unfortunately, the risk is huge. Especially if it is a growth entrepreneurship.'

And this is despite the fact that it has become cheaper and easier to start your own business. Nevertheless, we would recommend a lot of people to at least try, because if you know more about the task than others, the chances of success increase a lot. And after all, it has also become far cheaper to fail.

How can I reduce the risk?

There are numerous factors that can reduce the risk of start-up failure. Here are a few samples (they will, along with many others, be explained in more later in the book):

- Your chances of success increase dramatically if you have at least one co-founder, whom you have worked with before and know very well. If you previously have had a job in another start-up, it will increase your chances of success even further. All of this has been borne out by statistics (more on that in Chapter 10).

- In the beginning, you have no need for either a business plan or a lot of money, as you will typically spend the first several months or even years creating a 'minimum viable product', which you test with potential customers. Your plan can at this stage simply be on a large piece of paper and might consist of nothing else but bullet points. In addition, you should use a spreadsheet with some simple back-of-the-envelope calculations. And you will need some PowerPoint slides that tell your story, short and simple. Nothing else. You should review all this every week, if not more often. The purpose at the start is to learn, not to do (see Chapter 12 for more details).

- It is not embarrassing if you make some dramatic change of direction ('pivots') at the start. In fact, statistically, this increases your chances of success (see Chapter 12 for additional information).

- The statistics also show that it will further enhance your chances tremendously if you get a good mentor and/or follow blogs from entrepreneurial gurus (this will be further explained in Chapter 10).

- Your greatest commercial risks are (i) a poor product/market fit, (ii) internal strife, (iii) generally, investing heavily before you have clearly proven that you have a product that enough customers really love and want to pay for, (iv) accelerating parts of your project before other parts are up to speed, and (v) failed transition from early adopters (the earliest users) to mainstream customers (more about this in Chapter 14).

As mentioned, these examples are just a few of the many we will show throughout the book.

Alternative paths to the entrepreneurial life

Earlier, we wrote about the traditional view of the entrepreneurial life, which was suddenly getting a brilliant idea, then building a company around it. However, there are lots of different kinds of entrepreneurial life. The following 12 are probably the best examples:

1. *Working in a private equity fund.* Private equity funds buy large and often controlling positions in private companies and then typically implement several programmes to create more value, then sell their positions again. This work may sometimes be relatable to the traditional entrepreneurial life.

2. *Late co-founder.* A friend has founded a start-up and it is beginning to do well. You are invited to join as an investor and 'co-founder', even though the company has already existed for seven months, for example.

3. *Franchise.* You acquire the rights to become a reseller or franchisee for a growth company such as McDonald's (franchisee is someone who has bought the rights to do business with other people's trademark and products, etc.). As a franchisee, you may, for instance, build retail stores or other local distribution. Admittedly, it is based on someone else's idea, but it's still your business. And you are working as an independent in something that might be called an entrepreneurial project.

4. *Hobby-becomes-business.* You have a hobby that you think is more fun than your day job. Perhaps you decide to make a website about your hobby and build up a large network of like-minded people. One day you may conclude that since you now know a great number of potential customers within this area – and they know you – there is a basis for starting your own business.

5. *Internal venture.* Some companies actually work as serial entrepreneurs, thus creating plenty of opportunities for their staff to start entrepreneurial lives.

6. *Intrapreneur/spin-off entrepreneur.* You work in a large company and you – or someone on your team – have had a brilliant idea. You now propose that the management team implements this, but they respond that although the idea is fine, to fit it into the company's profile is hard. You therefore propose they make a new spin-off company to implement the idea there. The company may finance the first few months or years of operation, perhaps against a 50–80% stake, and you get the remaining shares, but at the same time your salary is reduced to a minimum. Thereafter, the rest is up to you. Incidentally, there are some businesses that are doing serial spin-offs, i.e. lots of them, giving plenty of opportunities for employees to become entrepreneurs.

7. *Consultant to start-up.* You develop on a consultancy basis a solution for a customer – for example, a software solution to a specific problem. Afterwards you start thinking, 'if the customer would pay so much for this, there are probably others who are willing to do so as well'. Thus, you're starting a business that turns this one-off solution into a scalable product. Or maybe you are wondering why the employer in the consulting firm you are working for bills the customer three times as much for the work you are conducting as you receive in wages. So why not become your own employer?

8. *Independent lifestyle entrepreneur.* You incorporate a little business to become your own boss.

9. *Lifestyle to growth entrepreneur.* You are a lifestyle entrepreneur but while being so, you develop an innovation, which allows you to scale your project.

10. *Skunk works.* The concept skunk works originated in Lockheed Martin during the Second World War and is still being used with great success today. This means that a company allows some of its employees to work on projects that run outside the normal management routines. Lots of successful companies – including many of the largest multinationals – have skunk work programmes and the work which is conducted there typically has a strong entrepreneurial flair.

11. *Sweat equity.* You work unpaid as a consultant for a start-up business, but only because you will receive stock options or shares in that business. Or here's a variation: you work for a start-up for a beggarly salary and stock options. The company goes really well and suddenly its stock options are worth millions. One day, with a few of the other people, you choose to quit the job and make a new start-up, financed with the earnings.

Oh, right, and then # 12:

12. *The brilliant idea.* You get a terrific idea during your morning shower, find investors and build your business.[7]

However, note that many of the 12 paths to entrepreneurship are far less risky than # 12. And many who implement # 12 have previously cut their teeth trying one of the other 11 approaches. Also, remember that many who have success failed once or several times before, and the horrible entrepreneurial statistics do not cover this aspect. So if, for example, 80% fail but everyone tries five times, most will arguably succeed eventually.

MANY WHO HAVE SUC-CESS FAILED ONCE OR MORE BEFORE SUCCEEDING.

Mads on how to practise entrepreneurial work as a young person

As a 14–15 year old, I bought a wholesale stock of discounted clothes with my pocket money – and then I walked into a store and tried to sell it. It cost me a lot of money, but it was one of many times when, while young, I practised my entrepreneurial capabilities – many years before I really began in earnest. Actually, my last time at Groupon and Rocket Internet was probably also a kind of 'sheltered workshop' for entrepreneurs, where I learned a lot by helping to create around 15 companies under a common framework. There is nothing wrong in practising – actually, quite the opposite. You wouldn't participate in a very difficult sports competition without training first, would you?

Lars on his first time as an entrepreneur

I had a lot of practice in business as a young man. During my studies in college, I helped a friend importing containers with cakes, which we distributed to supermarkets, and together with another friend I sold antistatic screen cleaners to computer companies. I also borrowed money and invested it in the stock market. At the age of 19, I bought a country house in Spain with a friend with money which in my case was earned during my leisure work. For me, buying the house was 50% about learning the ropes of buying and restoring a house. I just wanted to learn. And although none of my first businesses was a major success, I learned a lot from them and got familiar with the basic processes of running a business.

Risk is relative

Here is our take on start-up risk in a nutshell: when you think of risk, you must of course also think of the alternative. If you start a business, for a certain period you will live with extreme uncertainty, and it may well end up going wrong. But if it actually ends well, you get into a situation where you never – never! – again in your life need to have economic problems. Thus, you can achieve the ultimate financial freedom. And what exactly is the alternative? That you go through your whole life dependent on an employer to keep you financially secure – and if you do lose your job, you can get into quite big financial trouble rather quickly. Our point is that entrepreneurship is indeed risky, but the same can apply to a traditional career as an employee.

When you ask the elderly what they regret about their lives, they rarely mention something that they have done, it is usually something they did *not* do. Therefore, if you dream of creating a company, try. If it fails, then you know that you at least tried, you just couldn't make it work. If, however, you do not try, you might wonder to your dying day what it perhaps could have resulted in.

This ethos of trying for all the world is also very common among entrepreneurs: 'True failure is failing to try' has almost become an industry motto, and that is how we see it. When our days are about to be counted, we want to feel that we tried the best we could – even if some of the things we tried failed. By saying this, we certainly do not mean to say that failure should be glorified, as you sometimes hear in the entrepreneurial sector, but merely that it may be the biggest mistake of all not to test your potential.

THE BIGGEST MIS-
TAKE IS PERHAPS FAIL-
ING TO TRY.

What does it require of my personality?

Successful entrepreneurs have different personalities, yet we believe that there are some common characteristics that increase the likelihood of success substantially. Here we must admit immediately that we have never met a person – and certainly not ourselves – that lives up to all of these characteristics. But at the same time we would like to add that, at least in our opinion, you are able to train some of your personal weaknesses away. Working as an entrepreneur will most likely make you far stronger.

The first useful trait is *showing initiative*. When people are annoyed about something, they complain to their friends on social media, etc. We all do. But some people may afterwards say, 'OK, no more complaining. Let's fix it instead!' Then they come up with a proposal for a solution. 'Let's do it!' Such initiative is one of the typical features of entrepreneurs.

In parallel, entrepreneurs often tend to *think of continuous improvement*. When they enter a restaurant, for example, they immediately consider how they would change it. Therefore, there are constantly myriad possible projects running through their heads. Their attitude is that they typically do not improve anything by fighting the existing but by creating an alternative.

What else could help? One of the most important attributes among entrepreneurs is arguably that they are *self-motivated*, i.e. they can work persistently without being ordered to do so. This leads logically to the next property, which is to have a *passion for a project*. All start-ups include hard work, and it's difficult to be self-motivated in the long run if there isn't a significant part of the project which they really enjoy doing or are dying to see succeed.

With passion follows being *impatient to see the end result* – and when the results are achieved, entepreneurs immediately become impatient to improve this result. For the typical entrepreneur, everything had to be finished yesterday.

However, the impatience should not result in unproductive anger or irritation; instead it must play out through *ability to do high-speed work.* Great entrepreneurs tend to think quickly, decide quickly and get daily problems shot down as if with a machine gun. In younger start-ups, time is almost always a serious scarcity factor and therefore it is useful to have people on the team who can execute fast, fast, fast. A symptom of this personality trait may be that they took their education very quickly, had demanding jobs while studying, completed several studies simultaneously or started a business while they were studying.

Another qualification: entrepreneurs often have brains that are *optimized for speed, chaos and uncertainty,* just like in a football game, where everything can happen any time.

Every start-up has poor days (and poor months, plus probably poor years) and therefore entrepreneurs should also be quite *resistant to adversity.* Preferably very resistant. Part of this robustness or resilience should be that they don't care if they are looking like idiots, a trait which requires considerable self-confidence.

Typical entrepreneurs *look forward and do not dwell on the past.* When something has gone wrong, they draw their conclusions and remember them, but then they quickly forget the rest because it does not interest them. Thus, they look forward but still learn from their mistakes.

They have *professional pride* and therefore they do everything in the best possible way, even if the work is not interesting or particularly important for them. If, for example, they have boring jobs during their studies, they try to perform well anyway.

Entrepreneurs should be *able to immerse themselves in a task.* Entrepreneurial jobs require that they can familiarize themselves with a subject sufficiently well to see how things can be improved.

Also, many entrepreneurs are quite *curious.* They are 'what happens if I press this button?' types.

They are also typically *cooperative* types. People who think that everyone else is an idiot rarely find it easy to be part of teams or to build good social ecosystems. Trust but verify is a better attitude, which means that you should trust people but still conduct sanity checks.

In addition, an entrepreneur should be *persistent*. When everything starts to fall apart, they are still working – very hard. This accounts for most athletes as well. Think of how they might be up at 4 a.m. to train very hard just to have a small chance of receiving a medal in the future. In other words, strength of character and will to fight, even if the reward is questionable and at best very far in the future, are important and may actually have a bigger impact than intelligence, physique, training or experience.

Along with this strength of character is that you can *postpone a potential reward*; there is a willingness to work hard for years for a reward which may, or may not, come in the future.

It is also helpful if entrepreneurs in their youth have *tried low-paid jobs* as this makes them more earthbound and helps to put their struggles into perspective.

Are you able to postpone a reward?

'In the late 1960s and early 1970s psychologist Walter Mischel from Harvard conducted a famous study with children.'[8] They had a marshmallow in front of them and were told that if they could wait 20 minutes to eat it, they would receive one more.

It turned out that the children who did not eat it, and thereby exercised greater self-control, performed much better in later life. From childhood they could control their urges. An entrepreneur must possess a great ability to delay reward, and a 20 year old who, for example, is very concerned about work/life balance, is hardly an obvious entrepreneur.

Entrepreneurs are typically also more *optimistic* by nature than the average human being. Although they do not know what their job will entail, they have a fundamental belief that they will manage to grow and learn with the assignment.

There are some elements of the way in which people deal with information and decisions that tend to differ between typical entrepreneurs and non-entrepreneurs. The most popular professional personality assessment is probably the Myers-Briggs Type Indicator, which divides people into 16 personality categories. Regarding information, they are distinguished based on whether they mostly focus on the basic information they take in or are more interested in adding meaning to it. For instance, one historian may find it interesting to describe an event in history very carefully, while another may be more interested in fitting this event into a grand 'big history' pattern and thus giving it all meaning. The former is called a 'sensing' personality and the latter an 'intuitive' personality. CPP Inc., the company that publishes the Myers-Briggs Type Indicator assessment, in 2017 published a study showing that entrepreneurs were on average far more *intuitive* than sensing.[9] Entrepreneurs tend to focus on seeing the greater patterns and the bigger meanings.

Another main dimension in Myers-Briggs is the mental structuring of the outside world: do you prefer to take a final view of things once and for all, or do you prefer to stay open to new information and options? The former mentality is called 'judging' and the latter 'perceiving'. The study found that entrepreneurs were far more likely to be *perceiving* than judging.

They were also *thinking* rather than 'feeling'. Thinking people, according to the Myers-Briggs definition, will largely base their decisions on objective principles and impersonal facts, whereas feeling people are more moved by personal concerns and the people involved. Thinking people are thus more rational, and this applies to average entrepreneurs.

The other findings in this study were entirely as one would expect. Entrepreneurs showed far higher orientation for *creativity, extroversion, risk-taking, impulsivity* and, most of all, *autonomy* than did non-entrepreneurs. But interestingly, they were not more competitive.

Finally, it must be said that there is a significant preponderance of people with *personality disorders* among entrepreneurs.[10] A large psychological study of entrepreneurs showed a markedly elevated tendency to depression, substance abuse, ADHD and bipolar personality deviation, while half of them had close relatives with hereditary personality deviations. The consequence is that some of those who were perceived as a bit weird in school amazed their young friends by later becoming entrepreneurial stars. Perhaps many entrepreneurs also tend towards a fanaticism and savagery that makes them strive to achieve the target, regardless of the personal cost and the outside world's response. As an entrepreneur, you typically need to be able to piss off some people and keep going where most people would stop.

Who are most successful?

Of course, while one question is how entrepreneurs differ from the average population, another is which of them are most successful. One study from 2008 divided a number of entrepreneurs into two groups according to their personality and behaviour, namely the 'lambs' and the 'cheetahs'. The behaviour of the lambs was described as follows: 'graze in circles, feeding on the feedback and direction of others.' These were popular among investors and succeeded commercially 57% of the time.[11] Fine, but how about the cheetahs?

These were rougher, as their nickname implies. Cheetahs would move quickly and aggressively, work very hard, demonstrate persistence, set high standards and hold people accountable to those standards. Every single one of these produced high returns for their investors – each and every one.

The conclusion, which has been confirmed by other studies, showed that social skills were great, but only when combined with an enormous propensity to get things done. So perhaps a good question to ask yourself, when considering making or leading a start-up, is this:

'Do I have an exceptional propensity to get things done?'

The ability to get things done is obviously largely about *grit*. Navy Seals often learn that when your body tells you that you cannot do any more, you have actually reached only 40% of your capacity. Soldiers and sportsmen with grit continue beyond that. Beyond these professions, a number of studies have shown that grit is a better predictor of success in life than IQ or natural talents.[12]

Twenty-three Indications that You can Thrive as an Entrepreneur

- You show initiative
- You are self-motivated
- You are impatient
- You work quickly
- You are mentally optimized for speed, chaos and uncertainty
- You are resistant to adversity
- You look ahead, but learn from your mistakes
- You are thinking of sustained improvements everywhere around you
- You have professional pride
- You can immerse yourself in a task
- You are quite curious
- You are cooperative
- You are persistent
- You can postpone rewards
- You are generally optimistic
- You have had rather thankless routine jobs in your youth
- You are intuitive and interested in big pictures and broad patterns
- You are creative
- You are open to change and thus not inclined to seek a definitive answer to questions
- Your decision making is based on objective principles and impersonal facts rather than on people involved and personal concerns
- You can be impulsive
- You may have a moderate personality deviation
- You have enormous propensity to get things done

Can entrepreneurship be taught?

There is no shortage of people claiming that entrepreneurship cannot be taught – either you have it or you don't. Yeah right, and the same goes for music, acting and such. But we believe that as in any challenging task, the combination of practice, talent and, yes, instruction tends to be optimal. There are lots of colleges and universities that teach entrepreneurship, and they have got much better at it over time. Our opinion is that studying entrepreneurship can be useful. By the way, one of the best education programmes in the industry is the Kauffman fellow program, in Palo Alto, California, which takes two years. Each year, 20–30 students are picked from among some 200 applicants.

Do I need to be an expert within the sector?

If you are a lifestyle entrepreneur, it's probably easier to be an insider within your industry, but growth entrepreneurs are often outsiders or what are called 'outsider entrepreneurs'. Actually, this seems to be a rule more than an exception. For example, Elon Musk revolutionized the online payment, battery, aerospace and automotive industries (Zip2, PayPal, SpaceX, Tesla, SolarCity, etc.); Steve Jobs revolutionized the movie, computer, mobile phone and music industries (Apple, NeXT, Pixar); Reed Hastings revolutionized movie distribution (Pure Software, Netflix); Richard Branson revolutionized, among others, the aircraft industry (Virgin); Chip Conley revolutionized the hotel industry (Joie de Vivre Hospitality); Travis Kalanick and Garrett Camp revolutionized the taxi industry (Uber). These people were all outsiders to their industries.

What do the statistics say? In fact, they say that about 55% start their businesses within industries in which they had never worked previously.[13] Karim Lakhani from MIT said, after analyzing the activities of the innovation platform InnoCentive:

'Actually, we found that the probability of success increased in areas where they had no formal expertise'.[14]

Why? Perhaps insiders have too much tradition and reverence for the area. A degree of ignorant naivete can be a force.

A DEGREE OF IGNORANT NAIVETE CAN BE A FORCE.

Is it really as hard as they say?

Most entrepreneurs we know, and especially those from growth start-ups, describe their work effort as very intense. Think of it as a rocket that must reach stable orbit and uses an ultra-macho booster to get there – fast. A study of British entrepreneurs showed that a third regularly worked more than 70 hours weekly, and two-thirds did more than 50 hours per week. On top of this, half were planning no more than two weeks of holiday at all over the next year and 14% expected not a single day off.[15]

However, to deliver such enormous work effort within a short time requires not only dedication and tons of work hours but also personal efficiency, which we will address in the coming chapters.

Is it economically worthwhile to become an entrepreneur?

Bill Gates made tons of money starting his business, but from general risk-balancing principles, it is on average not worth it financially to be an entrepreneur.[16] Indeed, a study showed that entrepreneurs over a period of 10 years on average earned 35% less than what they – given their qualifications – could have earned in jobs per hour with the same effort. This was partly because of the hard work and partly the many bankruptcies.[17]

However, please notice the word 'average'. We have already looked at some factors that can improve success rates and we need to look more at business models in the next chapter, where it will be apparent that some models are on average much more promising than others. One study found, for example, that growth start-ups with original technologies/business types have better chances of success than me-too start-ups (companies that basically do the same as others).[18] Thus, if we could make statistics of competent entrepreneurs who went after thoughtful, scalable business models, the picture would probably be quite different and better.

You can think of it as follows: if you are a lifestyle entrepreneur and open a store, you must work 60–80 hours a week and have maybe a 75% chance of making your business survive the critical first three years. Alternatively, should you make an international software company, you will also have to work 60–80 hours a week and your company has only a 25% chance of survival in the long term. However, with the first kind of entrepreneurial project, you will probably not become rich, while the second, in principle, could make you a billionaire. And while the first wouldn't change the world very much, the other could potentially make a more noticeable difference by introducing new ideas to the benefit of all.

At what age should you become an entrepreneur?

We all know famous stories of very young people starting incredible growth companies. For instance, Bill Gates and Mark Zuckerberg were just 19 when they co-founded Microsoft and Facebook, respectively. Steve Jobs co-founded Apple at age 21, Daniel Ek co-founded Spotify at age 23, and Google was founded by Larry Page and Sergey Brin when they were both 25.

However, Jeff Bezos was 30 when he founded Amazon, as was Elon Musk when he founded SpaceX. Jack Ma was even older – 34 – when he founded Alibaba and Reed Hastings was 36 when he founded Netflix. Oh, and Charles Flint was 61 when he founded IBM.

On average, there is no evidence that people typically start their businesses at a particular stage of their life or career; instead it is rather widely distributed across age groups.[19] That being said, one study showed that on average people had worked 14 years before starting their own business, and 35% had worked at least 20 years before they chose to do so. Overall, according to this study, growth entrepreneurs (as opposed to lifestyle entrepreneurs) were on average 34–35 years old when they founded their business.[20]

The Startup Genome project, a study of more than 100 000 start-up companies worldwide, which we will refer to repeatedly in the following chapters, has also studied the average age among the founders of internet companies in the world's top 20 entrepreneurial cities. Here are the numbers:[21]

Average age of the founders of the world's 20 largest entrepreneurial centres

• Silicon Valley	36	• Paris	34
• New York City	34	• Sao Paulo	32
• Los Angeles	37	• Moscow	32
• Boston	35	• Austin	37
• Tel Aviv	34	• Bangalore	29
• London	33	• Sydney	40
• Chicago	38	• Toronto	37
• Seattle	39	• Vancouver	40
• Berlin	32	• Amsterdam	34
• Singapore	35	• Montreal	32

According to this study, whatever the place, the average age for founding a business is between 29 and 40 years old, with an overall average of 35 years. Incidentally, the researchers also investigated whether there was a significant difference between the average age of the founders who had success and those who had not. There wasn't – the average age was 35 years for those who were successful and 34 for those who failed.

However, in 2018, two scientists published a large study based not on a sample but instead on each and every one of the no less than 2.7 million people in the US who between 2007 and 2014 had founded a company and subsequently hired at least one person. How old were these entrepreneurs when they founded these companies?[22]

Overall, the average age was 42 years and as the figure shows, less than 1% of them were below 22 years of age. Moreover, a breakdown showed the following average ages of founders of companies which:

- received venture capital funding: 42 years
- made high-tech recruitment: 43 years
- filed patents: 45 years
- were among the 0.1% fastest growing startups: 45 years.

Founder age distribution: all start-ups and high-performance start-ups.

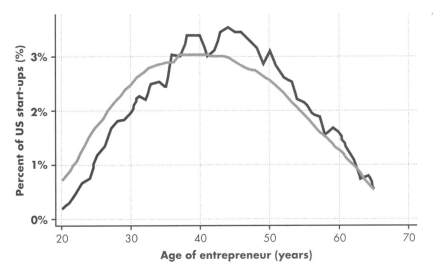

Overall US start-up founders
Founders of top 1% growth start-ups

So, in fact, those who created the most successful companies were a bit older than the overall average: they were on average 45. And just approximately 1% of the elite 0.1% founders were 25 years or less when founding their companies.

This brings us to something else: many of those who successfully founded companies at a very young age reached their zenith as founder-managers only when they were much older. For instance, Steve Jobs was arguably a far better entrepreneur when he returned to Apple at the age of 42 than he was when he co-founded the company at 19.

The conclusion is that as an investor in growth startups, all else being equal, you should have a preference for somewhat seasoned founders. Nevertheless, we recommend considering founding companies very early in your life if an opportunity arises.

Motives for starting early in your career may be that the idea simply is there, and the team as well. Or that you have not yet obtained a car, a dog and a family and thus the social and financial responsibilities that come with those. Funny fact, btw: when we give speeches on entrepreneurship around the world, we sometimes ask how many in the audience have a dog. When we speak to entrepreneur communities, the number is often almost zero.

Typically, during your youth, you are in better health and have no serious risk of ruining a great CV with a potential start-up disaster. And if you fail, then at least you tried and learned. As a youngster, it is also easier to say goodbye to one's ego – for a young person it is OK to sit in a supermarket to earn money until the start-up project is profitable. Therefore, it might be more acceptable to such a person to tackle all the small practicalities of running an early startup. In your younger days, you are also not too specialized.

Furthermore, there is a tendency as a young person to be better at spotting new trends and opportunities. This was what Apple's Steve Jobs and Microsoft's Bill Gates illustrated in the 1970s, and what Facebook's Mark Zuckerberg and Airbnb's Brian Chesky have shown in recent times.

Another consideration could be that the younger you are as an entrepreneur, the more impressed the rest of the world will be, whereas for an older entrepreneur, some might even think, 'Is this because he lost his job?'

Conversely, motives for older entrepreneurs could include better contacts, initial capital and experience. Or perhaps larger life changes such as having reached a glass ceiling in their career or even having lost their job. Overall, we believe young people have some advantages. Many would say that the best time to start is during your studies – if your project fails, you can fall back on those studies.

MANY WOULD SAY THAT THE BEST TIME TO START IS DURING YOUR STUDIES – IF YOUR PROJECT FAILS, YOU CAN FALL BACK ON THOSE STUDIES.

Lars on the benefits of becoming an entrepreneur during your studies

My oldest daughter co-founded a company selling a new type of hairband called 'Invisibobble' with a friend when she was 18 years old and just three months into her university study. When she graduated with her bachelor's three years later, they had two dozen employees, and two years later, when she was 23, they had a staff of 100. Furthermore, they received the Forbes 30 under 30 Europe prize. In her case, it was certainly a great decision to start early.

Does it require management experience to start?

Can you manage a start-up if you do not have management experience? Evidently. According to one study, only 18% of entrepreneurs in technology and life sciences start-ups had prior management experience.[23] However, the relevant experience many of these entrepreneurs had was from working in smaller companies and not as leaders. Thus, 64% of entrepreneurs came from businesses with fewer than 100 employees, although such companies accounted for less than 20% of the total workforce.[24]

THE RELEVANT EXPERIENCE MANY ENTREPRENEURS HAD WAS FROM WORKING IN SMALL BUSINESSES.

Does it require a lot of capital?

Do you have to be rich in order to create a start-up? Some manage to start up with very little or virtually no capital, either from their own pockets or from strangers. In the venture industry this is referred to as 'bootstrapping'. You can, for example, bootstrap by (i) generating very quick sales, (ii) saving money, such as by working from home and using cloud computing and crowd sourcing, etc., or (iii) earning money from consultancy income while you develop your product.

If you do not bootstrap and do not have enough capital, you need to obtain external capital, but this can be really time consuming for a young company. Actually, it can be just as time consuming as developing and selling a product, and therefore you should always consider other ways, so that you can avoid doing so – at least during the initial phase.

You should also consider the fact that having ample funding can have negative consequences as well, since the creativity may disappear if you can pay yourself out of all problems. With money in the bank, you will easily become too leisurely. 'You will not be hungry by being in paradise', as they say, and 'necessity is the mother of invention'. This of course does not imply that you are unable to start a business from paradise, and as mentioned, many previously successful entrepreneurs start new projects from their luxury villas. But they might adopt a more lenient approach now they have the necessary capital.

Should I wait for the brilliant idea?

The idea should be there, but, as we will get back to later, the idea is really by far a minor concern. Instead, it's the execution that is most critical. Besides, having a single great idea is often not enough – it is usually a combination of several ideas that creates opportunity. Let's say you get the idea to create a company that specializes in selling wines. Fine, but how do you find potential customers? Hmmm . . . maybe by creating a website and a magazine that is all about wine? Fine, but how do you then finance it? Hmmm . . . ads for wine and wine tours? And so on and on and on, until you have an overall story that could potentially make sense. A complex story rarely occurs to you one morning in the shower. It has many facets and is often developed over a long period of time. In fact, many companies can thrive only if they keep up the renewal process without end.

Simple often means quick

In 2005 scientists published a meta-study (study of other studies) of the correlation between how long it took companies to develop a product (concept to launch) and how quickly the product subsequently got a big market share (speed to market). They read 13 studies on the subject, of which 10 found a correlation where it was faster for companies to penetrate the market if the product had taken a short period of time to develop.[25]

2.
MY PERSONAL EFFECTIVENESS

Typically, entrepreneurs have a huge workload and a great sense of personal responsibility, and this combination can be both physically exhausting and mentally stressful. Therefore, in our opinion, you should consider your level of personal effectiveness carefully. People are obviously different, and everyone should find their own, individual way of doing things, but in this chapter we review a number of tools and approaches that may help you to deal with the work pressure and stress that being an entrepreneur might cause. These approaches have worked for both ourselves and others.

Our first and perhaps most important observation concerning workload and stress is that many entrepreneurs often have a partner and perhaps even children. Whether they like it or not, their entrepreneurial jobs affect these people and therefore we recommend you clearly agree with your partner on which parts of your private lifestyle you want to maintain and which you will have to alter. Perhaps you want to maintain almost exclusively everything that deals with your kids but might want to stop many of your dinners with friends? This you need to agree on with your partner. And if you have small children, one tip that has worked for both of us is to spend time with them in the morning because when you come home in the evening they are probably already asleep.

Decide how to tackle the unpleasant parts of your job

Especially at the beginning of your entrepreneurial project, you will have to deal with some of the things you don't like. Perhaps it is reading and revising long contracts, or listening to staff complaints, or maybe participating in endless budget meetings. Either way, make a mental agreement with yourself that you simply must do this, and that's OK, because the rest of the work is super fun and the company's success is extremely important to you. Think of it this way: authors must proofread their work, athletes must go through some horrible training days, skiing guides have customers when there is rain and fog. It's part of being professional that you go through efforts that are not all pleasant. And remember: eventually you

Lars on how to protect your health as an entrepreneur

In periods where I had an insane amount of work and a lot of travel activity, I felt very clearly that it gave me lots of energy to play sports and enjoy outdoor activities with my family and friends. Conversely, it destroyed my energy and broke down my health slowly to sit at a table for 4–5 hours with dinner and a deluge of wine. Therefore, I began saying no to invitations to such dinners, which I became quite unpopular for, until I – too late – explained why I chose to do so. I think it's important to inform people of what you can and cannot attend and, more importantly, why. The point is that people can often understand your decisions if you explain them properly. And if they cannot or will not, they should perhaps not be your friends.

will be able to delegate the work you are worst at doing or like the least (which is typically the same). Remember the great motto regarding these kind of tasks: 'Improve it, eliminate it or delegate it.' Eventually you can get rid of some of it – but probably not at the beginning.

Don't defer your life

It is quite common for entrepreneurs to front-load their lifetime work effort so that they can enjoy more fun and freedom later. We are not entirely opposed to this view, but while you can defer free time, it can actually become risky and inefficient to defer the happy life. Your chance of becoming a successful entrepreneur gets much higher if you can find a way of enjoying the road as much as the destination. After all, this is why successful entrepreneurs often start a new venture just after their last exit – they are successful because they like the entrepreneurial lifestyle and get bored without it. Their journey is a big part of their reward.

Optimize the combination of work, sport and socializing

It seems to be quite common for people to work until they become tired, after which they receive a 'much-needed vacation'. Obviously, this is understandable, and we've done it plenty of times ourselves, but in reality we believe it is much better to find a lifestyle that doesn't actually necessitate holidays, but rather you choose to take time out because you want to, which we have done.

Actually, we are not sure if it physically even relieves stress to go on vacation. Stress occurs in most cases, we believe, when you cannot cope with your tasks. Our experience tells us that if you work 60 hours per week but still fall behind with your tasks, then your stress disappears if you turn it up to 80 hours a week and in return get up to speed with the tasks. This is probably far too much in the long term, so over time you must find ways to delegate your tasks. In any case, your vacation should not be a necessary factor, but an optional enjoyment.

IT IS MUCH BETTER TO FIND A LIFESTYLE THAT DOESN'T ACTUALLY NECESSITATE HOLIDAYS.

How do you figure out how to create an optimal lifestyle? First of all, always consider the marginal efficiency of whatever you do. For instance, not doing sports at all is plainly completely irrational, whereas doing it 30 minutes daily is hugely beneficial and highly rational. Increasing it to 60 minutes adds to the effect, but the second 30 minutes are not as useful as the first. Add another 30 minutes and the marginal effect drops further while time spent begins to have significant opportunity cost. The same goes with everything else you use your time on. Working a lot is necessary, but working so hard that it breaks down your body, basic social relationships, etc., isn't. So we think it is always worth considering, 'Is my time now better spent on something else?' It is also useful to bear in mind the so-called Pareto Principle: 80% of the effect in anything typically comes from 20% of the effort.

Of course, a parallel consideration is this: 'Would it be more rational if someone else did what I am doing now?' Indeed, it might very well make sense to hire interns in your company for some of what you are doing yourself, and perhaps also someone to do your home cleaning, your shopping, etc.

Combine and time your efforts

Another good approach to efficiency is to do several things simultaneously. For instance, if your office is within running distance, why not run to work? This gives you exercise while getting you from A to B. Oh, and you could listen to a podcast while jogging to work. Now you are achieving three things simultaneously.

Another example: why not take walking meetings? Instead of always sitting in a room, take a walk in the park with your colleagues while you discuss business. That gives you fresh air, a bit of exercise plus often a more fruitful discussion. And a fourth tip: never waste a second while you are in airports, trains and on planes, etc. Read or work instead.

Another idea is to follow your energy – consider which times of the day you are best at what. Perhaps you find that it works best to do the intellectually challenging work in the mornings and the routine stuff towards the end of the day, or vice versa.

Finally, consider working from home sometimes, even if you have an office. Some kinds of work are best done in isolation, and it doesn't hurt to save the travel time.

Plan your work week before it commences

Take a bit of time out of your calendar Sunday evening to arrange a weekly schedule, including getting a travel plan in place, and find all the clothes and other things you need. Make a to-do list. What is important? What is not important?

A good day

One idea for a good day is to start quietly – take a shower, eat breakfast and do some exercise and/or play with your kids before you check your inbox. In other words, start the day really well. Additionally, you should remember that our bodies are optimized to get exercise and to see the daylight every single day. Without these you will easily suffer from back pain, stress, fatigue and so on. At least half an hour of exercise every day and, if possible, spending some time in the daylight makes an enormous difference.

Another issue: most people can tolerate both coffee and alcohol. But if you drink more than four to six cups of coffee and two to three glasses of wine a day, it will likely start to have consequences, such as decreased energy or waking up in the middle of the night.

This brings us to good sleep, which is essential if you want to succeed as an entrepreneur. Athletes understand the value of sleep for recovery from training, and so should entrepreneurs. Of course, people have different needs when it comes to sleep, but most require about seven and a half to eight hours of sleep per day. The probability of getting your optimal amount of sleep increases if you have exercised, seen the daylight and restricted your intake of coffee and alcohol.

Here is another discovery we have made: you need to get away from the office more often than you may think. It is best if you can have fun weekends, which work like small vacations where there is a very different scenario. Preferably, something fun and social combined with fresh air and exercise. In these settings, it is no problem at all if you occasionally bring your PC, tablet or smartphone and do some business. The 'office outside the office' can be just as effective for certain types of work as the office itself, but it enables a much-needed variation and has social benefits. In addition, it often triggers inspiration if you are working from different locations.

And finally, many entrepreneurs satisfy the need for a social life within the workplace. This works especially well if your partner is in the same workplace. Thus, the same people work, socialize and play sports together, and that way you can kill two birds with one stone.

MANY ENTREPRENEURS SATISFY THE NEED FOR A SOCIAL LIFE WITHIN THE WORKPLACE.

Read and listen effectively

If it is important for you to read books, blogs and articles or listen to audio blogs, etc. concerning your industry, or maybe a different one, you can improve the efficiency of this by using a variety of technical tools. First, drop following the news flow as presented in traditional media and drop chat except with people who really know what they are talking about. For instance, instead of turning on the TV news after work, read some structured and relevant analysis.

Next, as you optimize your information flow (which we will elaborate on later), an important task is to find the right blogs. These will also help you find the most relevant books. A good way to find blogs about your business is partly by doing a simple search on industry-relevant keywords including the term 'blog'. A second and potentially more targeted approach is:

- Find projects like your own on Kickstarter and other crowdfunding organizations.
- Do a Google image search on images of these companies' products to see which bloggers have written about them.

You can use apps such as Audible, Audiobooks, Overdrive or Pocket Casts to access books and podcasts. You can then listen to these apps, for example, when travelling, doing sports or preparing food. Another useful tool is Amazon's Kindle, which makes it easy to read electronic books and other electronic texts – even during a sunny day, as it uses electronic paper. Kindle has a feature where you can mark important passages of text and then later see those highlights on your computer and so easily copy them into Trello, Evernote (which has more than 200 million users worldwide) or Google Keep, technical tools we will explain further below.

Use voice recognition

If you need to create longer documents or have problems typing, use voice recognition. Just a few years back, this worked pretty badly, but that has changed. Today, for instance, you can dictate to Word on a Mac after preparing for it in Settings, and it works in more and more languages (tip: try to have clear separation between the spoken words). There are also various sites on the web with voice recognition, such as dictation.io/. And don't forget you can dictate to Notes on your iPhone, for instance. Samsung also has great voice recognition features.

Organize your thoughts and control your projects effectively

There are lots of brilliant and cool apps to store random thoughts, develop ideas and organize your life in addition to those mentioned above. There are also a huge number of apps and (especially) sites with templates for your marketing plans, legal documents, executive summaries, meeting schedules and a lot of other relevant documents. Check out the Word document templates that can be downloaded or found on Entrepreneur.com, Score.org, sba.gov, liveplan.com and bplans.com. However, please be aware that legal templates which you download from a foreign site may not be applicable in your country.

You can also create and sign simple contracts with legal apps such as Shake, scan documents using scanning apps such as Scanner Pro, and write invoices and handle online payments by using the Due Payments app.

Generally, it is all about creating an efficient workflow with simple systems that are neither expensive nor complex and that work on your applet (minicomputer such as your iPad) and smartphone. Also, note that in Appendix C we have made a list of 85 apps and websites including software extensions, which we find useful for entrepreneurs.

THERE ARE LOTS OF GREAT APPS TO ORGAN- IZE RANDOM THOUGHTS, DEVELOP IDEAS AND ORGANIZE YOUR LIFE.

Free up time for the most important and what you do best

As the founder, in a newly started company you are responsible for almost everything, but when the business grows, you need to constantly think of delegation. Some entrepreneurs seek almost no fixed personal tasks, so they can work as a kind of sweeper for the company – take action where it is most useful and important.

Gradually, you must reduce your time spent on the areas where you especially struggle. If your competencies do not include writing press releases, hire a freelance journalist to do it for you. If you do not fancy doing accounting, engage a bookkeeper. You need to constantly look at your challenges and get them resolved quickly, and this is often achieved by delegating and outsourcing. As we mentioned, a good motto is: 'Improve it, eliminate it or delegate it.'

Today, there are even large, global organizations which have almost no employees. There may be a headquarters with a few staff, but everything else is outsourced because this approach is more profitable. An extreme example of this is the American company Living Essentials, which produces an energy drink called 5-hour Energy. The company has only around 60 employees and it still manages to gain revenue of more than $1 billion while maintaining considerable profits.[1] This is possible because it has outsourced almost the entire business to partners and thereby kept only a tight core.

Keep track of the many invitations

Another important consideration is how you deal with the interviews, lectures and social events you are invited to. If your business is small and insignificant, the answer is simple, as you get no invitations – ha ha. But as your company gets a foothold, the situation can change rather quickly from no one wanting to meet you to everyone wanting to meet you – and then you get a lot of requests and invitations, perhaps even a deluge. Many of these will be very useful, others not at all. The most important thing in such a situation is to remember to keep enough time to be among your employees. One solution is to delegate a large part of these representative tasks for a single person with great social skills and flair for creating memorable presentations. For this to work, however, this employee must have a prominent title.

Streamline your travels

Today, almost all communication can be done virtually, but most business people still choose to travel to have personal meetings. Why? Because it is only via personal meetings that you can observe signals from people which you likely wouldn't notice if you were to communicate virtually – for example, signals regarding their personality, behaviour, state of mind, etc. The bestseller *What They Don't Teach You at Harvard Business School* is largely about this.[2]

Travel is often the most strenuous part of start-up projects (although not all of them). It is tiring to get up at 4:30 a.m. to catch a morning flight to Paris or LA – especially if it occurs frequently. One solution is to fly in the night before. That way you get to work in the office till 8 p.m., then go to the airport (after rush hour) while you continuously work with emails, plans, presentations and so on, both on the plane and on the train/in the taxi/Uber on the way to the hotel when you land. The advantages are (i) you get a 12–14-hour work day, (ii) you are guaranteed a full night's sleep, (iii) you are sure to be on time the next morning, (iv) you avoid rush-hour traffic and (v) you can have breakfast with a business associate at your destination. The downside is that you need to take clothes and other things for one night and pay for the hotel.

For overseas travel, you can sometimes do something else: take an evening flight (so-called 'red-eye' due to passengers' sleep deprivation), sleep on the plane, take a shower and dress in the airport after landing, conduct meetings all day, take another red-eye back and sleep on the flight again. That way you get a 12–14-hour work day, while it saves you checking in and out of the hotel – and you still get to sleep twice.

If you travel a lot to the same place, you can seek an agreement with a hotel that has laundry services to wash/clean your clothes and keep them for the next time. That way, you never have to take more than carry-on luggage on the flight while you also save time on cleaning. This solution is not yet widespread, but it exists. Some airports also have laundry services.

For air travel, check in online and when you get the electronic boarding card, transfer it into an app such as Wallet or take a screenshot of it so you can find it, even if you are subsequently lacking a telephone connection in the departure hall. If you fly a lot, you will get frequent-flyer benefits, which may include the fast track in security and access to lounges.

And then there is of course land transport. Download an Uber app and/or any taxi apps for places you visit often. Use GPS locators on your smartphone to find your venues and check them out in advance using the GPS. If you need to meet someone and you can't find each other, locate your position with your navigation app and forward it via SMS or email. There's even an app for that. It's called Glympse and it sends your real-time location to a given person. Finally, consider a train to the airport instead of driving your car if it is far away or you're travelling in rush hour.

Optimize the use of electronic productivity tools

Electronic communication is possible through a variety of tools such as email, Facebook, LinkedIn, Twitter, Instagram, WhatsApp and more. In your work, you need to use these effectively, but you can also use the more general tools that tie this all together efficiently:

- *Cloud data storage.* With Google Drive, iCloud, OneDrive, Dropbox or Amazon Cloud Drive you save your files on a cloud server, from which you can download and share them with other people via PC, smartphone and tablet – wherever you are.

- *Video conferencing.* This is used primarily for audio-video conferencing between two or more people, but also for video conferencing, where it also allows you to share your screen. Furthermore, you can use Ecamm Call Recorder or Zencastr to record Skype conferences so that you do not forget what happened. Alternatively, use FaceTime, Tango, Frint, Zoom, Facebook Messenger, Hangouts, Imo Free or WeChat. From smartphones, WhatsApp is especially easy to use. Skype, meanwhile, is good for external communications, as everyone has it. It might not always be as effective as a personal meeting, but the savings in time and travel expenses can be enormous.

- *File sharing.* You can share documents by sending a download link to anyone through services such as Dropbox, OneDrive, Sync.com, etc. However, most of the popular clouds such as OneDrive include simple file-sharing features, where you can easily (with one click) share a download link to one of your files.

- *Slack (or competing products).* This allows you to create many different 'channels' within the company where employees can chat about a specific project, share all types of documents, images and so on using drag and drop. You can also use Slack to search through all products and thereby stay updated and make notifications, among other things. These channels may be open to all employees or created for selected users, and they can also be made available, for example, for suppliers and customers that also use Slack. Effective use of Slack means that people can easily find relevant information and that new employees do not start with an empty email inbox but with access to lots of structured data.

- *Automatic personal website generators.* Lots of websites, such as wix.com and dozens of others, offer the possibility to design great websites for you within 10 minutes or less – typically bundling this with web hosting and often with suggested free domain names, if you don't have one already.

Keep track of contacts

Keep constant track of your network. For instance, when you meet people, immediately find out how you can get into each other's electronic systems. Connect on LinkedIn, Skype and other social networks, send the person your Outlook profile via SMS or email, and so on. Give out printed business cards and use a business card scanning app such as CamCard to get the business card into Outlook or whatever you use as contact software.

If, in the middle of a business process, you receive an email from someone who copies in other people within their business, get those people into your systems as well and find out why they were copied in on the specific email – they were copied for a reason!

When you email about a project involving more people from your company, attach your LinkedIn link and Outlook profile so that the parties can easily establish an electronic link. In your email signature, i.e. the automatic signature you create for emails you send out, you can include your LinkedIn profile and potentially your Facebook profile as well. Always invite contacts to connect!

Generally, we believe it is useful to develop your network when everything is running smoothly instead of waiting until you have problems and need help. Likewise, it is useful to help people when you have control of things, both because it is the nice and the correct thing to do and because they are likely to speak well of you and perhaps return the favour one day.

In addition, be aware that if you look at someone's LinkedIn profile, they can see that you have done so. So why not take the opportunity to send a connect request while you are at it?

When it comes to specific social media, they usually overlap with professional collaboration tools for businesses. Typically, these are better than email project-oriented communication. Snapchat is good for simple, ad hoc projects (single projects), while Producteev, HipChat, HiveDesk or Confluence can be used to manage more complex projects.

WHEN YOU MEET PEOPLE, IMMEDIATELY FIND OUT HOW YOU CAN GET INTO EACH OTHER'S ELECTRONIC SYSTEMS.

Be practical with emails

Social media surpasses emails for many purposes, but emails are still very important – for better or worse. One of the big problems with emails is that it can feel as though half of the world's population is filling up your inbox with tasks. At worst, you may feel as though you are sitting at a desk in the middle of a busy street where passing pedestrians are loading documents into your already overcrowded inbox.

Another problem with emails is that they often lack an organizational tool. However, there are some tools which can improve your effectiveness. Some of these are email plugins and we especially recommend the following:

- *Rapportive for Gmail* finds the LinkedIn profile of the person to whom you are writing an email.

- *Boomerang* allows you to schedule an email so it is sent at a specific time and therefore you do not have to remember to do it yourself.

- *FindThatLead and Email Hunter*. If you do not know the email of a person, these applications can often find it for you via the person's LinkedIn profile.

Another solution is to have an email policy where all mails must be answered within one working day (24 hours), for example. A lazy culture does not work in start-ups, and small problems can become huge if you do not react in time. It also gives a company a great reputation if all enquiries are answered promptly.

A typical email problem is that too many people are involved, or you are releasing too much information. Do not give people information they do not need. Delete possibly systematic parts of an email feed, so only the relevant part (the top of the mail) is sent to an external partner. This prevents irritation over a long email correspondence, and you also thereby prevent confidential material being sent unintentionally.

Moreover, it can be effective to write emails as bullet points, even if the message is very simple. It helps with understanding and facilitates a response. Many of your emails will be read by busy people, for example on a smartphone in an airport, thus messages should be as visually simple as possible. A great rule you can use when writing emails is KISS (Keep It Simple, Stupid).

Another tip: if an email you plan to send is very important, print it and read it on paper before sending it. You see errors on paper that you do not see on a screen.

And finally: do not check your emails constantly. It destroys your concentration regarding other tasks. Instead, take time to speak with people and to solve complex tasks, then check your emails in the intervals in between.

Manage your passwords

In modern times, we are connected to a variety of products and services that require passwords. These include social networks, cloud storage, frequent flyer memberships and much more. Additionally, we need to remember security codes, bank account numbers and so on. A busy person can easily have 50–100 passwords, etc., if not more. The easy solution is to have a single app on your smartphone where all these are stored. To open this app, you need to remember only one single password. iPassword is a popular example.

Sign on the Road When you build up a business, you sign documents all the time. It has become more and more accepted to use an e-signature, which is easily done on a smartphone or tablet. Download the free app Adobe Fill & Sign, for instance, which takes about a minute to learn to use and enables you to sign and send a document faster than in any other way while automatically filing copies, which evidently also help you maintain a record of what you have signed.

Use time-saving tools when designing documents

When you prepare offers and create presentations, meeting summaries, etc., you easily end up typing the same text passages, numbers and other things again and again. There is a solution to that. Applications such as PandaDoc make it possible to create a small toolbox of such things, so you can place various subcomponents in where they fit, with a single click for each. Thus, producing documents becomes similar to playing with a set of LEGO bricks that you put together without moulding each block again every time.

PRODUCING DOCUMENTS BECOMES SIMILAR TO PLAYING WITH A SET OF LEGO BRICKS THAT YOU

PUT TOGETHER WITHOUT MOULDING EACH BLOCK AGAIN EVERY TIME.

Organize meaningful meetings

Here are some tips on meetings:

- Create an agenda, clarifying what the meeting is about, and distribute it well in advance of the meeting.

- When you send out the agenda, indicate the duration of each topic.

- Make it clear who the organizer is.

- Potentially, make a penalty system for people who are late, where penalties can be contributions to a beer fund or the like.

- Do not invite people who are not important for the meeting – do not waste their time. If you see someone you don't know on an invitation list, check in advance on LinkedIn or elsewhere who they are.

- Everyone should turn off their phones (flight mode) at the beginning of the meeting. Take breaks during which people can check emails and then return to the meeting fully focused.

- Speak only if you have a purpose and something relevant to say.

- If someone mentions critical issues during the meeting but these are not relevant to the meeting itself, note them down for another time and move on.

- Do not take notes electronically, unless you are offline, otherwise you may be distracted by emails, etc. Instead, take notes by hand or keep offline while taking electronic notes.

- Do not arrange or allow parallel sessions during the meeting.

- Use only the time that is allocated.

- Meetings shorter than 20 minutes, for example, can be conducted while standing (people sit still for too long anyway).

- Consider walking meetings, for instance in a park.

- Send out a meeting summary with action points and responsibilities. Write this within 10 minutes of the end of the meeting and circulate it within 20 minutes.

Maintain a positive attitude

'Maintain a positive attitude' may sound like something some smart and fresh fellow would say, but you can deliberately create a positive attitude that provides more energy, which is contagious. Generally, think in favour of your project. Laugh at the problems. Start conversations by mentioning positive aspects, even if the topic of the conversation is a problem. Positive attitude gives energy, just like sport and coffee do, but it's free and takes no extra time.

You will be happier if you act happy

In a famous psychological experiment, people were commenting on how funny they found cartoons, while they had to hold a pencil in their mouth. Some were asked to hold it across, so they physically had to smile. Others were asked to place the pencil straight ahead, forcing a sour grimace. The result was remarkable: those who held pencils across their mouth on average found the cartoons funnier – merely because they had to smile since they could not drop the pencil. This phenomenon is also called 'priming' among psychologists.[3] It explains why conscious positive attitude creates more energy and well-being. It also explains why people who have good and high expectations tend to get further in life or with a given project – and why leaders expecting their staff to be productive are more likely to get the desired result. This self-fulfilling phenomenon is called the Pygmalion effect. Use it.

Maintain your social ecosystem

Your social ecosystem is crucial. We can start with the observation that some people are phenomenal at making things happen, while others are not at all. The significant difference often lies in the ability to stimulate cooperation – and as a part of this to build social ecosystems.

What are social ecosystems? Let's start with friends. Social scientists have found that on average people have roughly 50 good friends; they tend to know around 150 whom they would invite to a big party (if they could afford to do so); another 350 they merely know but wouldn't invite to that big party; and another 1000 whose name they know. This is their personal ecosystem.

These figures harmonize well with findings from 2012 when scientists found that Facebook users on average had 245 Facebook friends. But how many were there if you took another two steps, i.e. to friends of friends and their friends? The answer was about 160 000 different people![4] Of course, we should note that serial entrepreneur Elon Musk has several official and unofficial Facebook pages, including one in which he is followed by more than half a million people. Oh yes, and football player Cristiano Ronaldo is followed on Facebook by more than 100 million fans.

Now let's think about companies. Skilful managers can be great at creating events where many potential customers, suppliers and, for example, journalists and bloggers within the industry participate. These participants will obviously notice how many other important people are gathered around the business beyond themselves, and each person participating will thus become a part of the overall marketing message to everyone else. People with good social skills are adept at gathering people around themselves and their cause, but they also offer to connect people outside their own cause and they hope that others do the same for them. 'My friends can be your friends' could be their motto. Sharing friends is not only sympathetic, it is also a part of being effective.

Let's go back to social media and consider the following. You hold a speech in front of 100 people. The 100 people in the room will watch it – fine. But if you get it filmed and publish it on Facebook, your Facebook friends – maybe 245 people – can also watch it. That is a much bigger audience. And if you allow it, in principle everyone on Facebook is able to watch it, though of course not everyone will do so.

That's just Facebook. There are many other social media with enormous impact, such as Instagram, Twitter, Tumblr, Pinterest, YouTube, LinkedIn, Snapchat and Xing plus Renren in China, to mention just some of the biggest. Together they cover several billion people. None of the users is obviously interested in a boring, uninteresting message, but if you post something that is catchy, you can potentially get a lot of people to read your message through your social ecosystem.

Isn't it difficult to use such media? Not as difficult as you might think. First, each of the platforms is very user friendly and they all also work with social media management software (SMMS), such as Falcon, Hootsuite, Involver, SocialBooster, Buffer, Sprout Social, AgoraPulse, Viralheat, SocialClout and many others, which can help you publish a message on a variety of social networks at the same time.

Imagine that you have an exciting message – for example an entertaining video clip – and in minutes you can publish it on 10 different social

Roles within the network

Use people in your social network actively. An effective entrepreneur and a start-up project will often use a structured network of so-called ambassadors, beta testers and other test users, power users, influencers, evangelizers, bloggers, media contacts, pundits, market analysts and everyone else that they systematically nourish with information via social media and other channels. In addition, they might even prepare contests on social networks (e.g. design or innovation competitions) and thereby open parts of their product to make it easier for others to develop applications for it.

networks. Do you think this will increase your audience? In Chapter 13, on marketing mix, we will give you some practical tips about using social media.

Efficiency in other words

We have now studied personal effectiveness from a variety of angles, covering everything from the relationship with your family to your leisure, health, use of electronic tools, travel planning, delegation, networking, meetings and much more. This is important because start-ups have huge tasks but few staff and short runways to potential bankruptcy. However, there is another very important aspect of personal efficiency: the ability to make an impact and win. We will address this in the next chapter.

3.
MY PUBLIC IMPACT

Throughout Chapters 1 and 2 we looked at, among other things, the personal characteristics that may increase the chances of success as an entrepreneur and considered methods to increase the personal effectiveness in your everyday life. However, there is a third perspective to the personal factor, which is vital to entrepreneurs: the ability to break through – to be heard and seen in public. In this chapter, we will look at various practical aspects of this, as personal persuasion power can make an important difference as to whether you get the start-up project up and running or not.

People who work in well-established, well-known and profitable companies might survive without exhibiting the greatest personal impact, as the company does the job for them. But start-ups often depend entirely on the entrepreneur's personal ability to persuade and force change, and there are vast differences in how good people are at this. We have probably all noticed that some people really make an impression in the media, while others do not. Similarly, there are some sellers who could sell sand in the Sahara and others who could not sell ice in the self-same place. And some people are brilliant at negotiating, while others are not.

START-UP COMPANIES OFTEN RELY ENTIRELY ON THE ENTREPRENEUR'S PERSONAL ABILITY TO MAKE CHANGES.

Some might say that such capabilities cannot be taught, but we think they can. The ability to make a personal impact for sure involves a degree of innate talent, but certainly it is also a craft that can be taught and rehearsed. In this chapter we will therefore review some simple principles regarding how to approach media interviews, public speaking, corporate presentations, participation in exhibitions and trade shows, sales meetings and leading sales processes and negotiations – and get results!

How do I get invited to give speeches?

In our experience, an efficient way to get invited to give speeches at important events is to publish written articles about the subject, but also videos where you talk, so that event organizers can check whether you are an engaging speaker. Another way is simply to contact the organizers and propose yourself as speaker. Or you could get listed with corporate speaker agencies. However, there are obviously many more avenues, such as posting about your speaker activities on social media or offering them on your website.

How do I prepare great speeches and presentations?

Let's start with speeches and presentations. How do you prepare a great speech – a product tour, a business presentation or any other professional presentation? And how do you make a good appearance on a stage? Some decades back, ambitious speakers would largely take inspiration from great actors, and this is still a great idea. However, today we can also check out great speakers on forums such as:

- *TED Talks.* A forum where speakers are given at most 18 minutes each to present an engaging story.

- *PechaKucha 20×20.* A presentation format where you show 20 images, each for 20 seconds. These images (typically Power-Point slides) advance automatically while you talk, which means that you have 6 minutes 40 seconds to make an impact.

- *Ignite Talks.* Events where speakers each have five minutes to talk on a subject accompanied by 20 slides, each of which is automatically replaced after 15 seconds.

Of course, the most popular of these speeches are widely studied on the net, and many books, such as *Talk Like TED*, have been written to summarize what works best and why.[1]

The first important tip concerns the message. It is useful if mentally you can boil down your story to a single sentence including approximately three subsections. Tell yourself that two weeks after you have delivered your speech, everyone present should still remember your main theme and your three messages – because if they can, then you have probably succeeded.

But how do you achieve this? A good starting point is to connect your messages with something memorable because it is dramatic and speaks to the emotions, such as an engaging anecdote or a visualization. Six minutes after your speech is over, people might remember many of your shown data; six weeks after, they remember most of your anecdotes and visualizations – but probably not the data; six months after, they probably remember *only* your visualizations and anecdotes. So work on those. They are vital. Really!

If you have enough time for it, and you are a novice, here is another tip: film yourself doing your presentation. Once done, look through your recording – first without sound where you take note of all your movements, your timing, your bad habits, etc., then with sound but without picture, where you notice your tone of voice, your way of speaking, and so on. List what you need to change. Then practise.

How do I structure a good speech?

Let's say that you are comfortable with your message and disposition and you are now preparing the actual speech. How should you structure it?

A rule of thumb says that a good presentation should contain around 10% that builds credibility – why do you know anything about this subject? Around 5% should cover your motives for preparing the presentation. Approximately 15% should be documentation and evidence of your claims. And most importantly, around 70% of the speech should focus on the emotional aspect. This distribution should not be taken too literally, of course.

But there is one thing that can make or break a presentation: the beginning. This is incredibly important because if you do not connect with the audience during the beginning of your speech, you might never connect with them. Indeed, during the first few minutes you must convince the audience that what you are going to say is interesting and important, and that you are worth listening to.

As a part of that – and this is really important – you should probably include why the topic motivates you: why do you do what you do? Why is your company doing as it is doing? What is your motive? (Also consider whether the speech is taking an 'I' or 'we' approach. It is good to be personal occasionally, but if it is the company speaking, you should use 'we'.)

It can prove effective to use an anecdote very quickly. This can be about other people or a personal experience. For example, it may be about an experience that led to a surprising result. One success story is good, but it can be even better to tell a story that follows the Hollywood model: it went really badly before it went really well (at least half of all movies seem to follow this model).

After this anecdote, it is often a good idea to summarize what you want to talk about. Maybe something like the following: 'Within the next 15 minutes, I want to walk you through . . . and I will show you why x, y and z is true and important.' A good rule of thumb is therefore: (i) explain what you are going to talk about and why, (ii) talk about it and (iii) summarize what you just talked about.

After the introduction, you get to the subject matter of your speech and now it is important not to become boring and unengaging. Therefore you should include multiple anecdotes in your story and it might be relevant to include visual or verbal examples of your messages. However, from time to time you might deviate from your main storyline and insert a little entertaining tale. That way you give your audience a small, fun, mental break before continuing with the more serious stuff. Consider these as being similar to coffee breaks.

You can also include surprises in your story – unexpected turns. And if you have something important to present visually, such as a vital statistic or a product, mention it before you show it. In other words, create some positive mental tension. Just think of how new cars are launched at car shows: first, they are covered by a cloth, then the cloth is pulled off. Tension works.

How do I use illustrations during my speech?

You may make great speeches and presentations without PowerPoint, but if indeed you do use this tool, beware of the concept 'death by PowerPoint', which means that your audience dies of boredom if there are too many slides.

But is that always the case? No. A TV documentary has a speaker most of the time, but it also includes visual images – all of the time. And that may work very well – no 'death by images' there. Why not? Because a skilled video producer ensures that the spoken word and the visual images do not compete but instead reinforce each other. How? First, the typical TV documentary imagery does not require you to read. In other words, the spoken language and pictures can work well together if the former brings facts and the latter arouse emotions. A similar effect is created when a movie has background music: this rarely confuses the viewer but rather reinforces the impact.

So, the conclusion is this: too many slides are a problem only if they make the audience focus on something different from what you are saying. If the slides are in fact amplifying your message, all is good.

THE SPOKEN LANGUAGE AND PICTURES CAN GO VERY WELL TOGETHER IF ONE BRINGS FACTS AND THE SECOND AROUSES EMOTIONS.

This leads us to another important tip: generally, you should not have too many words on a PowerPoint slide, or maybe none at all. Why not? Because words on slides make people concentrate on reading rather than listening, or on listening rather than reading, and in either case they will be distracted. However, the exception is if the written words literally reflect the spoken words *while you say them* and you use this technique briefly. If this is done synchronously – words pop up on your slides the moment you start saying them and disappear as soon as you have finished – it works very effectively.

Bullet points can be used, but great speakers usually avoid them. Should you do it anyway, for example in a summary of the three points that your speech focused on, you can let each bullet fade out as you read the next. Again: if there are words on your slides, it should be because you say those exact words at the same time as they appear on the screen. The exception – the only exception – may be a headline, for example on a graph so that your audience understands what it illustrates. Again: slides should predominantly be pictures without words, and if they are structured like this, you can have many slides.

Slides can also serve another useful purpose – by using them, you avoid having to look down at prewritten text to remember the speech. People who read aloud from a paper frequently do not involve their audience, unless the speaker is particularly skilled at this.

Incidentally, there is a simple aid that many speakers often forget: blank slides. It is a huge but common mistake to have a slide showing for some time on the screen while you are in fact speaking about something else. Therefore, at many presentations you will need several blank slides, and for the same reason, black or very dark is the best background colour. An alternative is to press the button 'B' during your presentation (if you have a keyboard) – if you do so, you will get a black screen.

When you have almost finished your speech, it is usually a good idea to summarize. This summary must be strong enough to ensure that the audience does not forget the perhaps three key points. If this is done properly, it will cause them to remember the speech for the next 30 minutes. But as already mentioned, what can make them remember the speech after three months are good anecdotes or something similar, which spoke to their feelings.

As the very last thing, you can end the presentation by giving people tips on how they can follow up. Put your website address and maybe also your email or LinkedIn address on the last slide, and if you later need to submit the PowerPoint electronically, you should add your email address. If you are speaking at a conference, mention that you or your employees will be found, for instance, in the room in front of the conference hall after the presentation – this is appropriate for people who want to know more, look for career opportunities, etc.

The good speech

What You Say:
- Open with an anecdote and what motivates you
- Summarize what you will talk about
- Go through the main story, but insert anecdotes and perhaps funny deviations
- Perhaps build in surprises
- Summarize what you said and draw around three conclusions
- End by leaving people options for how to follow up with you.

Your Slides:
- Show text on slides only if they don't take attention from your speech. Best is only text that you quote verbatim. The rest of the slides should be pure images.
- During parts of your speech when you are not referring to anything on a slide, show a black/neutral slide.

How do we optimize our presence at exhibitions and fairs?

Let's move on to exhibitions and fairs. It is often overwhelming to participate in such events since there are people, noise and chaos everywhere. Our experience is that you must have a system for how to operate at such events, otherwise you will not get enough out of them.

First tip: make copied electronic or printed forms to be used by all your team members. Fill out a form for each important contact that each person has met, whether it is a potential customer, supplier, employee or otherwise. Write down the name and contact information, with notes on what was discussed, as well as who within your company is to follow up and

Lars on how to get something out of your participation in exhibitions and fairs

In one of my companies, we were very good at participating in exhibitions for almost no money. For example, we convinced Intel to give us a free corner of their stand. Of course, lots of people came by to see what Intel had to show and then we took it from there. However, we were also great at making new contacts.

How? We made it into a game. During each day we all completed many contact forms, but each evening, after a long day, we met and alternately put today's 'hottest' leads on the table, as when one is showing his hand in poker. One of us was asked to be a judge and award gold, silver and bronze for that day's lead generation, which triggered the premiums, typically consisting of beer. The number of leads counted, but if someone could introduce a lead, which, for example, was the CEO of a large company that was interested in a major purchase, it was like putting a royal straight flush on the table. The overall effect was that everyone ran around like hungry hounds and brought home tons of leads and had fun all along.

when. Get business cards or other information that you can transfer to LinkedIn. Have a stapler available on the stand so that business cards can be attached to forms. Alternatively, do it electronically on smartphones.

How do we get set up on social media?

Here is how we think you can set up your company up to be efficient on social media:

1. *First, secure your company's brand presence by opening accounts on all potentially relevant social media.* Make accounts for your company and thus brand with at least LinkedIn, Instagram, YouTube, Facebook, Skype, Twitter, SlideShare and Vimeo. Do this just to ensure that no one else does it. Each channel has advantages and shortcomings – you need to find the best.

2. *Activate the most important social media accounts.* Choose accounts or channels that you want to activate and make use of early. Within each of these, use your corporate logo plus nice background pictures and add relevant descriptions of your business in each of the profiles. To get inspiration, check out some companies you admire. Also, if you happen to be an author, create author pages on Amazon and Goodreads. Please note that you can link your Instagram to your Facebook account, since the latter owns the former.

3. *Create a presence on Wikipedia.* If there isn't one already.

4. *Open employee social media accounts.* Ensure that all employees have individual LinkedIn accounts. Key staff may also use personal accounts on Facebook and other media to post about your business. Profile photos should ideally be at least 600 pixels wide and asymmetrical. And please, use the same personal photos on all your accounts in order not to confuse people.

How do I use social media to become better informed?

Social media provide an invaluable door to a lot of content, but also for you and your company to communicate. However, in order to be inspiring, you need to be inspired. So we suggest that you dedicate perhaps an entire day, if not more, to arranging your information inflow from the web and social media.

Entrepreneurship is very much about empowered people and teams taking control of their learning. Your use of social media is about not just finding information but also connecting to people and sharing viewpoints, insights and experiences. This is often referred to as the Seek–Sense–Share framework:

- Seek information through networks of people who provide and filter data for you, just as you do for them.
- Sense what it all means.
- Share not only information but also its deeper meaning.

Through this process you develop 'communities of practice' with people who add real value to each other. For instance, you may share a new practice first with a professional community of practice before publishing it to your general social networks. It's a holistic approach, not one that compartmentalizes work and life, but something that helps us to make sense of the whole messy, complex world we live in. As such, it's always a work in progress, but it starts by connecting to others.

The first step in order to follow the brightest minds is to sign up to respected outlets such as CB Insights, The Economist or MIT Technology Review and list yourself as a follower of the most inspiring people and organizations in your industry or ecosystem. If they post on blogs, sign up to feeds or mails.

Next, we recommend setting up profiles with feed aggregators and content curation platforms – these are services that filter and aggregate content from hundreds and thousands of sources and create a filtered or personalized news and feature service for you. This combines the seeking and the sense making of quality knowledge, information and data sources.

Here are some feed aggregators and content curation platforms that we like (new ones keep coming up):

- *flipboard.com* and *feedly.com* provide personally tailored news feeds and feature stories for your tablet, smartphone and computer.

- *Scoop.it*, *RebelMouse* and *Paper.li* are other services you may take a look at and consider depending on how you want to make the most of the social media content that you find useful. All three are content curation services that can help you have a powerful voice on social media.

- *futurity.org* aggregates great university research within your personal areas of interest. You can also use *alltop.com* and *Google Trends* services, which give you the most popular and trending stories within different segments.

- *Google scholar* is great for nerdier academic research.

- *LinkedIn influencer* is a list of important people writing longer posts – you can choose who to follow.

- *TED.com* is famous for TEDTalks; high-quality speeches that are a maximum of 18 minutes long. The talks are divided into main subject areas and are searchable. There are also smartphone/tablet apps.

- *getabstract.com* provides 10-minute abstracts of 1000 popular business books. Also available as an app.

- *audible.com* offers a range of audiobooks that you can listen to while travelling, jogging, etc.

- *Podcasts* – Google your areas of interest together with the word 'podcasts' and you will find a lot of links to audio blogs which you can typically download for later use alongside audiobooks.

- *Kindle* is a great way to read books and make highlights in them, which makes it easy to read electronically in broad daylight.

- *Google alerts, commun.it, Hootsuite, Sprout Social, Social Mention* and others enable you to track mentions of your company, products or key people, for instance.

Once you have found a good setup of seeking information and sense-making, you should share your messages and your curated content. A couple of tools in this respect are:

- *Buffer.com.* It lets you schedule and manage social media posts across all of the most widely used channels and you can individually customize each post for all of the different platforms it gets posted to. Buffer also shares your content at the best possible times throughout the day and tracks links so that you can see what content gets the most traction.

- *Hootsuite.com.* Hootsuite makes it easy to manage the sharing across all your social media accounts. It's easy to add accounts, easy to schedule posts across all major platforms and easy to add account managers. In addition, the company has a robust training platform that teaches not just the tools but how to think about social marketing as a whole. As a package, it is one of the best out there for the price.

How do I promote my social media presence?

Next steps are about making it easy for people to find you on social media. The first thing to do is to create so-called 'vanity URLs'. To explain, on Facebook, LinkedIn and some other platforms, you can change your account URL (internet address) from the standard long list of letters and numbers to something shorter and nicer. You can change your Facebook URL at facebook.com/username and for all the other networks we suggest you Google how to do it. If someone has registered your obvious vanity URL without using or deserving it, you can contact the network and complain to get it.

Second step is to upgrade your email signature – paste the relevant vanity URLs into your email signature. For instance, each of your emails may have a signature that includes your name, email, mobile phone number, LinkedIn address, personal or corporate Facebook address and corporate website URL.

Finally, we recommend you cross-reference what you do on social media – for instance, list on Facebook where else you have social media activities, if possible, by providing the links.

How do I become a blogger and make webinars?

Perhaps you also want to become a blogger. This can be done via WordPress.com or other sites such as medium.com. Medium has a WordPress plugin, which enables you to post on both simultaneously. Also, import stories from, say, Facebook straight into medium.com. You can subsequently use the blog to make long-form posts and then social media to promote it. Another idea is to become guest blogger on someone else's platform. If they have a big audience that you don't have, use their platform to reach this audience.

Another efficient tool is a webinar – an instruction video clip relating to your business. For this, you need to set up a webinar account – we recommend using Webinarjam.com as the content engine, Simplero.com as the platform for selling the content and Stripe.com as the payment gate.

Which equipment do I need for multimedia posting?

Now you are set up with the networks. To make popular posts, you need to buy basic hardware – the two pieces we think are close to mandatory are (i) headset(s) for Skype calls and for listening to audio in aeroplanes, etc.

and (ii) selfie stick, if you want to distribute your own photos and video takes. Additional equipment for making your posts more professional includes (iii) wireless microphone for your phone, (iv) tripod for your phone, (v) cell phone holder for your car so you can attach the phone to the windscreen for selfie videos and (vi) steadicam for stabilizing video takes when you are moving. You can buy all of this on, for instance, Amazon.com for a couple of hundred pounds max.

If you want to travel with a professional mini-studio, we could recommend, for instance, a Zoom H6 Six-Track Portable Recorder, which can be bought on Amazon for a few $100, perhaps combined with DT297 headsets, which cost a few $100 each. The combination of professional compact mobile recording equipment and headsets for, say, three participants in an interview would cost around $1000.

How do I make compelling social media posts?

So now you are set up with accounts and equipment and thus ready to post, but how do you do that most efficiently?

The first important point is that your themes must be interesting and should not be like commercials. Instead, you should post about things that are not only informative but also odd, fascinating, funny, charming, or in other ways engaging and creating curiosity.

Second word of advice: always (always!) include photos or (better) video. You can do this by linking to illustrated stories or by attaching your own visuals. If you are a frequent and professional poster, you may use a tool like canva.com, which has graphical templates and single graphs that you can drag and drop directly into your post.

Please note that if you upload your own video, it will start playing as people scroll over it – and at least in Facebook, the algorithms will probably distribute stories with video wider than other stories, since they want to compete against YouTube, which is owned by Google. As an aside, the main reason that you need a Vimeo account is that if you have recorded a rather long video with your smartphone and need to send it somewhere, Vimeo will compress it on your phone and then generate a download link.

Apart from graphics, it's important how you structure your post. Explanatory headlines can work, whether it's a single word in **bold** or a short sentence. Below this headline, get to your conclusion within the first one to two lines. If what comes after is long, try to divide it into bullet points. If you do that, then the headline might be something like '12 steps to get set up with social media'. An illustration plus a list tends to be really popular.

Hyperlinks are also good. For instance, in Facebook you cannot make notes in normal posts, but from the left bar on the homepage you will find a little menu item called 'notes'. This feature allows you to make hyperlinks. Another useful feature is found on ClickToTweet.com, which enables you to make a part of your text on social media into tweets – users with Twitter accounts just need to click on the highlighted text and then they get a tweet, which they can share with others.

Of course, there will be people who disagree with some of your posts or generally dislike your company. Perhaps they are right, but perhaps not, and no matter how unfair or annoying this then might be, it's normally not a good idea to write rude answers. And if you want to remove their comments, don't delete them as this will damage your reach; hide them instead.

How often should I post?

A summary of 14 studies of this question led us to the following conclusion about when you should post (assuming you know in which time zone most of your target audience lives):[2]

Platform	When to post (time zone for your main target audience)	How often to post
Facebook – best for high-quality, low-frequency activity. Content can mix personal and professional	Thursday, Friday, Saturday and Sunday are best days. Early morning works for 'likes', 1 a.m. is best for clicks and 3 a.m. is best for engagement. The most efficient for mid-afternoon posts and most efficient for engagement.	1–2 times a day or 5–10 times per week
LinkedIn – for high-value/low-frequency content. Content is rarely personal and may be technical	Best days are Tuesday, Wednesday and Thursday. Best times are 7–8 a.m., 12 p.m. and 5–6 p.m. Hashtagged keywords increase reach.	Once per day
Twitter – for high-value/high-frequency professional, curated and augmented content. Great for links to high-quality, relevant articles	Daily – Twitter is global in nature, going beyond friends and local networks. You may repeat posts to optimize for normal working hours in, for example, Europe and the Americas.	Three times a day or more – perhaps much more
Instagram – a photo palette with short text annotations	Best to post every day. Posts between 2 p.m. and 5 p.m. get most likes and engagement.	1–2 times per day or perhaps more
Blog – a platform for original in-depth content	No general rules	Approximately twice a week

Please note that if you have lots of friends and followers, they won't see all of what you post, nor will all of them get access to everything that you post. This is decided by algorithms developed and constantly revised by each network.

However, there are some things you can do to increase effect. The first is to hang around after you have posted something and respond to the feedback. The algorithms will notice that you tend to do that and consequently promote your posts more, which makes sense.

Another tip: as your network expands, you should try to learn more about who the friends and followers are and how they react to your posts. SocialBro, Likealyzer or the tools in Hootsuite or other cross-platform publishing tools can give you that information. Also, use Facebook Analytics and Facebook Insights to check when your reach and user interaction are greatest.

How do I use social media at corporate events?

Whenever something interesting is happening in your business – a speech, a promotional event or a product launch, for instance – don't forget to use social media to cover it. Take out your phone, stick it on a tripod or selfie stick and make a recording! If you want to livestream it or take photos for Instagram, then you are likely to get more coverage. Twitter, Instagram and Facebook are especially good for this.

Note that if you take photos with somebody else, they might post them and tag you, which will promote the event even more, since all their friends will see the tag. Of course, if you tag other people, it will have a similar effect: their communities become available to you, and vice versa. You may get a similar effect by tagging companies.

A particularly efficient communication tool can be a live ask-me-anything (AMA) session. The method is simple: you livestream over Facebook, for instance, preferably using a wireless microphone and a tripod for your phone, then you let people write questions. A few tips though: it's good to have some questions ready beforehand, in case you don't get enough during the session.

What is the 70:30 rule?

Both for sales and marketing, you should bear in mind the so-called 70:30 rule, which says that 70% of the time regarding your media activities, you should have dialogues with the customer where the customer speaks and takes the initiative. This 70% can include bidirectional communication between two or more clients discussing your product via a platform such as a corporate forum on Facebook or a dedicated website. The remaining 30% of the time, you should control the communication and provide the information.

It can also prove to be effective to use so-called search engine marketing (SEM). Google AdWords is probably the most well known and it is clever because you pay only per lead or click, which is a great advantage, especially for new businesses. Many companies also use Search Engine optimization (SEO) to become more visible on the web. However, in our opinion, this has become less and less effective.

In any case, this is all about making your website present on the internet, so it is more likely to show up in people's searches for relevant topics. You pay for SEM, whereas SEO is free (except for the time spent on implementation).

How can my business become well covered by the press?

Let's talk a bit about the art of tackling the media. First, if you would like to make yourself interesting to the media, it is rather simple: be interesting.

You must have an interesting personality, or your company should do something that seems generally interesting. Thus, you should have a good story, which is entertaining and/or informative to others. Also, consider how you might tie your story to something that is widely covered by the press at the moment.

Then of course you should make sure that bloggers or journalists discover you. A good place to start is on social media, where you have every possibility to tell your story, even if no one is listening at the beginning. But it can also be useful to gain technology or entrepreneurship awards. And if no one bothers to speak about your company and its products when your company is still very young, make them speak about you personally instead. For instance, elaborate on your career journey and the triumphs and difficulties you have had on the way. In other words, make yourself into an interesting story.

What should I do when I am contacted for an interview?

If you are contacted about a media interview, you should first do some research on the journalist and the media. You can of course spend a long time on this, but 5–10 minutes can be enough for you to get a fairly good feeling of how they work – even two minutes is better than nothing. The easiest approach is typically to ask the journalist for relevant web links or examples of similar productions – they usually have no problem providing these.

Before the interview, you should consider that the journalist has a job just like you do. And this is a job as a journalist, of course, not as your advertising agency, and hopefully nor as a sort of public prosecutor. The journalist and you can help each other in the process. If you do this well, you might get a lasting relationship with the journalist and the media, which most likely will help you in the future.

At the initial contact with the journalist, it may be good to ask about his or her job, speciality and purpose of the interview. This does not take more than a few minutes, which is good, since you probably both are busy.

You can also offer to send some reference material such as potential research material, photographs, resume and other background data. Also, let the journalist know in advance what you know and are passionate about. Finally, tell them what you cannot or will not talk about (because you do not have the relevant insight or do not wish to/cannot speak about exactly that subject). Thereby you will prevent a 'no comment' situation.

You should ask about the extent of the interview. Ask, for example, how much column space or airtime there will be for your contributions. If the interview is very short, you should express yourself in one-liners; if it is longer, you can offer more extensive reasoning, evidence and anecdotes. If it is electronic, is it then live, re-live or canned? It is obvious what live means, but re-live means that it will be transmitted entirely as if it were live, meaning unedited, only at a later time (though possibly with the start or end being shortened). 'Canned' is journalist slang for something that is recorded for a later broadcast which might be edited.

IF THE INTERVIEW IS VERY SHORT, YOU SHOULD EXPRESS YOURSELF IN ONE-LINERS; IF IT IS LONGER, YOU CAN OFFER MORE EXTENSIVE REASONING, EVIDENCE AND ANECDOTES.

Now think further about the interview and imagine that you are a typical viewer/listener/reader. Which statements would get *you* hooked? Perhaps prepare 1–3 key messages that you think are relevant and which will also catch the audience's attention – and which are also suitable for the journalist's mission. Also think about whether your language must be technical or not.

Should I make an agreement with the journalist?

Agreements with journalists are very common and they are typically made either orally or by email; in more rare cases, they are even on signed paper. Such an agreement will almost never involve a lawyer.

For a written article, the most frequent topic of an agreement is that you get the right to read it through, either for its overall content or (more common) for checking any 'factual errors'. Most journalists are willing to accept this if they do not propose it themselves, since it may also be in their own interest to avoid errors. If during the inspection you propose to reformulate some of the quotes, this is often acceptable; after all, they are your words. Furthermore, you can agree that the journalist can rephrase your quotes at will on the condition that subsequently you read and approve them. Other elements of an agreement with a journalist can be an embargo date for release and that some of what you tell them is off the record.

You should be aware that headlines/titles usually are created later in the process by an editor or producer and are quite often misleading. Thus, you should try to get the right to see those headlines/titles, although this is usually more difficult.

You can also suggest an email interview where you will be sent the questions via email and then you will answer them via email as well, after which the journalist may follow up with supplementary questions. Journalists rarely suggest this on their own, but it can often work brilliantly for both parties.

Regarding radio and television, you can ask for editing rights, i.e. veto regarding the editing, but this is relevant only if you have reasons to suspect manipulation – editing right is an exception and is rarely given.

For photos, you may want to ask for veto regarding which photos are being used, although only very few journalists do this. Remember that many photographers put pictures of you on stock photo libraries, from which others can buy and reuse them, unless otherwise agreed. If this is a problem for you, then say so. Finally, you can agree that material from the interview cannot be reused for other purposes.

Are there practical issues regarding the interview that I need to consider?

Before the interview takes place, it is good to check the location and the format. If it takes place in a studio, check what attire does not work. Too much jewellery, for example, may reflect in the spotlights. If it is taking place somewhere else and you can choose the venue, be creative – walking down the street, driving, on a fishing trip, in an office, a factory, a library or somewhere else. A good choice can contribute to a better interview.

Before the interview commences, think about a possible final note: many interviewers will finish the interview by giving information about your company website, for example, or where people can buy your product, but if you are unsure, you can suggest it before the interview starts. It doesn't hurt to try.

Be aware of how you are introduced – it is quite common for people to be introduced incorrectly. Check this with the journalist because they often overlook this and leave it up to the editors or producers, who then make mistakes.

As the time of the interview approaches, it is a great idea to practise what you want to say before you say it into a microphone. For example, in a taxi on the way to the television studio, tell the driver the story you intend to tell the journalist. Do the same with the makeup-artist in the media

Sell the truth

We all make mistakes and journalists often like to cover them. Think about the following motto: 'Tell the truth.'

Is it a good motto? Yes, definitely, but in business, here is one that we think is better: 'Sell the truth.' This means say it like it is, but explain it very well, so that the journalist and the audience can put themselves in your place and maybe even realize that they would have done the same thing as you if they were in your shoes at the time.

By the way, your story is often much better for both the audience and yourself if you (also) speak about what is *not* going very well. Thus, you should explain why something went wrong and what you did or will do to make up for it. By telling the truth you prevent the attack, which would occur sooner or later if you were to present a false picture. And by selling it well, you defuse a bomb.

building. Why? Because it becomes a kind of warm-up and it also prepares you for some of the questions you might get. If you can meet the journalist before you walk together to the studio, tell your story again, not only to practise but also because it gives the journalist a feeling of what they have to work with. It should be mentioned that many electronic media make use of pre-interviews before live and re-live, but this is not entirely the same as practising a few minutes before you go on stage. Pre-interviews are usually the day before or earlier.

How do I make journalists come back for more?

Here is something to think about: if you want repeated presence in public media, you probably need to be interesting, unless your product is so fascinating that it doesn't matter what you do and say. So here is a clue: you are not particularly interesting if you present a cold, calculated façade preoccupied only with not making mistakes. Instead, be yourself, a person with a personality, and tell the journalist about what motivates you or your workplace or industry. Why did you start the company? What is the purpose of the product? Include feelings, when relevant. And anecdotes, if time permits. Even better: tell them in re-live format, such as:

> 'And he said: "What you sold to me does not work". And I stare at him and think, "What on earth have we done wrong?" I do not know how to answer him. I am speechless. But the next morning, while I am eating breakfast, it strikes me suddenly that . . . '

Some people can really make the audience listen. The entertainment value can also increase if you say something completely unexpected, of course.

Regarding preparation, you should obviously keep track of your message, but it is better if your words come naturally and spontaneously. However, you should bear in mind one rule: do not respond in long phrases where the conclusion first comes at the very end. Instead, when you get a question, answer in a simple way and if possible in a single sentence. Thereafter, you can elaborate. If you do the reverse, especially in live interviews, you risk being interrupted before you come to your conclusion. For printed media there is a particular need for short, concise answers, and if you have answered with long sentences, in the editing process the journalist will often shorten what you said, so your main point might be omitted or the meaning might change completely.

Unconsciously, a lot of people use sign language in a dialogue, for example by nodding their head when they complete an answer, raising a hand when they want to interrupt, and so on. If a journalist has a habit of interrupting in the middle of sentences, you can suggest before the interview that he instead makes a signal with his hand when he wants to interrupt, then you can finish your sentence or point quicker.

Another tip: you will have far more credibility if you present serious sources to your claims. However, it may seem amateurish and distracting to look down at notes while you are being interviewed on TV – unless you read them out loud. If so, you can easily say: 'The figures are here. I will now read the numbers for you.' You can also bring something up in front of the camera, so that everyone can see it, though this may require prior agreement with the cameraman or team to function optimally.

Empty stomach, full lungs

Most people perform best when speaking on a fairly empty stomach. If you need energy before a media interview, coffee, grape sugar and just enough water are better than a burger with everything. In telephone and radio interviews, some people perform better if they stand up. In TV, you can ask how the photographer would like you to present yourself – should you lean forward, back, or some other way?

Is there anything I should be careful about in interviews?

Interviews with entrepreneurs are rarely aggressive or negative. Nevertheless, we should mention some possible pitfalls you should be aware of.

The most innocent one is the silence trap. If the reporter is silent when you complete an answer, it is typically a technique to get you to say more. But whether to continue is entirely up to you and you can choose to remain silent and indicate with a nod or gesture that your answer is finished.

Another typical trap is that the journalist tempts you to make a generalization that is not (entirely) true, then you are confronted with counter-evidence. 'You just said that you appreciate your workplace to be clean. But we have been out to visit your business and here are some pictures of what we found. Do you think this looks clean?' The best method is, as we said, to sell the truth.

What if the journalist is posing unreasonable questions or violating an agreement? Normally, the reporter in the interview is not the protagonist – it is you. However, if you think a journalist is going across the line with a question, then pull him out of anonymity: 'I don't know if your editor has told you to ask this question, but I actually don't think this is within the framework of fair journalism.' Or: 'You are asking me about this because you want to create a journalistic angle, which is populistic. However, it is also untrue.' If the journalist asks you something even though you agreed you could not speak about this during the interview, you may answer: 'As I told you before this interview, I cannot answer this because xyz. So I don't know why you are asking it anyway.' In other words, reply as a professional who is speaking with another professional rather than as a child who is insulted.

Additionally, pay note to the way the interview is filmed. Normally camerapersons/photographers are innocently filming you in a way that works well for everyone. However, in rare cases, the recording style may be fishy. For instance, if they use up-light on your face, you may look evil. If they use worm's-eye view (filming from below), you can appear arrogant. Who knows, maybe it is OK like that, but you have the right to say otherwise if you do not feel comfortable. For example, you have the right to ask to look through the lens, to see how everything looks. 'It is our product,' the producer might say, but it is your person being recorded.

When the formal part of the interview is over, you may be chatting with the journalist, which in itself is fine. But remember that unless otherwise agreed, everything that is said can be quoted. The classic error is the politician who forgets that the microphone is still on and then says something that is definitely not suitable for prime time.

One more thing: before you leave the interview setting, you can suggest that a journalist and cameraperson verify that the equipment actually worked. If something needs to be changed, it is probably easiest to do it there and then.

Generally, remember that your style is your reputation. Journalists, sources and the public discuss journalists and their work and therefore these typically take care of their reputation. But journalists also discuss their sources and the sources' professionalism and media appeal, and if you are unreasonable, boring, untruthful or unnecessarily cumbersome, you will get less access to media in the future than you might want. Show respect to media people and be professional when working with them, then they will probably treat you the same way.

How to make social media posts compelling

Often, people decide within a split second whether to read a social media post or not, and if they don't like the beginning, they never reach the end. Here are some tips for effective posts:

- *Use a compelling headline.* Perhaps either very funny, click-bait-surprising ('man bites dog') or a promise: 'Read about the seven ways to close a sale.'
- *Get to the main point instantly.* Just after the headline might follow an exceptional quote, summary or anecdote.
- *Make it super easy to read and scan.* Each paragraph should include only a few sentences. Add frequent subheadings so that the reader can scan these visually in a few seconds before deciding to dig in. The first paragraph should be only four lines because if it is too long, people may not even read it to check whether the rest is any good. You may break up with bullet points and quotes.
- *Use visuals.* Include either a video clip or an image. If an image is embedded in the text, make it right-adjusted to ease continued reading of the left-adjusted text.
- *Optimize for keywords.* Use one or several keywords repeatedly in, for instance, the URL, headline, opening paragraph, closing paragraph, subheadings, body of the articles and image captions.
- *Interlink.* Make your different posts link to each other.
- *Create interaction.* Request feedback or other action.
- *Use tags.* Tag relevant people and sites – this will increase your reach.

What should blog posts contain?

Some blogs are far more widely read than others. Here are some tips about what works – mostly, it is great versions of either so-called massive value posts or good filler posts.

Massive value posts are posts that are extremely useful and might have been sold for money:
- a large practical checklist or list of useful references/links
- the ultimate resource to a subject, such as a scientific meta study that summarizes all other studies, or a video that shows how to solve a task in such a way that nothing is left out or can be misunderstood
- a case study of how to achieve something
- words from successful people, which you tag (they will then perhaps share to their own audience)
- series of connected blogs that gradually gives you a much wider picture, as if they were single chapters of a longer handbook.

Filler posts are short posts that can be easily read on, say, a smartphone while on a train:
- a short, simple explanation of a subject
- a short description of an opinion or feeling
- an interesting little anecdote
- a product review or product comparison
- multimedia content such as infographics, videos and podcasts
- short expert interviews
- lessons from the experts
- contests (use SurveyMonkey or WordPress Polls plugin)
- updates on events.

4.
MY FACE-TO-FACE IMPACT

The last chapter was about how to make an impact in speeches, on social media and with/through the press. However, there are lots of situations where you as an entrepreneur are not trying to have an impact on many people but on only a small group or perhaps a single person. Yes, we are talking about sales and negotiations.

Either you are a salesman or you are not. And either you are a great negotiator or you are not. At least that's what we hear people say. But the fact is that while each and every normal person tries to sell ideas and negotiate terms frequently in their daily lives, being able to do it in business when large sums are at stake depends partly on training.

How should I run sales processes?

Now we will look at sales, starting with the structure of an effective sales meeting and then moving on to the overall sales process in an organization.

In principle, everyone is a salesperson at least some of the time because we all need to persuade someone to do something from time to time. For instance, you might have tried to sell the idea that it is your partner's turn to cook tonight. Indeed, we would argue that it is difficult to obtain much success in life if you do not possess at least some ability to sell, whether it is selling ideas or products. Sales is neither superfluous nor bad – it is a necessary form of communication. Born salesman types sell constantly – also to friends, their partner and their family – but everyone does it sometimes. Some people are very good at it, others are not, but it is not terribly complicated.

There are rather simple sales, such as when a cashier sells a shirt in a store. Other products are more complicated and in those situations you can make use of different techniques, which we will refer to here as the sales compass – we will get to that in a moment.

Selling techniques are not used only for products

The art of selling is not only about selling products but also, for example, about achieving major distribution agreements, convincing media to cover your company, getting VCs (venture capital funds) to give you money, or getting smart people to work for your fledgling start-up. Many of the most successful entrepreneurs can sell all sorts of thoughts, ideas and products from morning to night – and love it. Being able to sell is a gift; if you are poor at it, you should probably try to learn while also partnering up with someone who is extremely good at it.

The sales funnel

How do you organize the company's overall sales flow? Think of a sales funnel, starting with marketing and PR. Today, people who are exposed to this PR and marketing are, rather comically, often called 'suspects' by marketing pros. The next phase of the sales funnel – if you do not have purely online sales – is to create the first two-way communication between your company and the customer. This is where you proceed from shouting into the darkness to having a dialogue with a potential customer.

The sales funnel.

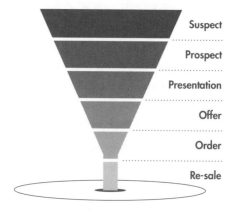

The efficient sales meeting

A sales process starts with a so-called sales opening, which is a process aiming to create curiosity and interest, as well as to inspire credibility with the many suspects. The classic sales opener is a person who is articulate and perhaps charming or charismatic who, for instance, through his or her performance at your booth at a trade fair or at a speaking podium can stimulate the first dialogue with potential customers. If your personality is that of a typical sales opener, you might, for instance, perform the company's speeches at conferences, after which people will approach you. However, as they do, you quickly redirect them to other people in your organization who can take it from there. When this happens, the people who approached you are no longer suspects in your sales funnel but are now 'prospects'. It should be noted that skilled sales openers easily can be introverted people who nevertheless have an exceptional ability to make good speeches or introductions.

Prospects are those who know about your company's product and have already shown a minimum of interest. They receive a presentation and if they like it, they get an offer, which then may become an order and later perhaps a repurchase.

Sales processes must be planned

The way through the funnel is a challenge for everyone, and in our opinion entrepreneurs with a purely technical background – engineers, for example – tend to underestimate how much planning and training are required to organize and run the sales funnel. Likewise, people often underestimate how to plan professional sales meetings. Think of it like this: if you were a film producer for a big Hollywood production company, would you start filming without a plan and a set of procedures? Probably not. Sometimes, technically oriented entrepreneurs tend to approach sales as if they were film producers with no plan at all.

Sticking with the idea of movie production, would you make a movie without casting for the roles first? Again, you probably wouldn't. Planning sales is about planning who does what. And it is also about planning what happens when they are in action. An example: some customers even have a tactic where they deliberately try to provoke you – this is called 'kicking the tyres'. Sales training often involves sales people taking turns being on each side of the desk – one kicking the tyres and the other trying to close the sale. That way, they learn to deal with different tricky situations.

What is the customer's decision-making unit?

If you make enterprise sales (business-to-business, or B2B), you should identify early on the so-called decision-making unit, i.e. the team that together can authorize a purchase. Incidentally, this may well also apply in sales to private people, where several members of a household influence many purchase decisions. In these situations, it is important that you speak with all the right people; otherwise you will waste both their time and your own. Many sales people forget to check whether they are speaking with the right people, or if so, *all* the right people.

Methods concerning the sales opening

How do you work most effectively as a sales opener? Speaking at many exhibitions as well as in the media can be very effective. Therefore, if your main job is to be a sales opener, you should offer to speak at many events. It's important to know that people who organize exhibitions often have trouble finding great speakers and therefore are open to suggestions. You could introduce yourself by referring to a YouTube video that shows how you present and what your message is, for example.

If your company deals with complex sales such as system sales of enterprise software, the sales process may include a prolonged middle phase, which is quite different from the opening phase. Here you will exchange lots of technical and commercial information while trying to build confidence in your company and product.

Important tip: if you are dealing with a technology-intensive product, we recommend that at meetings with the client company you split the technical team from the commercial team. Why? Because it can be difficult for a commercially oriented executive to understand the complexity and technology of your product. Therefore, you should make this separation because in that way you will have a technical team which focuses on explaining how the product works and a commercial team focusing on the business and the sale as well.

The final phase of your sales process is closing. If the sale is complex, the client should ideally meet a senior person such as the company's CEO together with the seller in charge. The perfect closer is a charismatic, almost hypnotic person who can quickly bond with people.

How to prepare for a sales meeting

A sales meeting is highly dependent on individual psychology, but nevertheless, it is important to have a good presentation ready and to have rehearsed beforehand. In addition, you need to have thought through the obvious questions and objections you might encounter.

Some sales people choose to deliberately exclude something in their presentation, thus indirectly encouraging the other person to ask about it. When clients then brings up the subject, they will most likely be surprised by the articulate and accurate answers they receive since they do not realize that the seller has already thought about this. Conversely, one must be careful with this strategy as it can seem as if you are poorly prepared if you do not include vital aspects. Therefore, if you adopt this strategy, you need to find a balance; if the other person does not pick up on the subject, you can then do so yourself.

Another tip for your preparation: you should have sent only parts, if any, of your presentation beforehand – that way your oral presentation can arouse more enthusiasm and you avoid having your audience keep looking at a printout instead of at you and your slides as you present them. If you are forced to send a presentation beforehand, make it much shorter than the version you will use at the meeting. That way you have a surprise for the meeting.

Using sales crutches

Material such as a PowerPoint is usually referred to as a sales crutch. A sales crutch is an element you can use as a supporting document during a meeting, for instance presentation material.

Important sales crutches in complex sales are meeting summaries, or protocols. Here we have a rather unusual proposal: before a crucial meeting, you should write a draft of the protocols, but of course without showing it to anyone outside your company. This is because it can be used as a psychological road map for yourself that you can follow during the meeting. Particularly if you are the type who thinks best by writing, drafting these will force you to think about the goals of your meeting as well as the complications that may occur as it proceeds.

And here is the kicker: if the meeting subsequently proceeds roughly as expected, you can immediately update your draft and send it out maybe 20 minutes or less after the meeting has ended. By doing this, people will note that you are very effective and at the same time you can run the meeting with a clear plan based on a good analysis.

Lars on how to use simple sales crutches at meetings

In relation to the use of sales crutches, one should generally use PowerPoint as a presentation document – certainly not Word, the reason being that in Word, one typically tends to write long, confusing explanations, whereas in a PowerPoint one is forced to get to the core of the issue.

If I have a meeting where I need to explain something important, I do not like to show diagrams and stuff on a laptop. Instead, I often print perhaps 10 pieces of paper with diagrams or text in large letters, with a maximum of two to three sentences on each paper. Then I turn it face down and turn one page at a time during the session. If useful, I can also draw and write on the pages while I walk through my story. After the presentation, I sometimes leave the pages behind. This makes the session clear and comprehensible.

When you need to present your company and your product, it is important that you have thought through the whole process. You can benefit from practising on people before you present your business for someone that really matters. Then learn from people's objections, misunderstandings or maybe their lack of engagement. By doing this, you will learn to handle people's objections and predict what they typically are looking for.

In a way, a sales meeting can be compared to a court trial. Who are the common winners in trials if the case is not obvious? They are often those who can tell the best story. If the customer is to believe that your product is great, you must think about how you should structure your story – you need to convince the jury, so to speak. Some people are better at this than others, but even if you are not the perfect salesman, you can make thorough preparations and think everything through. That way, you still have a good chance of closing deals.

Mads on how to practise before crucial meetings

When I went to MIT in the US, I decided that most of all I wanted a job in the consultancy company McKinsey. Therefore, I practised on several other consultancies first. So, I did not go directly to the European Championship final, so to speak. The other interviews were kind of friendly matches, which prepared me for the final interview.

Lars on how to practise for important speeches

Before I make an important presentation, I always try to get a chance of presenting it for a smaller, less important audience, and I recommend this to others. Back in 2015, my then 21-year-old daughter Sophie was invited to make a TED talk, which was broadcast on YouTube. As she had never held this or any other public speech before, I suggested she practise in front of a smaller audience first. She had the opportunity to practise at two schools, which probably contributed to a great and confident presentation later at TED.[1]

How do I find out about the organization I am selling to?

When you have prepared the agenda, tactics and sales crutches for the meeting, it is important to find out how employees are organized in the target company, including identifying the decision-making unit. In our experience, this is usually easy. If you can get friendly with just one single employee in a huge company – what you might refer to as an 'ambassador' – that person is often willing to elaborate on the structure of the organization, its approach, its problems and its priorities. You might also be able to find information about how the people you are going to sell to within the organization generally behaves, and whether each important person learns best by listening, talking, reading or writing. Furthermore, you might glean some information on their attention span (i.e. how long you can keep their attention).

What is the sales compass?

The sales compass is based on a sales approach originally developed within IBM. It looks like this:

Sales compass.

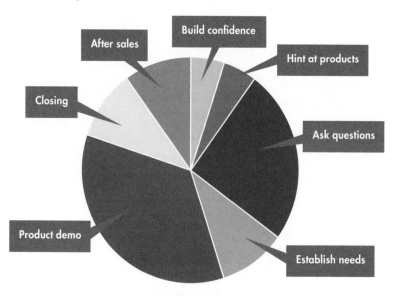

Let's start with the very first few minutes, where your goal is to build trust and interest. The premise is that you are dressed appropriately for the situation and are confident, positive and enthusiastic. It can be effective to be a bit happier than the customer, but do not exaggerate it too much.

If the customer is depressed, it is most effective if you are a bit less depressed; if he is happy, be slightly happier. It is important to remember here that if you believe the conversation will lead to a sale, it will increase your chances of converting the customer significantly. Being happy makes you more likely to believe in yourself. And remember: most smiles are initiated by a smile.

When you begin your actual presentation after maybe a little small talk, you should state from the outset what the purpose of the meeting is. A good way is to start with an anecdote that covers this. Then say something that convinces the customer that what you represent is solid and potentially attractive – perhaps a story about how great a customer found the product or the company's overall success. You should include what motivates you or the company. Imagine that you were the customer – what would impress you?

During this phase, you may imply something about the product – but just a bit and not more. Think of it as when someone unbuttons a single button on their shirt at a first date to become a bit – but only a bit – more sexy. Why only a bit? Because the most important rule in the sales compass is that *you must not describe the product before you have sold it.* Of course, this may sound ridiculous, but we shall explain shortly.

THE MOST IMPORTANT RULE IN THE SALES COMPASS IS THAT YOU MUST NOT DESCRIBE THE PRODUCT BEFORE YOU HAVE SOLD IT.

After the sales meeting's two opening phases, the vital discovery/qualification phase is next. This has two primary purposes: first, to identify the customer's needs and second, to make partial closings. Thus, you should ask about the client's current situation so that you can understand what product he possibly needs and eventually might buy. Your questions can cover everything from workflow and spending habits to budget and preferences. In some situations it is important to identify the exact decision-making unit. It's obviously best to ask these questions in an empathetic way so that the customer wants to have this conversation with you. A key rule is that the customer should do at least 70% of the talking.

To make the dialogue work, you should primarily use open questions – the so-called wh-questions that begin with 'what', 'where', 'who', 'when' or 'why'. In between these, you can add a few closed questions, which typically start with 'do', 'are', 'you' and 'can' and which may be answered with either a simple 'yes' or 'no'. These can begin with 'Do you mean that . . ', for example, to move the conversation in a desired direction.

Everything must be in moderation and never mechanical, however. If you only ask questions, you can easily sound like a CIA interrogator, and that is not a good approach. Therefore, you should occasionally bring some information on to the field which is relevant for the product. But the main point here is that you are seeking to identify what the client actually might buy and why.

Part-closings

You will also seek to do so-called 'part-closings'. In principle, it is about asking: 'What would it mean to you if I can fulfil your need?' If in some way or the other the customer responds, 'It would be attractive', he or she has opened the door to a final closing of the deal and you have made a part-closing. Why is that? Because if you can later show that you actually do have the desired solution, the customer has already given you an acceptance, as he or she previously said that this would be of interest. A good technique to get such partial or contingent acceptances is to use one simple word: 'Right?' By ending a sentence like that, you invite the customer to give you a partial acceptance. You might say, for example: 'As I understand it, you weigh low power consumption very highly, right?'

With part-closings you create trust between the customer and you and at the same time you create a rhythm with several part-closings. As a rule of thumb, we recommend that you aim for something like 5–7 part-closings before you start presenting your solution to the customer. In other words, don't talk about the product until you have – almost – sold it.

WE RECOMMEND THAT YOU AIM FOR 5–7 PART-CLOSINGS BEFORE YOU PRESENT YOUR SOLUTION TO THE CUSTOMER.

Additionally, it is important to remind the user of your role before you present the solution. This may be by saying that you only intend to offer the customer the absolute best or something similar. This will once again provide reassurance and thereby ensure that the customer reaches a decision more quickly when you present the solution.

When this discovery/qualification phase is completed, the conversation moves on to a new phase, where you as a seller must clarify the identified needs to the customer. This is for two reasons: (i) to avoid misunderstandings that can damage the sale when you are going to present the solution and (ii) to set in stone what the customer's needs are and to make sure that you have understood them correctly. We call this the requirement phase.

After this, you finally move on to demonstrate the product. How you do this obviously depends on what you are selling. However, we have four tips that are quite general: (i) you must have rehearsed the demonstration/ description multiple times until it is perfect, (ii) it must be 100% understandable, (iii) you must relate it very closely to the identified client needs, and (iv) you must engage the customer in this presentation phase. Regarding the fourth: in the ideal demonstration, it is eventually *the customer* who shows *you* how the product works.

Sell what you have

A good rule of thumb regarding sale is not to fantasize about how the product could be adapted to the customer's specific needs until you know which adjustments – if any – the customer really needs.

Imagine, for example, that you are a real estate agent and you are trying to sell a house. You are now showing the customer around, perhaps telling them regularly how it could be improved by tearing down walls, replacing the roof, etc. A great salesman, however, would call this a big mistake as the customer perhaps thought that the house was perfect from the beginning – but now you have made it sound like a restaurant project!

Closing the deal

The next phase in the sales process is closing. So how do you close a sale? A simple method is obviously to simply ask, 'Do you want the product?' If you have prepared yourself well enough and landed, for instance, 5–7 good part-closings beforehand, the customer in most cases will answer yes.

Alternatively, you can close the sale by assuming it has already happened, which is called 'assuming the sale'. This may be expressed by something like 'Should we send it on Wednesday?' Thus the customer does not make the decision because you have already made it for him or her. A variant is to assume that the sale has happened but then offer the customer two options, such as 'buy or lease?' or 'red or blue?'.

A third possibility is to tell the customer what will happen now, such as, 'What we will do now is send an invoice to your email and then . . .' That way you get an acceptance without being too direct.

After-sales

When the job is done and you have closed the sale, you should avoid another big and frequent error – stopping the meeting as soon as the customer has agreed to buy the product. If you disappear right after this, the customer is often left with a strange feeling and unanswered questions. This does not mean that you necessarily must talk more about the product – rather the contrary. However, you now have the possibility to build the relationship by talking about something that has nothing to do with the sale, since there is no commercial game between the two of you any more.

In addition, customers can often refer you to other potential customers and are often willing to do so right after they have made their initial purchase decision. Therefore, you should ask whether the customer knows someone who might also be interested in your product. Now is the best time ever.

About objections in the closing phase

One way to handle objections to your offer is to ask the client to list all doubts and objections they have before answering any of them. That way you avoid fighting against something that has no end – and if you manage to tackle the objections, you have closed your deal.

Managing complex sales

If you do complex solutions sales, a useful tool after sales meetings, besides writing the protocols, is to make a sales-oriented 'letter of intent' (alternatively referred to as 'heads of agreement'), which outlines the essence of the agreements without complex legal language. In such a document, using large, simple letters, you can write what the other company is doing and what your business can contribute, plus what you can do together. This will show the potential synergy between you and the other company. The document can then circulate in both companies and act as an effective communication tool. Note that such a document does not have to be signed and should in any case not be legally binding – it is used purely for communication and is essentially a sales crutch. Moreover, such a sales crutch can later be used to brief the lawyers who should rewrite the agreed intentions into a legal, binding contract.

What do I do if sales turn into negotiation?

The simple and positive outcome of a sales compass process is a completed sale. A negative one is an outright rejection. However, in some cases, the process leads to a third outcome: the beginning of a negotiation. For example, the discussion of an investment round in your company, a sale of a complex technology, a major distribution agreement, renting premises for your business or something similar often include a negotiation.

This is a very important observation to make because once you enter a negotiation and not a straight sale, you must immediately stop selling your product. Why? Because if you keep on trying to sell to a person seeking to negotiate, you will seem both weak and praying. In a negotiation, it is all about *not* pushing but rather holding back and making concessions only when the counterpart is doing so. The one who is quiet during a negotiation will typically come out better than the one who is trying to sell.

Can a negotiation process be scripted in advance?

In the previous section, we became familiar with how one can plan and script a sales process in advance. Negotiations are far more difficult to script because they are a game with many unpredictable twists and turns. If anything, they are similar to mind games such as chess or poker. And while you can train for these games, you cannot script what will happen.

However, you can know about the basic principles before beginning the negotiation game. The first one is this: just as in a traditional sales process, in negotiation it is really important to obtain the maximum knowledge of the other party's situation and preferences. For instance, in a commercial negotiation, this often involves understanding the customer's calculation of revenue, expenses and profit margins. An example of what you want to know is under what conditions a deal would no longer make commercial sense for the other party. This is called their breaking point.

There is much more. For instance, can you find out which previous agreements they have made with others? And how much they have paid previously for similar products? Under what conditions? Is there a critical time factor? Are there prestige-related factors? Technological dependence, perhaps? The more you find out about such matters, the more effectively you can negotiate.

Likewise, if you do not know your negotiation counterpart personally, it is useful to seek information about how he normally behaves in negotiations. Like Obama or like Trump?

Another good piece of preparation is to submit a proposal to the meeting agenda before a negotiating session. By writing the agenda you can affect what you will talk about and what is omitted, which is an advantage. If the other person makes corrections to the agenda, it gives you an indication of what they are looking for. Here we recommend that price discussions are scheduled roughly in the middle of the agenda. Why? Because if price is at the top, you risk the negotiations never getting beyond this point. And if it is at the bottom, all the other items that could be used as a set-off in price negotiations have already been negotiated and agreed on. So again: put the price discussion around the middle of the meeting agenda.

The fourth important thing to do in negotiations is to clarify how big a mandate your counterpart really has. In other words, what is the decision-making unit? Is there an absent manager who needs to be consulted? A board?

Where necessary, it may be a good idea to break negotiations into several steps so that the customer can consult its hinterland and get the support of all the decision-making units before moving to the next step. Here you must be careful not to end up in a 'good cop/bad cop' game, in which you successfully negotiate a complex agreement and then you must start over with the counterpart's boss.

What if the negotiation counterpart does not have a full mandate but still is the only one you can get access to? Your best defence is to match him by saying that you do not have a full mandate either. If he has an escape, you must also have one.

Your fifth important move in a negotiation is to seek a BATNA. This is an acronym for Best Alternative To a Negotiated Agreement and means that you have negotiated with others and therefore know your best alternative in the market.

THE NEGOTIATOR WHO HAS THE LEAST TIME PRESSURE IS MOST OFTEN THE ONE WHO ENDS UP WITH THE BEST DEAL.

One last thing: try to avoid time pressure. The negotiator who has the least time pressure is most often the one who ends up with the best deal. Try to make sure that you are not under pressure of time during negotiations.

When the actual negotiation begins, it is useful to clarify the type of negotiation that is about to commence. There are two basic types: partnership development and horse trading.

THERE ARE TWO BASIC TYPES OF NEGOTIATION: PARTNERSHIP DEVELOPMENT AND HORSE TRADING.

Partnership development

Partnership development is a discussion between two parties who from the start both indicate strong commitment to future cooperation. Such a debate has a win-win nature; it is important for both sides to create a strong, mutually beneficial alliance, or to increase the overall value and thus extent of an increasing cooperation, for example by addressing common problems or expanding the scope of cooperation. An example would be that the buyer of your products posts a person in your company to ensure continuous quality control, thus taking joint responsibility for the production.

This type of negotiation can be done in an honest and positive spirit, but your benefit often depends on the ability to think creatively. For example, it is advantageous if you constantly think about all the types of cooperation, which we will review in Chapter 13 regarding the marketing mix. The names of the typical elements include co-branding, co-packaging, co-pricing, co-promotion or joint marketing campaigns, joint marketing organization, joint production and joint product development. The negotiation can also involve financial aspects such as a joint venture or the sale of product rights, patents or companies.

Are there special tips and tricks in such negotiations? Perhaps most importantly, if you want to sell an idea to your counterpart, try to see whether you can get them to discover the idea before you have even mentioned it. If the other person mentions your own idea, you have probably achieved your goal.

If you cannot sell a little, you might instead sell a lot

The creative negotiator who discovers that it is difficult to achieve the smaller deal he originally tried to obtain will sometimes instead bring up a more comprehensive agreement, which then will be accepted. For instance, if you cannot sell your product, how about selling your business?

Horse trading

Unlike partnership development, a horse trading is a win-lose transaction. If, for example, the case is a price discussion, a gain for one part will result in an identical loss for the other.

In horse trading, all sorts of ploys and tricks are often used and we will now mention just a few. The first is that it is usually a significant advantage to be the one who makes the first move. Just as you normally have an advantage by sending over the first draft of the meeting agenda for a major debate, you have an advantage in being the one who comes up with the initial offer in each of the main negotiations. The reason is that you are throwing the mental anchor (which is called anchoring by behavioural psychologists). It should be added that you may be using your BATNA as an inspiration. And obviously, you throw your anchor as close as possible to the counterparty's breaking point, but without going beyond it.

You might be extreme, but not unrealistic. For instance, if the potential buyer of your product has a break-even price of $95 and therefore will lose money if you require more than that, you may start out by making an offer of $100. Then the counterparty will address the heavy task to negotiate you down, which would be like dragging your anchor through heavy sand. And here is what then happens: each time you move your anchor, you ask for something in return and ultimately your anchor's location is what determines your overall negotiation dividends. You have gone down in price, but you received a lot of other things in consideration during the negotiations.

EACH TIME YOU MOVE YOUR ANCHOR, YOU ASK FOR SOMETHING IN RETURN.

However, this might not always be as easy as it sounds. If your counterpart is just as tough a horse trader as you are, he might try to neutralize your first anchor roll with one of two popular methods. The first is to throw his own anchor far from yours and then keep quiet. You say '$105' per unit, to which he immediately says '$10' and then remains silent. Thus, you should be the next to speak, and if you are not careful, you will find that you are now in the process of pulling *his* anchor! The solution is not easy, but it is to ignore the counterproposal and add other requirements to your opening package.

The second neutralization of a radical bid is to accept it, but with prohibitive conditions. Your counterpart may say, 'OK, we accept your price of $105, if you give us a marketing subsidy of one million'. If you are very tough, you can consider outlining your entire negotiation terms at once.

Instead of these games, why can't you just open with a fair bid instead? Could you just not say, 'I believe $70 for the product is the price that is most appropriate for each of us'? Well, if you know your counterpart well and know that he is likely to agree, you can. But if you do not, you run the risk that the customer thinks the $70 was in fact your attempt at an extreme bid and thus the customer will be annoyed when you will not subsequently meet him halfway to his counterproposal of $10. You may be perceived as unfair, even though the opposite was your intention.

Lists of requirements and deadlines

If a negotiation involves more than a single area, each party will initially start out with their own requirements list, which then gradually will be negotiated down or away. Here, it is advantageous that from the outset you ensure the counterparty does not have any requirements other than those mentioned, so you do not end up fighting against something endlessly. Be very specific. Ask: 'Are you sure that these are all your requirements? There are no more? I will not negotiate them if I do not know whether there will be more requirements along the way.'

ASK: ARE YOU SURE THAT THESE ARE ALL YOUR REQUIREMENTS? THERE ARE NO MORE? I WILL NOT NEGOTIATE THEM IF I DO NOT KNOW WHETHER THERE WILL BE MORE REQUIREMENTS ALONG THE WAY.

Regarding the requirements lists, you should know that experienced and tough negotiators sometimes include so-called phantom requirements, which are requirements that actually mean nothing to them. The purpose is obviously to use these as negotiation objects.

Usually, the purpose of negotiations is that each party gradually decreases or removes their requirements. Here, it is essential that you never give a specific concession without taking time to record *why* you are doing it. For example, you withdraw your requirement number five *because* the other party withdraws his requirement number seven, and so on. In this way, you can prevent the counterparty later beginning to bring up earlier withdrawn claims. If towards the end of the process they say, 'We will still maintain claim number seven', you can answer, 'As it says in the summary of our last meeting, we withdrew our requirement number five because you withdrew your requirement number seven. Thus, if your requirement seven is back on the table, our requirement five is too.'

It is generally a key rule to take a break in negotiations each time one party has withdrawn about three requirements. This gives both parties time to think about everything before proceeding.

A common negotiating tactic is also to introduce deadlines, but you should bear in mind what we stated previously, i.e. that the strongest party is usually the one who has the most time.

An example: Let us assume that one Monday you say that the counter-party's last chance to accept your bid is on Friday at 3 p.m. What will the counterparty do? Probably disappear until Monday the following week, i.e. *after* your deadline. Unless you then actually choose to walk away from the negotiation, you will look like a poker player whose bluff has just been called. And after such an episode you will be significantly weakened during the rest of the negotiations.

PART 2.

ABOUT MY COMPANY'S IDEAS AND FUNDING

You want to become an entrepreneur. You think you have enough of the important personal characteristics for success. You imagine that you can also work efficiently enough to cope with the workload, and that you will have enough clout, persuasiveness and impact when it really matters.

But what should your product be? How do you develop the combination of ideas that can make the project a likely winner?

We will now study these questions. We will also undergo a series of more practical considerations for entrepreneurs – for example, where should you locate your company? And how do you deal with accounting standards, company names, trademarks, logos and so on?

And then there is the value creation and business model. How do you make sure that these elements will work?

Finally, there is funding. How do you fund your growth? Are you going to raise capital from others?

5.
MY COMPANY'S BASIC IDEAS

Simply put, an entrepreneurial project requires four main components: a business idea, a team, capital and execution. In this chapter we will focus on the first: the idea. Or rather on the ideas, because a successful start-up typically combines multiple great ideas. We will look at how you become good at getting ideas, but also at how you sort and analyse these.

You might have a few friends or acquaintances in your network who have an incredible number of ideas but who at the same time are working in unstructured or unsystematic ways and therefore cannot bring their ideas to fruition – 'all hat but no cattle', as they say in Texas. These types are usually quite hilarious to dine with because they are constantly mentioning new ideas, and they may be both funny and inspiring, but it will probably be you who ends up with the bill because these hyper-creative people are often penniless.

You might also know people who are good at running a business but at the same time are not the ones who get the great ideas. They might not be the most hilarious people, but at least they can execute on a project.

Whether you naturally belong more to the one or the other of these groups, the challenge as an entrepreneur is to be reasonably good at both things – ideas and execution – to achieve major success. Often, however, you must learn some of it; just as you can be taught marketing and logistics techniques, you can learn plenty of methods to get and develop ideas. Think of it as follows: if you play chess against a bad player, this person may test a maximum of three to four ideas in his head before making a move. But the good, experienced player runs intuitively – almost unconsciously – countless scenarios through his head before he makes his move. A Grand Master is great at getting ideas in the game because he has a unique pattern recognition based on a deep knowledge of the game's options.

Like the chess player who evolves from beginner towards Grand Master, you can develop capabilities when it comes to innovation and business; you can *train* your ability to develop and sort ideas.

Business idea generation

How? We can start by considering what a good idea really is. Roughly speaking, there are two kinds:

- *Unresolved problem*. Something in the world is annoying, poorly solved or missing. Your idea solves the problem.

- *Improved business model*. You implement an improvement on, for instance, an existing product, service, speed, promotion or distribution model. Your improvement might be radical, but it can also be a minor feature/benefit, which simply makes the end result better or cheaper.

But how can you create a new business model? And how do entrepreneurs find their hopefully great business idea? This question has been studied widely. The typical course is actually, as we wrote earlier, that an idea develops gradually over time and then later changes – often beyond recognition – when you start to implement it in practice.

Studies also show that entrepreneurs often forget how their idea evolved. While they will often say that it came to them in a single instant, the reality is often that it evolved over time in fits and starts. For example, Darwin described his understanding of evolution as coming suddenly, but his diaries told a different story – that actually he had circled around it for years. So yes, people tend to remember their ideas as having occurred more suddenly than they did in reality. And when entrepreneurs tell the media about their idea, they probably forget how it actually changed along the way.

Now, you may ask: "Are there any good ideas left? - has everything not been invented already?"

'No' is the short answer. As new ideas are predominantly new combinations of already existing ideas, mankind can get more new ideas the more ideas we have already invented. So if there is something that keeps you from seeking a way to entrepreneurship, it should in no way be the belief that everything important and useful has already been invented. Never have more new ideas been possible than now.

Most business ideas don't work

The fact that you have a business idea doesn't necessarily mean that you have a hidden gem in your mind. A large study from 1997 indicated that only one idea out of 3000 led to a successful business.[1]

ENTREPRENEURS OFTEN FORGET HOW THEIR IDEA EVOLVED. WHILE THEY WILL OFTEN SAY THAT IT CAME TO THEM IN A SINGLE INSTANT,

THE REALITY IS OFTEN THAT IT EVOLVED OVER TIME IN FITS AND STARTS.

Techniques to develop ideas

Our impression is that basic ideas are not really so much something you *make* as something you *find*, like truffles in a forest. Steve Jobs once expressed it very well:[2]

> 'Creativity is just connecting things. When you ask creative people how they did something, they feel a little guilty because they didn't really do it, they just saw something. It seemed obvious to them after a while. That's because they were able to connect experiences they've had and synthesize new things. And the reason they were able to do that was that they've had more experiences, or they have thought more about their experiences than other people.'

So how do you get to see something that can be combined into a new practical idea? By travelling a lot, for instance, and living in many different places. Or by working within different functions in different industries, meeting many people, reading a lot and listening a lot, much like a truffle hunter who roams constantly in the forest. Such people gather an enormous number of impressions and find lots of patterns that can be combined in new ways. Thanks to their experiences and information, they develop an open mind to change.

This also means that if you move into a tent in the desert to study your inner ear while you are waiting to get a good idea, this will most likely not happen. No, *do* something! Seek out the truffles – they will not come to you. That is certainly our experience.

So the creative process is about learning by doing. Another aspect of getting good ideas is simply to talk a lot about them. Some people are concerned about keeping their ideas secret, and to some degree they might be right, especially if it involves a patent application that has not yet been filed. However, typically, it is far better to discuss your idea with a lot of people before you start implementing it. By talking about it and listening to feedback, the idea will gradually mature.

THE CREATIVE PRO-CESS IS ABOUT LEARN-ING BY DOING.

Get inspiration by reading about entrepreneurship

A good preparation for a later life as an entrepreneur is to read about the new technology and entrepreneurship in media such as Wired, The Next Web, TechCrunch, The Verge, Engadget, Mashable, Gizmodo, TechRadar or VentureBeat.

Another way is to follow websites from leading venture capital firms such as Andreessen Horowitz, crowdfunding platforms, and accelerators such as Kickstarter, Techstars, Alchemist, Launch-Box, DreamIt Ventures, Y Combinator, Seedcamp, Bootup Labs, AngelPad, Capital Factory, 500 Startups, Startupbootcamp, Wayra, Bethnal Green Ventures, Entrepreneur First, The Founder Institute, etc.

We believe that most entrepreneurs who begin to implement an idea probably had countless other ideas. The ideas that they choose to implement are simply the best among many.

And here is something interesting: if you are constantly looking for ideas, you become much better at it over time, just like an experienced truffle collector develops a sense of where the truffles are most likely to be found. However, the following 12 systematic techniques might help you as well:

1. *Get away from your normal place of work.* Go into another room, go for a walk, do sports or something else when you are trying to envision new great stuff. It can be in such situations that you suddenly remember some experience which can be combined into a new idea.

2. *Use crowdsourcing.* Via the internet, ask the whole world which thoughts and suggestions they have regarding your idea.

3. *The long list method.* Together with your team, make a 'long list' of wild and crazy suggestions and associations. These might all sound stupid, but some may be stepping stones to something that isn't.

4. *Role storming.* Imagine that you discuss a problem with a famous, hyper-creative person. What do you think this person would tell you? This mental game can be effective.

5. *Use associations that are far-fetched.* Choose a few words from your problem and think about other problems containing the same words. Or think about how nature solves similar problems. Or check how similar problems are solved in other sectors.

6. *Use the 'five why' method.* Ask why the problem exists and then make a deep dive into the existing poor solutions with five layers of 'why?' until you get to the core of the problem. Then think of a possible solution.

7. *The poker chip method.* Everyone in a room can come up with suggestions and everyone has some poker chips, which they can give to the suggestions they prefer the most. Repeat this a few times. The richest player in the room has the best idea.

8. *Draw trees with associations.* When a branch on the tree sounds particularly promising, you set it as a new sprout next to the tree and keep repeating until you find the brilliant idea in your forest.

9. *Use the so-called Hemingway bridge.* When Hemingway had finished a chapter in a book he was writing, he would immediately write the first section of the next chapter before resting for the day. This procedure helped him to get started the next day.

10. *Write down all the ideas you get during your life and save them.* Maybe you cannot use an idea right now, but it could be relevant later in your life, or – more likely – it could be part of something bigger, you just have not realized yet. It can be a piece of a puzzle you slowly finish without even knowing what the end result will be.

11. *Think of problems as gold mines.* A known problem often has an unknown solution, and if you find this nugget, you probably have a market. So think of the problem as a positive opportunity rather than as a pain in the butt.

12. *Identify known and hyped trends – and find problems associated with them.* 'Everyone gets drones – what problems does this cause?'

Lars on a few of his methods to get ideas

I think everyone has their own methods to get ideas, and one that works especially well for me is to wait to get out of bed in the morning until I have thought for 10 minutes about a specific problem I worked with the day before. Incredibly often, I see a solution when I do so. It has something to do with being entirely fresh after a good night's sleep. My second method is to start writing on the subject. When I start writing, I have some rudimentary thoughts about it, but when I finish, these are often highly developed. And I always try to use the Hemingway bridge when I write.

Some of the most compelling business ideas involve network effects, where people or businesses connect with each other over a network created by the start-up – these types of ideas are so important that we will address them separately in the next chapter. However, there are plenty of other business models, and you will be much better at getting great business ideas if almost intuitively you can combine your thoughts with a quantity of possible business models. Appendix A contains a list of 116 business models covering network strategies, products, promotion, marketing, alliances, pricing, speed, timing, distribution and more. In the following we will just introduce some of the best.

Examples of product ideas to consider

Let's start with product ideas. How about making the ultimate luxury product? Or maybe the contrary, a product tailored for the poor? Or a no-frills version of a product for the cost-conscious middle class, perhaps enabled by a low-cost business design?

Here is another idea: you could fuse some products or services that were never merged before – just like they did in Cirque du Soleil, when they merged concepts from restaurants, sports, circus, dance and rock concerts to great effect. Again, these strategies are all described in Appendix A.

You could pursue a blockbuster model and boost it with the profit multiplier whereby you repurpose the same assets in multiple ways. Or alternatively you could use the trash-to-cash model, which is about reusing old stuff.

Here is another idea: make a deliberate counter-trend product – if everyone goes left, you go right. Or use a secondary sales model, whereby some parts of your products are free or very cheap, as you use these to lead people to other parts, on which you can make money.

Or how about doing mass customization like many of the car manufacturers do? Cool? Alternatively, you might choose to make the product simpler than ever to use. This is the 'one and you're done' strategy.

Ideas regarding speed and timing

There are many other product strategies, but some business approaches focus more on speed and timing than on the product itself – McDonald's, for instance. As an example, you can pursue a first-mover advantage or alternatively the foxier second-mover advantage strategy. Then there is trend spotting – predicting a big trend or discovering it in its infancy. Then dominate it. Alternatively, you can enable your company to always develop and launch new products faster than your competition. This is the so-called turbo-business model. Or do like McDonald's and deliver the product to the client faster than the competition.

Ideas regarding marketing

What about marketing strategies? Here are some ideas: brand building, self-service/self-ordering, direct selling, franchising and affiliate marketing.

Some companies build commercial eco-systems stimulated by revenue sharing. Others use shop-in-shop concepts or supermarket models such as in financial supermarkets, niche supermarkets or e-stores with broad product scope.

Many people don't like shopping, but some vendors apply so-called experience selling, whereby the shopping process becomes a great adventure – like when you buy a nice car and get the option to pick it up at the factory after a tour of the facilities.

More ideas? There are lots, including some relating to how you think about value and profits. To name a few: you deliberately aim for your company to become an acquisition target (build to be bought). Or your game is to consolidate an industry (consolidation play). Or you are systematically cloning other people's businesses, perhaps in different geographical areas (business model cloning). The latter model may involve combinations of second-mover advantage and first-mover advantage. First mover is in prime position to capture key deals and perhaps create network effects, but second mover can copy what first mover does while avoiding its mistakes. You can also aim for niche dominance or base your business on using idle capacity, such as Airbnb or Uber do.

More? How about cross-selling or crowdsourcing? Or you could make your company into a so-called layer player which becomes extremely good at solving the same practical problem for a lot of companies.

Of course, one of the biggest and fastest expanding business models these days is to use social media services to collect vast amounts of user data, which is used for offering highly targeted advertising platforms as well as any service where detailed client information is important. Facebook and Google are masters at this mass customer data-mining model, but there are tons of other players and market opportunities in it.

How to think about ideas

When considering such models, there are some more practical considerations that may be helpful:

- *Find models that scale.* Can your idea support massive scaling, and will profit increase per customer if the project grows like that? If you sell work hours, the answer is probably no, but if you sell software products and electronic media subscriptions that are virtually free for you to copy, maybe yes. Also, remember that the work effort to create and manage a company that can scale enormously does not necessarily have to be greater than for one that cannot.

- *Dominate or die.* Successful entrepreneurial ventures must almost by definition have some kind of market dominance; otherwise, they will compete to the point where they do not make money. Dominance is achieved by being best at something for a specific audience, and it can then be supported by patent, the lowest costs, a critical local presence, etc. Remember, customers and distributors will often find it safest to work with the dominant firm, and in times of recession, the weaker often drop out of the distributor's product lists.

- *Amazing timing.* Lots of huge start-up success stories can largely be explained with one single fact: they launched a good product at the exact time the market was ready for it. As Victor Hugo once said, 'There is nothing more powerful than an idea whose time has come'. This readiness often follows developments in core technologies – for instance, when bandwidth became cheap and powerful enough for Skype and later for Netflix.

- *Collaboration is easier than fighting.* People often speak about 'disrupting' a market, but be careful not to start a fight with the big ones if you can avoid it, because in the real world, sometimes it's Goliath who beats David. Bearing this in mind, it is often better to work with some muscular companies than to fight them.

- *The 10× rule.* As a rule of thumb, your product must be at least 10 times better, faster or cheaper if you go into an existing market with something new. If you beat the competition 10 times, you will have the market for yourself for a while. If instead you improve the product with only 10%, you will be in competition with everyone.

- *Simple is good.* The shorter time it takes to develop a product, the faster it will penetrate the market. This, as mentioned before, is a statistical observation, but the explanation is that the faster you can make the product, the simpler it is, and the simpler things are to distribute, explain and use, the easier they are to roll out.

- *Think of the need before you think of the product.* **Some inventions are solutions looking for problems. This rarely works. Therefore, all else being equal, you are better off by starting with a problem looking for a solution. You could think of a target market and a needed target price, much like Nicolas Hayek did when he revolutionized the Swiss watch industry with the Swatch Group. Thereafter, work your way back and see how this can be achieved, i.e. 'If we could make X at a price of Y, it would be able to sell Z. So how do I make X at that price?'**

- *Features are not a company.* **Many start-ups are based on ideas that actually are features instead of complete solutions. These can survive only if they rather quickly are sold to someone who has a broader solution. Launching a start-up based on a feature alone may be OK, but it is risky. 'I have developed a new video compression algorithm' doesn't sound like a promising basis for making an up-start company, in our opinion.**

- *Search barriers to entry.* **If your strategy has 'barriers to entry', i.e. factors that make it difficult for your competitors to penetrate the market and which last at least a few years, you are more secure. These barriers to entry can, for example, be distribution agreements that keep others out, patents or switching costs for the customer (i.e. it is complicated to replace the supplier), etc. This gives room for you to constantly develop the business fast enough to maintain leadership.**

- *Find a big 'whitespace'.* **A whitespace is an area where there is a need but no solution. For example, there is something that annoys you and others in your everyday life. In such cases, there is rarely an articulated demand for the product, since people have not thought about a solution to this problem. However, they will use the solution, if you can create it. As Steve Jobs said, 'It is not the** customer's job to tell me what they want. It is my job to know'. Originally, there was almost no demand for an iPad, but when it was invented, people did use it.

- *Use a rapidly developing core technology.* If performance in a core technology grows hyper-exponentially, think about where it is in about 3–4 years. Create, for example, software for hardware, which will exist only within a few years.

- *Follow the money.* If the market you want to change already exists, try to position your company around the ordering and payment processes because that is where money is most easily made. Thus, you should always consider where the money is flowing. Get straight into this part of the value chain if you can.

- *Spot a big profit pool.* Find an industry where the players combined earn a lot of money. Then innovate your way to some of those profits.

- *Bet on habits.* Can you create a product that people almost automatically will buy again and again once they have become accustomed to it? This is often possible for interdependent products and for the so-called 'experience goods'. For instance, if parents have found a nappy that works well, they will probably not change brand.

- *Capital is expensive.* If your project requires significant capital, you are going to spend a lot of time to get it and your equity position will be diluted along the way. Projects that are less capital intensive are therefore better.

- *What worked for one may work for many.* If you have just solved a problem for a paying customer, for instance by developing a software solution for them, there may be a business opportunity in scaling what you just did. Solve the same problem for thousands of others, but this time with a scalable standardized product.

- *Category kings are typically the greatest winners.* Many companies, such as Xerox, Apple, Google, IKEA, Netflix, Salesforce.com, Airbnb and Amazon, have enjoyed being in the position where a whole product category has been associated with their company and products. Such companies typically earn a large part of the overall profits in a given category.

Branding can be a core competency

The founder of Red Bull bought the rights for a drink in Thailand and made it into a global phenomenon with a great talent for branding. The core competency was therefore not the product itself but instead the very skilled branding of it.

But can it make money?

We meet lots of people with business proposals that have one little snag: there is no clear plan for how to make money on it. The typical case is someone who wants to make an app or website that doesn't seem to have any chance of ever generating a profit. However, we also meet people who make one profitable company after the other who confess that they have never created a proper budget.

In start-up business, you do need to have a clear idea of how to make money. But no, you do not necessarily need a detailed budget forecast, unless your project is capital intensive. Often, detailed budgets for start-up companies are nothing but fancy fables. However, what you *always* need is at least a 'back-of-the-envelope' calculation. And this calculation must be more than just wild guesswork; there must be some clear assumptions to test it against.

Then you need to reflect. What does this calculation show that you can earn on the project if it ends up being somewhat reasonable? £100 000? £100 million? Billions?

Some people do not have a great flair for numbers and calculations; in that case, they get someone who has the time and they can rely on 100% to spend a few hours on it. Does it make sense? Is it a big business opportunity or a small one? Tiny, perhaps? Or huge? Always think of proportions.

ALWAYS THINK OF PROPORTIONS.

We are not saying that the size of earnings is everything always because money does not have to be your motive – or at least not your main motive. But it is easier to deal with highly profitable projects because money allows freedom and flexibility. In addition, profit signals that what you sell is worth more than what you buy – which again means that you create value. A loss-making project, however, essentially destroys value. Therefore, you probably create massive value if you earn a lot of money.

So earnings are nice, and they give you money for product development as well as working capital in order to compete better if you are one day faced with tough competition. It is therefore no wonder that successful companies often call their possible money bin a 'war chest'.

There is one more thing: when thinking of financials, think also about the downside. When Richard Branson founded Virgin Air, he leased a plane from Boeing but included in the contract that he could give back the plane should his business not work. Thus, he thought of both the upside and the downside. The question is, therefore, how much can you limit your downside if your project is not going well? Can you, for example, minimize it by renting or borrowing most of your equipment rather than buying it?

Five mental tools

Above, we had some thoughts concerning the great business idea. So how do you proceed from these fundamental ideas onto actual business development? We like five mental tools for this:

1. What would be great to look back at?

2. SWOT analysis.

3. Core competencies.

4. What is it that I do not know?

5. Lasting competitive advantages.

With the first tool, you simply try to imagine what your company will look like in 5 or 10 years. Close your eyes and dream. What problems has the company solved by then, do you imagine? What market position does it have? What can you look back on with pride? What great vision has it achieved? After imagining these things, ask yourself how much you actually like that dream. Is it worth the risk and effort? And how plausible does it feel?

The second tool, the SWOT analysis, is a simple procedure to assess the market position, whether your company is already up and running or exists only in your imagination. SWOT stands for strengths, weaknesses, opportunities and threats. The task is simple: list your main conclusion about the company in this figure.

SWOT analysis.

Strengths	Weaknesses
Opportunities	Threats

After the SWOT analysis, the natural next step is to analyse the core competencies: what does the business and its team want to be really good at, i.e. better at than others – so much better that there will be a lasting market opportunity for it? By extension, you must also consider whether these skills can be threatened. For instance, are they dependent on certain founders or employees and their continued participation? Or could they easily be jeopardized by an expected development in core technologies? And if you think about your combined strengths and opportunities, does that give you some new business ideas?

The fourth step is to consider the difference between what you know now and what you need to find out before you finally can start the business. What studies need to be done? Which hypotheses need to be verified?

Finally, it may be helpful to define lasting competitive advantages. How can your company stay competitive? Should it, for example, have critical patents, distribution agreements, etc., which will both now and in the long run make it difficult for others to compete on equal terms? Or how else can it remain competitive?

Leveraging a brand

Companies with strong brands often create so-called 'brand extensions' where they sell other companies the right to use their brand against a royalty. They can also leverage their brands through co-branding, joint branding or simply by having it placed on a screen or a piece of hardware, for example, that they make. Breitling watches in Bentley cars are co-branded because Bentley would like to have a sportier image and Breitling would like to seem more luxurious.

Why do big companies often fail to implement disruptive innovation?

'It is not the owners of horse carriages who build railways', the famous economist Joseph Schumpeter once said. Often, management in large companies in an industry are perfectly aware that there is a technological quantum leap on the way, which ultimately can make their products obsolete, yet they are frequently incapable of doing anything about it. Indeed, very often, the revolutionary innovation typically comes from start-up companies. Just think of who revolutionized many of our big sectors with new products:

- *Online shopping.* Walmart or Amazon?
- *Smartphones.* Nokia or Apple?
- *Car sharing.* The taxi industry or Uber?
- *Movie streaming.* The movie industry or Netflix?
- *Large-scale accommodation sharing.* The hotel industry or Airbnb?
- *Media.* Newspaper companies or internet start-ups?

A typical reason is that well-established players are driven by short-term profit motives, causing them to postpone the time when they change. In addition, they suffer from what Clayton Christensen refers to as 'the innovator's dilemma': should they innovate and thereby risk competing against their own products?[3] The inability among many, if not most, large companies to adapt to paradigm shifts provides openings for young start-ups.

About intellectual property rights

Start-ups often make mistakes regarding intellectual property rights such as patents, trademarks, contracts and outsourcing, where they forget to secure copyright. This problem can also apply to NDAs (non-disclosure agreements) to ensure that information, which was meant to be confidential, will not be leaked.

How do I apply for a patent?

Patents are not relevant for every start-up, but if and when they are, they can be challenging to work with. Each patent can cost between €20 000 and €50 000, and the procedure can take 1–4 years. However, it is cheaper to take a provisional patent, which gives the right to write 'patent pending' on a product.

Typically, a patent lasts for 15–20 years. The invention must, however, be 'non-obvious', i.e. not self-evident. Additionally, you must be 'first to file' and there cannot be prior promotion and/or publicity of the concept. In the US, you should usually exploit a patent in less than 12 months from the filing – otherwise, you lose it. In other countries, there is typically no such limitation.

Finally, if you do not want to file a patent but want to prevent others from doing so, you can publish a description of the product or process in an obscure medium where hopefully no one important will read it. If a competitor files a patent for it later, you can challenge this due to 'prior publication'.

6.
MY STRATEGIES FOR NETWORK EFFECTS

The most powerful business models often build on the creation of efficient networks between existing entities. But why is this often so effectual, and how do you achieve it?

In the hyped dotcom bubble in the 1990s, many start-ups were following a mantra saying that you had to gain lots of 'eyeballs' first and worry about revenue models later. Many of those companies disappeared after the bubble burst in 2000, thus closing their access to new funding. However, among the survivors, it was often a powerful trait that saved the day: they had strong *network effects*.

So what is this? A network effect means that the utility of participating in a network increases when more participants join in. For instance, it's pointless to be the only one in the world with a telephone, but great when more and more others get one. Today, these effects are especially well known from social networks, which of course will be better for each user, the more other people are using the platform – Facebook is an obvious example. Often, when a network effect starts to kick in for a company, it will experience explosive growth without needing too much marketing, if any. Why? Because the clients or users are recruiting each other.

Viral effects

One of the consequences of network effects can be so-called viral effects. Among the best-known examples are video clips on YouTube, which sometimes are so good that people on average share them with more than one friend, which makes them spread like wildfire.

In such cases, marketing people refer to a 'viral factor'. If people are watching a given video on YouTube, for example, and on average forward it to 0.5 others (for instance, every second person shares it with a single friend), the viral coefficient is 0.5 and thus the distribution will gradually die out as follows (if we ignore the overlap between receivers): 10 000 → 5000 → 2500 → 1250 → 625 → 313 → 156 → 78 → 39 → 19 → 10 → 5 → 2 → 1 → 0

The sum of these figures is 19 998, so if your company sends 10 000 people a link to a video clip via YouTube, and if that clip has a viral coefficient of 0.5, it will, due to viral effects, reach nearly twice the original number of receivers.

Ok, let us now take 14 steps again, but this time where the viral coefficient is 2.0. Here we go: 10 000 → 20 000 → 40 000 → 80 000 → 160 000 → 320 000 → 640 000 → 1 280 000 → 2 560 000 → 5 120 000 → 10 240 000 → 20 480 000 → 40 960 000 → 81 920 000.

Wow! If we again ignore the effect of some people receiving the clip multiple times, this video will be shared with the sum of these figures, which is 163 830 000 people! In fact, here you don't need to send it to 10 000 people to start with – probably sending to 100 or even 10 will have exactly the same result, just a bit slower.

The point is, of course, that quite small differences in viral coefficients can have a huge impact on the overall impact you create.

The combination of network effects and viral effects explains why Instagram was sold for $1 billion when it was 15 months old and had 13 employees: its tremendous value was justified by the fact that it had network effects plus some viral effects as well.

INSTAGRAM'S TREMEN-DOUS VALUE WAS JUS-TIFIED BY THE FACT THAT IT HAD NET-WORK EFFECTS AND/OR VIRAL EFFECTS.

This is an example of business models – or parts of comprehensive business models – that can be very effective, where the keywords are *network effects* and *viral effects*. Because of these, you may quickly obtain a dominating network position and/or become a de facto standard for a lot of associated businesses.

Multi-sided platforms

A special case of network effects occurs when you have multi-sided platforms. For instance, a platform such as the company Just Eat connects two different types of entities: restaurants and consumers. This is a two-sided network, enabling interactions between interdependent groups of customers. A network effect will thereby build up, but only if both sides grow big. This is challenging to build up because you get a chicken-and-eggs problem, but it can become very robust, once it works. Credit cards, online market places and stock exchanges are other examples.

Another special case of network strategies is peer-to-peer (P2P) networks, whereby you set up a platform such as an online database or other communication service that connects players with each other – eBay, Craigslist, Airbnb, Uber and TaskRabbit are examples.

The third special case of networking strategies is to use an open business model and/or open source software. This is where you deliberately give external access to your business or software platform, so that others can add to it or build on it. In software, this is ensured by releasing the software source code and perhaps a system development kit, so that anyone can understand what it does and can manipulate it.

Finally, we should add that many large businesses end up operating complex multi-sided networks combining, for instance, app providers, content providers, third-party resellers, advertisers, and end users. Just as you can do a detailed financial analysis or legal audit of a complex company, you may also do an audit of its network effects and find how they drive the growth and give it its robustness.

The chicken-and-egg problem

From the time that you begin the task of creating network effects, as a rule of thumb you have 1–2 years to achieve 'ignition', which means self-perpetuating growth in network-motivated sign-ups. If you don't, people who previously signed up will start dropping out and then it may all unravel very quickly. Here are 10 traditional ways to increase the likelihood of ignition when you launch multi-sided networks:

- *Self-supply.* You sponsor one side to ensure its presence. For instance, new nightclubs might initially offer free drinks to girls to attract men. Or when YouTube was launched, the founders posted the first videos.

- *Free/paid.* You make the service free for one side, then charge the other. For instance, on a commercial 'yellow pages' network you charge the sellers but not the buyers.

- *Two-step.* You deliberately focus entirely on one side first and approach the other only when the first is reasonably populated. For instance, OpenTable focused initially entirely on signing up the best restaurants for online booking before then turning to the consumers with targeted advertising.

- *Scarcity by design.* Make it attractive to sign up via selectivity, for instance: 'During the first year we will have only what we believe are the 10% best restaurants signed up. Do you want to be included in this exclusive group?'

- *Trojan horse.* You give potential users a free tool, product or service, which happens to connect them to the network. Once there are enough passive network participants, you try to activate them.

- *Piggyback.* You launch your network as a service within another network that already has critical mass. For instance, PayPal got its ignition because it was launched within eBay.

- *Niche approach.* Choose a small market niche and get it to work there. Then expand. Facebook, for instance, was initially available only for students at Harvard.

- *Encourage bilateral recruitment.* Pay all participants from one side of the network to recruit people for the other side. For instance, the mobile payment system M-PESA in Kenya paid senders of money to recruit receivers.

- *Early sign-up benefits.* 'It's free now; if you want to sign up later, you will have to pay'.

- *Pioneer stakes.* Tattoodo initially offered some of the best tattoo artists in the world stock options for signing up.

In addition to these traditional strategies to build up complex network effects, a new one has emerged, especially through 2017: blockchain.

Using initial coin offerings

A fairly new way to build network effects in start-ups is to use Initial Coin Offerings (ICOs), an approach that solves several issues simultaneously. It usually works like this:

1. You write a white paper describing the business you are planning (typically one depending on network effects). It describes that you will fund the development and the build-up of the network with 'tokens', and you describe how these can be bought by the

initial investors and during which period. Technically, your tokens will be based on blockchain, and they will in many ways be rather similar to cryptocurrencies such as Bitcoin or Ethereum.

2. The white paper also describes the purpose of the business, how it will work and its expected funding requirements and revenues.

3. Then you start the campaign and people buy the tokens. If you fail to raise the minimum required according to the plan, all investments will be returned to the backers.

4. Since the token will be based on blockchain, it becomes instantly tradable across the globe, 24/7. This is like taking your company public from day one, but on a global, decentralized, unregulated exchange. If you issue the tokens from California, someone in Korea can trade them instantly after. This is because cryptocurrencies and thus tokens work entirely P2P and independent of banks, exchanges and borders.

The first ever such token sale was held by Mastercoin in July 2013. In 2014, the Ethereum project raised $18 million in Bitcoins, or $0.40 per Ether in an ICO. The project went live in 2015, and in 2018 the value of the coins broke above $700, giving initial investors a gain of more than 17 000%. For the issuer, the tokens have many advantages:

- Buyers have no voting rights.
- There is not a huge contract with venture capital (VC) or angel investors.
- There is an immediate global market.

This is obviously countered by less protection for buyers, and it seems that a large proportion of early ICOs have been based on very bad ideas, if not fraud. Having said that, ICOs give investors the advantage of being able to invest directly in start-ups and get an immediate market for their investment. You can think of it as a combination of (i) crowdfunding through, for example, Kickstarter and (ii) an immediate global market for your tokens, which makes it easy to sell and makes it more likely that their price goes up.

Token network effects

However, here comes the point about the network effect. Blockchain is based on a system of anonymous participants automatically managing a 'distributed ledger' of every transaction anywhere (they act as if they were collective notaries). But what do they gain by doing that? The answer is that they benefit from a related right to 'mine' new currencies by letting their computers solve mathematical puzzles. For instance, please note from the description of the Filecoin ICO: '70% being held for miner rewards'. This means that 70% of the coins are given to the people who build up and run the network.

This overall structure is called a 'shared incentive network'. In reality, you can view the tokens/cryptocurrencies issued in connection with ICOs such as the Ethereum project as bets on the expectation that the organization will be able to create an efficient network effect. However – and this is where it gets really smart – you can be a miner only by contributing to this network effect, which you do by running a part of the distributed ledger.

What happens in a successful project is that you initially have a lousy network effect but issue a lot of tokens to initial backers and miners. Then, as the network effect kicks in over time, the value of the tokens goes up and the numbers issued to the miners go down.

7.
FOUNDING AND STARTING MY COMPANY

You have decided to create a company. But where should it be located? Should it be where you live today, or somewhere else? What kind of legal company structure should you choose? Which accounting system? And how do you quickly and cheaply make your logo and website, etc.? So many practical questions! This chapter brings some answers.

When you feel comfortable with your idea, vision, strategic set-up, etc., the next step is to start making it real. The first practical question is perhaps this: 'Where should the company be located?'

Where should the company be located?

For practical reasons, most people probably locate their company roughly where they live – this is the easiest in terms of family, language, housing, colleagues, etc. And through this decision you have not turned your entire life upside down, should it go wrong.

However, there are often good reasons for locating the company elsewhere and we think these are the 10 most common:

· Access to external financing · Access to qualified experts · Access to cheap labour for routine work (if you need it) · Flexibility of labour laws · Access to people who have tried to work in start-ups previously	· Market attractiveness · Attractiveness for staff and their spouses · Local costs levels · Tax environment · Travel infrastructure.

Regarding external financing, this speaks for locating your start-up in an area where there are large concentrations of venture capital firms. The map shows the cities and regions in the world where most venture capital was invested in 2012 – each circle indicates the amount invested in millions of US dollars.[1]

Venture capital invested per region, 2012.

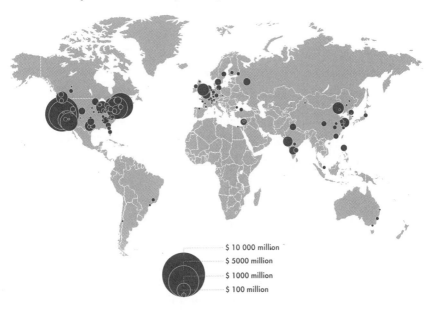

$ 10 000 million
$ 5000 million
$ 1000 million
$ 100 million

As the map shows, the largest VC concentrations are found in (i) California, (ii) the Boston–New York–Washington corridor on the American East Coast, and (iii) North West Europe. Additionally, Texas, Western India and parts of China are large venture powerhouses. Below is the breakdown between the 20 major cities, which together account for almost two-thirds (63.6%) of the global VC investment:[2]

Twenty major cities for global venture capital investment.

San Francisco	15.4%	Chicago	1.6%
San Jose	9.9%	Toronto	1.5%
Boston	7.5%	Austin	1.5%
New York	5.0%	Shanghai	1.2%
Los Angeles	3.4%	Mumbai	1.2%
San Diego	3.3%	Paris	1.1%
London	2.0%	Bangalore	1.0%
Washington	2.0%	Philadelphia	1.0%
Beijing	1.8%	Phoenix	0.8%
Seattle	1.7%	Moscow	0.8%
		Total	63.6%

It should be noted that San Francisco and San Jose are geographically close to each other and both are often described as part of the Silicon Valley environment. Together, these account for roughly a quarter of global VC investments.

Why is the proximity to VCs so useful? Because VCs in practice show a clear preference for investing close to their physical location, as they usually expect to join the boards of their portfolio companies so they can follow and guide them properly. They do this to monitor, advise and help. In other words, to receive funding, it is a huge advantage to be located close to a strong venture finance community (unless you intend to fund yourself with an ICO).

TO RECEIVE FUNDING, IT IS A HUGE ADVANTAGE TO BE LOCATED CLOSE TO FINANCING COMPANIES.

Investors do not want to travel too much

A study from the US has shown that the probability of a given VC investor joining the board is 47% if the company is located within 8 km of the investor's office.[3] Conversely, if the distance is more than 800 km, the probability drops to 22%. Thus, there is a practical aspect in the election of directors, which explains why it is easier to raise capital if the company is located physically closer to the funds' offices.

Other location criteria

You almost certainly prefer to be close to a lot of people working within your sector, mainly for recruitment purposes. Of course, it also increases the risk that your staff members get headhunted or your business secrets leak out to competitors, but all experience shows that the former benefit is far bigger than the latter risks.

For some positions in a start-up company, the right people are sometimes those who have previously filled management positions in other high-growth start-ups. This generally speaks more for California than for Athens.

For some business types, low-cost labour is an important parameter, whether it is factory workers in Mexico, software developers in Romania or something else. However, for these and other employees, it is important to consider labour laws and especially how easy it is to fire people. Flexible labour laws are almost always essential. First, start-up companies need considerable financial flexibility so that they can downsize more cheaply and instantly, should the need arise. Second, because working in start-ups can be extremely demanding, they often need to fire people who can't or won't cope.

You should also consider market attractiveness. Is it useful for your company to have a large domestic market very close? If so, this speaks, for instance, for the US rather than Lithuania.

Then there is the cultural and natural environment that can attract the best people. Of course, the key team might be willing to live in the world's worst dump if your business succeeds, but how about spouses and children? And how about the creative people you will need to hire? American urban studies theorist Richard Florida, who heads the Martin Prosperity Institute at the University of Toronto, with co-workers has made numerous statistical studies of what attracts creative workers.[4] This includes aspects such as high concentrations of other smart, creative people, good nightlife, access to nature and sports facilities, tolerance towards sexual minorities, etc.

According to Florida, evidence suggests that many of the greatest developments of regional power centres have occurred where the smart people were in the first place, not where the smart buildings were erected to attract them.

Two other factors can be important: local cost of living plus local tax levels. There tend to be far more smart people where tax levels are lower, but this is sometimes also correlated with higher property/rental costs. However, as your company matures, it does pay to consider how big an impact these two factors may have. When you start a business, taxation is arguably often secondary in one's thoughts – after all, most start-ups lose money in the beginning. However, it becomes important over the longer run.

The main taxation considerations are corporate income tax (of the profits), dividend tax (of dividend payments), tax on stock options (in particular of non-realized capital gains in employee shares) and capital gains tax (of all liquid gains). Please also note that many countries have about 40% capital gains tax or higher, whereas others do not charge taxes on capital gains at all. The OECD, for example, prepares regular summaries of this.[5]

Similarly, you can run into complicated considerations of possible transfer pricing if you have subsidiaries in different countries. Transfer pricing happens when your company and its subsidiaries trade with each other besides trading with the outside world.

The last factor we need to mention is travel infrastructure. Are there good airports with a good number of direct connections close to your office? Does road and rail traffic work efficiently?

The quality of the overall start-up environment

Is it possible to make a meaningful comparison and ranking of the quality of entrepreneurial environments? The Startup Genome project has tried comparing the main locations based on how well entrepreneurial environments provide access to finance and talent, the market's immediate reach and the amount of start-up experience among people within the area. Below is the ranking from 2015; however, cities in China, Japan and Korea have been excluded as essential data was missing.[6]

Attractiveness of the top entrepreneurial environments.

1. Silicon Valley	11. Paris
2. New York City	12. Sao Paulo
3. Los Angeles	13. Moscow
4. Boston	14. Austin
5. Tel Aviv	15. Bangalore
6. London	16. Sydney
7. Chicago	17. Toronto
8. Seattle	18. Vancouver
9. Berlin	19. Amsterdam
10. Singapore	20. Montreal

Once again, we notice that Silicon Valley is in the top position. It is also quite outstanding on exit value, i.e. what the start-up companies ultimately are sold for. In 2013 and 2014 Silicon Valley was accountable for 47% of the total exit value among the 20 largest start-up powerhouses, and Los Angeles, which lies just south of Silicon Valley and has an entrepreneurial 'silicon beach' environment, took another 6.6%.

When you study the returns on VC in different locations, it is easy to see why the moneys are concentrated in Silicon Valley because whereas it accounted for 'only' about a quarter of the investment, it drew in roughly half of the exit value. This indicates that Silicon Valley venture firms on average utilize their capital almost twice as well as the average of the rest.[7] Meanwhile, it seems that exit markets in Europe experience the fastest growth.[8]

As seen, four of the above powerhouses are in Europe: London, Berlin, Paris and Amsterdam. When it comes to so-called unicorn exits, i.e. exits for start-up companies that are traded at more than $1 billion, Nordic companies accounted for 9% of the world's such exits between 2005 and 2009 – that is very good.[9]

How successful are different venture scenes?

There is a general tendency in life for success to produce success and it is therefore interesting to consider how successful different venture scenes are.

VC, as we know it, is largely an American innovation, and the US VC market is well developed and quite successful. For instance, one study of 17 000 financing rounds in 8000 VC companies found an average annual return of 57%.[10] It should be added that this study covered the period 1987–2001, which included some exceptional years for the industry. However, another study from 2017 covering the much longer 30-year performance spanning 1996–2016 for the venture industry, including 1718 US VC funds, showed an average annual return of 18.3%, which was still far higher than returns from equities and bonds.[11]

Another study compared VC funds to public stock markets and found that VCs on average from 1980 to 2010 had produced 1.45× the annual returns of public equity markets.[12] This measure is called PME in the industry, meaning 'public market equivalent'.

That would explain why the US venture market is big. In 2015, 4380 VC deals totalling $59.1 billion were made in the US, approximately half of which were attributable to California alone.[13] In comparison, 3006 deals were concluded in Europe, but for a total of only $4.4 billion. This was less than a tenth (!) of the volume in the US, even though total European gross domestic product (GDP) is comparable to American. Only Israel has a VC investment intensity to GDP that compares to the American figure, whereas Europe is far more 'VC light'. One way to put this is that US VC investments amount to 0.211% of GDP per annum on average, which is more than seven times the EU average.[14] Closest to US VC investment intensity to GDP in Europe are some of the smaller Nordic nations plus the UK, which because it also has a substantial GDP accounts for approximately a quarter of overall European VC activity.[15] This is illustrated below.

Rank	Investments as % of GDP by location of the VC company	Investments as % of GDP by location of the portfolio company
#1	Denmark	Finland
#2	Luxembourg	Switzerland
#3	Finland	Sweden
#4	Switzerland	Ireland
#5	Ireland	UK
#6	Portugal	Austria
#7	France	Portugal
#8	Sweden	France
#9	Netherlands	Denmark
#10	UK	Germany

The European venture capital market

The main venture markets in Asia are still so young that it is difficult to obtain reliable long-term statistics for their performance. However, we do know a good deal about conditions in Europe. Between 2007 and 2015, approximately half the European VC money was allocated to dedicated early-stage funds, about 20% to later-stage funds and the remaining 30% to balanced funds.[16] Unlike in the US, in Europe balanced and later-stage funds performed best (the number in the right column is internal rate of return (IRR)). This is a measure for average annual return of all the money deployed at any given time; there is more explanation in the endnote:

Category	Number of top quarter funds	Top quarter pooled IRR[17] (%)
Balanced	30	17.89
Seed/early stage	112	12.36
Later stage	26	17.77
All venture funds[18]	107	18.51

According to a study covering 752 European VC funds from 1980 to 2013, venture funds in the top quartile reported IRRs of 18.51% for their lifetime.[19] In other words, investors in those funds earned on average more than 18% annually – a great return.

For a broader sample of top-half funds, the number declined to a still very healthy 11.28%. However, when including *all* European VC funds, i.e. also the lower-performing half, the aggregate average 'pooled IRR' dropped to a measly 1.68%. In other words, returns were highly dispersed, and whereas the better half did very well, the lower half did very poorly.

Why are European venture capitalists earning less than American VCs?

A large study analyzing VC profitability in Europe and the US confirmed the large gap between the high average venture returns in the US and the much lower ones in Europe. It then went on to propose four main explanations:[20]

- US VCs were far more likely to provide more funding to emerging winners. Indeed, they might supply up to several billion dollars to a start-up company that showed exceptional promise. European VCs, meanwhile, tended more to 'throw good money after bad' when a portfolio company disappointed while not riding the winners all the way.

- US VCs were better at cooperating in investment 'syndicates'. These in turn enabled them to fund the winners all the way.

- US VCs were more likely to provide contingent funding – meaning staged funding frameworks whereby financing was provided in pre-agreed stages upon portfolio companies meeting certain milestones.

- US VCs included more highly specialized funds and funds owned by tech companies.

However, within the European start-up scene, there exists an interesting phenomenon. As already mentioned, the Nordics are fairly VC intense by European standards. Furthermore, when analyzing unicorn exits, the Nordics shine.[21] Indeed, when comparing fraction of global unicorn exits to fraction of global GDP from 2000 to 2015, the Nordics accounted for 7% of these exits globally while only 2% of global GDP. On this measure, Nordic unicorn exits equal American, as both regions were 3.3 times better at producing unicorn exits compared with GDP than the world average.

To put this into further perspective, while the Nordic nations accounted for only approximately 5% of the European population and 7% of its GDP, between 2000 and 2015 they produced *half* of its unicorn exits. This means that Nordics were around 20 times better than other Europeans at producing unicorns per capita, and approximately 15 times better than the rest of Europeans when controlling for GDP.

NORDICS WERE AROUND 20 TIMES BETTER THAN OTHER EUROPEANS AT PRODUCING UNICORNS PER CAPITA AND APPROXIMATELY 15 TIMES BETTER THAN THE REST OF EUROPEANS WHEN CONTROLLING FOR GDP.

All the considerations above can be important in your choice of company location.

Where can I follow the venture markets?

Some of the best news sources on global tech investment activity are CB Insights and PitchBook, which both have excellent free email news services. Also, we recommend downloading the Flipbook app or similar to your smartphone and at least follow the entrepreneur and technology sections there. Furthermore, many leading VCs produce great podcasts – try, for instance, the Andreessen Horowitz site.

Which accounting system should I use?

Companies do accounting in primarily two ways – financial accounting and tax accounting. The methods for tax accounting are established by local law, but regarding financial accounting, you can select several alternatives. A European or Asian company may, for example, choose to skip local standards and instead report after the IFRS (International Financial Reporting Standards) or US GAAP (generally accepted accounting principles). Why would it do so, if the company is not American? Perhaps because it plans to be sold to an American company or to move to the US, or to be listed on an international exchange where US GAAP is widely used. In all these cases, there will be international investors, who will feel more confident when the reporting is done by a system they know and understand.

How do I make a shareholders' agreement?

Shareholders' agreements are vital documents, and no serious investor will invest in your start-up without them. You can easily download good templates from the net and what you will find there are suggested rules about how shares are allocated between the founders, what is expected from them, under which conditions continuing founders can buy shares from departing founders, and more. There may also be rules that dedicate, for instance, 20% of the founders' shares as preferred, so that they can be sold to investors during the company's non-profitable growth phase to enable the founders to take some chips off the table. There may be provisions that reserve one or two board seats for the founders, even if they have left management.

How do I choose a company name and a web domain?

Oftentimes, the choice of name will be driven by your ability to find a web domain that suits it. For instance, Apple has the obvious domain www
.apple.com. Before choosing the names of companies or products, you can

use The Name App or similar to check whether others are already using a given name or something that is almost identical.

If you find an obvious descriptive name, it may indicate that no one else has thought of your idea. That sounds great, but the more likely outcome is that almost everything that sounds suitable is already taken – at least as .com. Or alternatively, that the best name is reserved by a domain squatter (speculator) who is asking too high a price. You can typically find contact information for the owners via the domain searching apps and then start negotiation.

In case you need to buy your domain from a squatter and are concerned whether the rights will be transferred, if you transfer the money, you can use a service such as escrow.com (which works with PayPal), so that you transfer the money to this neutral platform first, while the designated receiver cannot get the funds until you have received the web domain rights.

Regarding the best naming, you should perhaps not think as much about whether the name is logical regarding the company's activities as you should think about whether:

- there is an available web domain you can register or buy
- it is easy to say in any relevant language (something people often forget!)
- it is easy for people to remember
- it is easy to spell
- it has a different, unfortunate meaning in another language
- it is already being used on Facebook and LinkedIn.

Simplicity works. For instance, Apple and Amazon are examples of names that not only met the criteria above but also said nothing about what the companies actually did – which did not matter at all. What mattered was that they were easy to say, spell and remember.

A strong concept can also be to name the company and the products the same thing, just like Amazon and Apple do. For instance, Michael

Bloomberg's company was called Bloomberg and so were his products; Enzo Ferrari founded the company Ferrari, which made the cars called Ferrari. In short, when it comes to branding, less is more, so keep it short, sharp and simple.

WHEN IT COMES TO BRANDING, LESS IS MORE, SO KEEP IT SHORT, SHARP AND SIMPLE.

How do I create a logo and website quickly and cheaply?

Every company – big or small – has a visual/graphical appearance and this should preferably be consistent and effective. Typically, one would first create a 'style guide' for how the company should present itself visually on websites, in brochures, in PowerPoints, on exhibition stands, etc., followed by the actual execution of, for example, a website, PowerPoint presentations, etc.

Large companies can spend fortunes and a great deal of time on something like this when they launch product lines or subsidiaries, but start-ups rarely have that privilege. Instead, we recommend doing the following:

- Start by using crowdsourcing to get a logo and subsequently style guide designed (perhaps both for the company and for product lines). For these tasks, you can use websites such as themeforest. net, 99designs, Template Stash, Tongal and DesignCrowd, which are cheap and quick.

- Then use crowdsourcing to create a slogan (you may also do the slogan before the logo, of course). Try, for instance, Sloganslingers.com.

- You may also use crowdsourcing for product names through, for instance, squadhelp.com.

Regarding the design of the first website, you can save time and money by choosing a standard template on either WordPress or the Squarespace platform, which also offer hosting for websites and blogs. If you are not familiar with these tools, it may be better and cheaper to hire a web designer or a small, inexpensive web agency to navigate between them, but you should have the final say regarding the design.

A good idea for many start-ups is to start a periodic newsletter for stakeholders almost from day one. If this is set up in, say, MailChimp, you can see who opens the newsletter and how long they have it open on their screen.

Printed business cards are becoming a bit old-fashioned, but if you want them in small quantities, we suggest using sites such as Vista Cards, Biz Card Creator or Business Card Land. Some of these also provide you with templates to print business cards yourself but where you subsequently cut them out of your print sheet. That makes it *really* cheap.

What if I need a webshop?

Lots of start-ups need to set up a webshop for selling their products or even just an e-book, for instance. Instead of making this yourself, you can get it cheaply as a service from companies such as WooCommerce, Magento, Shopify or PrestaShop.

The benefits of small teams

Jeff Bezos, the founder of Amazon, once said: 'If you cannot feed a team with two pizzas, it is too big'. Virgin founder Richard Branson does not believe that a huge enterprise with thousands of employees is the way forward. When one of his companies grew to more than 30 employees, he would often split the company into two different companies to maintain the creative culture.

Ten important legal mistakes entrepreneurs make at the beginning

- Start to operate commercially before they have founded a company and transferred the whole project to this.
- Do not make a shareholders' agreement.
- Make handshake agreements on important decisions.
- Give equity to the founders without the condition that these co-founders remain in the company for a given number of years and deliver the expected work.
- Use a lawyer who does not have experience in start-up companies and the relevant contract areas.
- Do not protect their 'intellectual property rights' such as trademarks, copyright and patents.
- Tell people about an invention before the patent application is filed.
- Hire people without checking whether they break competition clauses.
- Forget to submit legally required information.
- Use outsourcing without ensuring all the copyrights to the work produced.

What if I cannot afford attorneys in the beginning?

When your company is young and your savings are meagre, you might not be able to afford lawyers to help you with licensing requirements within the sector, for example, or consideration of the structure of your company, preparation of a shareholders' agreement between the founders, protection of trademarks, copyright, employment contracts, stock option agreements, supplier contracts, etc. Here you might benefit from innovative environments such as incubators and accelerators (more about them later), which often offer free sparring with lawyers and in addition legal support. Alternatively, you can use template contracts (and other documents) that can be downloaded free from the internet. Here we recommend using the following sites:

- bplans.com. A website with Word templates for various aspects such as marketing plans and legal documents.
- creativecommons.org. A website where you can download standardized contracts.
- entrepreneur.com. A website with Word templates for various aspects such as marketing plans and legal documents.
- liveplan.com. A website with Word templates for various aspects such as marketing plans and legal documents.
- nvca.org. A website that contains a range of standard legal VC financing templates.
- seriesseed.com. Contains standard templates for seed financing contracts, initially developed by Silicon Valley lawyer Ted Wang and promoted by VC firm Andreessen Horowitz, it has since improved and simplified through crowdsourcing.
- wsgr.com. The law offices of Wilson Sonsini Goodrich & Rosati provide an online term-sheet generator, where you simply answer several questions and then get a complete term sheet.

Also, if you google 'how to check trademarks', you will get a lot of sites where you can check existing trademarks in many countries for free.

8.
MY SOURCES OF FUNDING

For most start-up companies, funding is a big problem – in fact, it is often the big problem and thus the reason that they never really get started, or later fail. And even if as an entrepreneur you have a great business idea and the right team from the start, it is almost impossible for you to get the necessary funding if you do not understand the structure of the relevant finance markets, both in relation to start-up companies' situation and especially to investors' very different motives and limitations. In this chapter, we will review all of this.

As start-ups grow, they change their structure at a rapid rate and therefore they must continuously change their ways from development phase to development phase. Which phases are we talking about? In our view, one of the most practical phase descriptions are the six Marmer phases, named after Max Marmer,[1] of which phases 1–4 are especially relevant to the start-up problem. These are described below, where the indicative amounts refer to the cost levels in the US.

Phase 1: Discovery. Here you start with your basic idea and need to further develop it by looking for a commercially viable product/market fit, i.e. a product that has a market. If this fails, you should stop the project to limit losses. Remember, if you keep your business very small at first, the cost of failing will also be very small. According to Max Marmer's Startup Genome project, the discovery phase takes on average about seven months, which by the way is much more than most founders expect. On average around $150 000 is spent to finance this phase; this capital often comes from friends and family. Normally, there are no employees, and the founders may even be unpaid. In other words, there might be no salaries yet. However, along the way, a 'minimum viable product' (MVP) is being developed and tested with users. The biggest challenges here are partly to get someone to spend and possibly pay for the product, and partly that the founders are typically lacking income. To facilitate the process, you can seek support from a mentor as well as the previously mentioned accelerators or incubators.

Phase 2: Validation. This where the product/market solution must be integrated into a broader business model, which you typically make using a 'business canvas' – more on that later. At the same time, you start using selected business metrics to follow the progress of your business and you maybe make fundamental strategic changes – the 'pivots'. This phase typically takes 3–5 months, but it may last longer and it may require about $4.5 million in capital, which is usually very time-consuming to raise as it probably needs to come from professional and demanding investors. The number of employees may now have risen to a handful, maybe 3–5. This phase should be used to show that you can effectively increase the number of customers.

Phase 3: Efficiency. You are now spending a lot of time on building a strong team and the number of employees may increase further, to perhaps 15–20. They primarily work to streamline the product and its value to the users, as well as to better understand the market and its sub-categories – and to build up sales and marketing. In this stage, considerable efforts are spent on product rights, sales and payment systems, etc. Additional capital is being raised during this phase, perhaps in the order of $700 000, which as in the previous phase is quite time-consuming.

Phase 4: Scaling. The company has now proved that the product, market and organization work, which is why it is shifting up in gear. Several million dollars might be raised in a so-called A-round and the number of employees is raised to perhaps 25 or more.

However, regarding the above, it should be added immediately that companies in, for example, biotech and hardware often need a lot more capital than mentioned. The time and money requirements cited are averages, which cover huge variation.

Anyway, after these four phases, the company comes to phase 5, 'maintenance', which is dealt with extensively in traditional management literature and is less relevant to this book. Then, finally, it reaches phase 6, 'sale or renewal', which we will discuss in Chapter 15. Phase 6 is essential for this book, because obviously, almost no external investor will invest in a start-up company without a later exit opportunity – and start-ups may in fact provide exit opportunities even before reaching phase 5.

The valley of death

A lot of start-ups die simply because they cannot raise additional money between their first funding and their first commercial revenue. The first funding is based on a dream, but it can very well be that the next will be possible only when there is a commercial reality – and the first is too small to get you to the second.

Bootstrapping via free labour

Typically, much of the company's funding in the initial stages is not through cash deposits but comes indirectly from you, your co-founder and your key employees, because you all work for artificially low wages or even for free against having stakes in the company. The founders themselves can do this by choice or necessity, but they must sell the idea of doing it to others, which is one of the reasons why even if the company has a product that in principle sells itself over the internet, the founders will benefit from sales skills to be able to convince employees to work below market rates.

EVEN IF THE COMPANY HAS A PRODUCT THAT IN PRINCIPLE SELLS ITSELF OVER THE INTERNET, THE FOUNDERS MUST HAVE SALES SKILLS TO BE ABLE TO CONVINCE EMPLOYEES TO WORK BELOW MARKET RATES.

Types of funding in various growth phases

Some companies manage to bootstrap, i.e. to be profitable almost from the beginning, perhaps, among other things, because the founders work for free. However, as mentioned above, companies with high growth potential often require plenty of start-up funding.

Investigations in the United States showed the following average sizes for different investment rounds, called series A, B, C, etc.:[2]

- Business angels: $1 million
- Venture capitalists series A: approximately $7 million
- Venture capitalists series B: approximately $12 million
- Venture capitalists series C: approximately $21 million
- Venture capitalists series D: approximately $31 million

This adds up to a total of approximately $70 million. However, many companies do not take that many rounds and a few take none at all because they manage to bootstrap entirely, or cannot raise money.

This brings us to the term 'burn'. Burn means burning (in this case banknotes) and it covers how much a start-up company loses per month or year. The monthly cash drain is your monthly burn and the accumulated burn until you start earning money is called 'max drawdown'.

If you really have a great growth project, you can easily burn $30 million before you reach your first profitable month, and perhaps even more. In fact, burn and max drawdown can be extremely high. There have been examples of successful start-up companies such as Amazon, which had a max drawdown of several billion dollars before the trend turned – and yet, they were astounding investments.

Which sources of capital can you choose between?

A US survey has shown the following distribution of sources of funding to US start-up companies (by amounts raised):[3]

- The founders themselves: 60%
- Friends and family: 20%
- Venture capital: 7%
- Angel investors: 7%
- Banks: 5%
- Crowdfunding: 1%

However, this was done before an explosion in the use of a new funding concept in 2017: Initial Coin Offerings. By the end of 2017, these contributed more capital than angels and VCs combined although this since reversed.

Funding sources of American start-up companies.

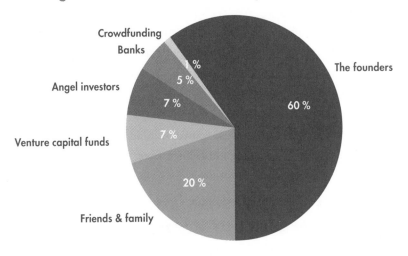

In any case, most of the total funding by far comes from the founders themselves and from friends and family – probably because the vast majority of start-up companies do not have a growth potential that may interest other investors. The funding can be of various types:

- *Share/equity capital.* Investors buy shares in your company with expectations of share price increases and/or dividends.
- *Loan/debt/bond capital.* A loan to be paid back according to an agreed plan.
- *Tokens.* Blockchain-based electronic participation certificates.
- *Convertible notes.* Loans where the lender has the option of converting to shares or simply buying shares.
- *Initial coin offerings.* Issuing tokens based on blockchain, which in principle are instantly tradable.
- *Grants.* 'Free capital', which typically comes with some clear expectations of what the money will be used for.

In addition to this, there are two other ways to generate cash:

- *Working capital optimization.* This means that you make your working capital more effective to avoid raising capital.
- *Sales of intellectual property (IP).* You sell some of your intellectual property rights to gain more working capital.

We will now look more into these sources of funding, but with the most focus on the former, i.e. issuing and selling shares.

How do investors think about return from my company?

For you to raise capital, you need to understand investors' thoughts and priorities, which can vary from category to category. Let's start with the situation where a skilled investor considers buying newly issued shares in your company. Such investors will be perfectly aware that there are huge uncertainties associated with start-ups, especially in the early stages. The investors know that such companies are more likely than not to run into, for example, product problems, conflicts between founders, other management problems, tactical marketing mistakes, new competitors, contractual errors or an overlooked patent. Therefore, the early-stage investors will have astonishingly high expectations for their return *if nothing goes wrong* – basically because the seed investors assume that something probably will go wrong.

THE SEED INVES-
TORS ASSUME THAT

SOMETHING PROBABLY WILL GO WRONG.

It is important to know that virtually no start-up companies raise their entire capital in a single round – you normally raise enough to take you to the next milestone. If you don't reach that milestone, it may mean game over. However, if you do make it, then you raise a bit more, hopefully at a higher share price, and so on.

The table below shows the names of the different investment rounds as the business grows, as well as (here it comes!) an indication of how many times an investor will expect to return their capital *if everything goes well*. The expected return is the 'multiple', where 30×, for example, means an expectation of getting the invested amount back 30 times. This expectation does not include the cost of running a VC fund, which is why expected net multiples for investors in the funds are smaller than gross profits generated by the funds. Note that in the table, IPO stands for 'initial public offering'. This means listing a company on a stock exchange.

Investment rounds as a business grows.

Development phase	Financing stage	Typical formal name of funding round	Typical expected return in multiples of the investment
Discovery phase	Early seed	Pre-seed round Seed round ICO	50× 30×

Development phase	Financing stage	Typical formal name of funding round	Typical expected return in multiples of the investment
Validating phase	Late seed/ start-up	Seed round/ angel round	20×
Efficiency phase	Early growth	A-round	10×
Scaling phase	Growth	B-round	8×
	Late growth expansion	C-round	5×
	Bridge/ mezzanine/ pre-IPO	D-round, etc. Mezzanine round, Bridge loan	2×
	Growth capital	Growth capital	1.5×
	IPO	IPO funding	1.5×
Maintenance phase	IPO		1.5×

An A-round will be obtained when the company has proven its product/ market fit and receives its first significant venture round, then any subsequent rounds will be given an alphabetically continuous name, i.e. B, C, D, etc. The multiples given in the outer right-hand column of the table are of course loose indications and depend, among other things, on the investor's concrete assessment of the uncertainty in each case. But think about it: an 'early seed' investor may not want to invest in your project unless a 30× return is expected, assuming nothing goes awry.

A bit later – in early growth – uncertainty has fallen somewhat, but investors might still demand 10× return in the base case before investing. If your plan shows a realistic return of 5×, it may be good in your mind, but perhaps not good enough for the investor.

These are major barriers, and that is not even the whole story, because investors often expect large returns – *rather quickly*. VC funds, for example, have a typical duration of approximately 10–12 years, within which they are contractually obliged to return all capital plus/minus returns to their investors. In the first 3–4 years after a given fund's start, they typically invest their capital. In the next few years there may be add-on investments as well as sales of shares (exits), and in the last four years or so, only exits plus perhaps cleaning up the mess after investments that failed. This means that their average shareholding time in a given portfolio company often spans just 4–6 years. For you as an entrepreneur, the consequence may be that if, for example, they come in at an A-round, they actually expect you to tenfold their investment within 4–6 years!

Where does the capital come from?

Professionals sometimes split investors into three groups:

- dumb money (have no expertise)
- money only (have expertise but do not make it available)
- smart money (have and use their expertise in the specific investment).

'Dumb money' generally refers to friends and family or others who invest even though they do not possess a comprehensive analysis apparatus or experience. However, while the term literally means stupid money, of course this does not need to be the case.

Money-only investors can be professional foundations or individuals who have the competencies to analyze your business, but in the particular case not the time. Instead, they typically because they trust that a co-investor has analyzed the project on their behalf.

Smart-money investors analyze the business and then follow it closely, typically trying to help it, for example via board work. If your company has skilled smart-money investors, such as leading VC funds, it may be easier to raise more capital later.

What types of investors exist?

The table below shows the typical investors in the company's different development phases.

Typical investor categories through various stages of start-up growth.

Development phase	Name on funding round	Typical investors
Discovery phase/ Validation phase	Pre-seed/seed Seed round/angel round Crowdfunding ICO	Founders Family and friends Business angels Crowdfunding community Incubators Accelerators ICO investors Pre-seed and seed VC funds

Development phase	Name on funding round	Typical investors
Efficiency phase/ Scaling phase	Early growth (A-round) Growth (B-round, etc.) Late growth/expansion (C-, D-, E-round, etc.)	VC funds Growth funds
Maintenance phase	Bridge/mezzanine/ pre-IPO Growth capital IPO	VC funds Growth funds PE funds and private strategical investors Venture debt companies
Sale or renewal	IPO	PE funds Privates

There may partly be a cycle in this, where some of the earliest investors are often not very professional, and many of the ultimate shareholders after a public listing are not either. However, in between, the outside investors are mainly smart-money/money only investors. This does not apply to ICOs, which bypass the entire process with an instant sale of tokens to anyone.

The founders' investments

Let's now take a closer look at each investor category. We'll start with the founders. Studies show that the average founder brings in approximately $25 000, and often far less (41% invest nothing, 33% invest up to $25 000 and only 27% invest more).[5] However, the larger investment is often the free work hours provided by founders.

Investments from friends and family

Many times, the founders receive help from direct acquaintances – our so-called dumb-money investors. In the table above (and in industry jargon) this is called 'family and friends', but the category can also cover professional acquaintances who do not have investment in start-ups as a career (sometimes for fun this is referred to as 'FFF' – family, friends and fools). These typically invest very early and the amounts range from a few thousand dollars to perhaps a few hundred thousand. And as mentioned, they need not be dumb at all.

Very often, friends and family do not invest in the project but instead in *you* – they do this because they will help *you* personally or have confidence in *your* skills. But often they do not know how risky this investment is and therefore it is important that you check (i) whether they can afford to lose their investment and (ii) whether they are aware that it is distinctly possible that this will happen. You should therefore ask them what it will mean to them if their investment is lost. You must also make it clear to them that even if it goes well, it may well take between 5 and 15 years before they can sell their shares and score any profit, which, however – maybe! – can be huge.

Likewise, you should carefully consider the valuation by which they invest in your company. How would you feel if the next round was carried out at a lower valuation than what your parents and your uncle got?

Funding from business angels

The term business angels derives from Broadway, where producers and directors often looked for funding among wealthy individuals, which they then began calling 'angels'. Angels are private investors, who invest in start-ups other than just their family's and friends' projects. Between 2001 and 2009 there were 49 000 angel investments made in the US and there are far more angel investments than VC investments.[6] A study of 539 North American angels experiencing 1137 exits and a significant number of complete write-offs showed aggregate 2.6× return in 3.5 years, or 27% IRR.[7] Other studies have shown similar results, which of course are far higher than for public stock markets. One of the more recent studies, this one from 2016, showed average annual angel returns in the US of 22%.[8]

However, while some win big, others lose their shirts. Indeed, some angels are quite unprofessional, while others are 'super angels', who operate almost as VC funds, just on earlier stages. Super angels will most likely invest only in industries they already know well from the inside, perhaps because they made their own money by starting or running companies in that sector.

In addition, there are 'angel groups', where many angels invest within the same network. An angel investment can therefore often come from five angels, for example, who cooperate and know each other. One of the angel investors will typically be the most active in the group and therefore also their 'investment lead', and the investment round will then be syndicated. The reason angels frequently work together is partly to see more opportunities, partly to have more people to evaluate a case, and to have enough cash to jointly close a funding round which may be too big for each of them alone. Many angels prefer a portfolio of 5–10 smaller investments to a single large investment and syndicated investing facilitates this.

The pros of having angels in a round are that (i) they typically have earned their money through entrepreneurship and therefore understand well what you are battling with, (ii) they are willing to take risks and (iii) they are quick in making decisions. According to a US study, the average angel round in the US is $450 000.[9]

Angels can invest from a purely financial motive, but frequently they have a personal desire to work with the project and its people. Why? Some angels do it because they have personally experienced what it is like to be a desperate entrepreneur who really needs capital. Therefore, they want to help someone else in that situation. Others believe that your company's product or service is charming, fun or beneficial to society and therefore they want to support it and would enjoy contributing with their special knowledge, experience and network. Therefore, do not pitch angels on return on investment alone.

Oh, a final note on angels: just as there is no shortage of people claiming to be entrepreneurs while they actually aren't, quite a few 'angels' don't really invest. To avoid wasting time on perpetual window shoppers, we suggest asking how long they have been angel investors and – more importantly – what they actually invested in and when.

AngelList

AngelList is a useful US website where start-ups can offer jobs and seek funding from angels free of charge.

How do seed rounds work?

Angels normally invest around the seed phase. This is when the company either has not been started or it has an early prototype of its product but very little or no turnover. Nowadays there is also the pre-seed phase, where the investor comes in when there is nothing more than the founders and a PowerPoint. Seed capital's purpose is to support the company until it has a proven product/market fit showing that there is a real business case to build on. The typical size of seed investment is shown in the table below.

Average seed round in the world's 20 biggest entrepreneur centres ($ thousands).[10]

Silicon Valley	900–950	Paris	650–700
New York City	850–900	Sao Paulo	450–500
Los Angeles	750–800	Moscow	550–600
Boston	750–800	Austin	900–950
Tel Aviv	700–750	Bangalore	300–350
London	700–750	Sydney	750–800
Chicago	650–700	Toronto	700–750
Seattle	800–850	Vancouver	550–600
Berlin	550	Amsterdam	450–500
Singapore	450–500	Montreal	600–650

Angel investors also cover more industries than venture capitalists, as the latter operate almost exclusively in life sciences and IT, and sometimes (rarely) in cleantech.[11]

As the typical pre-money valuation at seed rounds is $2–2.5 million, and as angel rounds often are in the $6 800 000 range, the angel investors tend to get some 25% of the company.

Funding via convertible notes

The preferred instrument among angels is convertible notes, which are also common among VC funds. The notes typically work like this:

- The investor lends the start-up company x amount, say $100 000.

- This has a modest interest, perhaps 3–10%, which accrues so that it doesn't need to be paid out annually.

- The initial amount plus accrued interest can be converted to shares at a pre-determined percentage discount to the share price at the next fundraising, given this round is of a pre-determined size or over (there can be other triggers). The most common discount is 20%, but it is not uncommon to see discounts up to 30% or even 35%.

- The notes contain a maturity date provision at which point they must be repaid with interest, if they have not been converted. This is typically after 18–24 months and happens if the company has failed to make a capital increase triggering a conversion. Such scenarios will often threaten bankruptcies and leave the note issuer in de facto control of the company.

The main purpose of this structure is that if the company fails, the angel, as a creditor, has a claim on any assets in the estate. Another purpose can be to keep the investment secret from the public until it is converted.

Ok, let's say that you have a 20% discount. What does that mean? If, for instance, the next fundraising happens at an enterprise value of $5 million, you convert at the cheaper valuation of $4 million, which means that you get 20% more shares per dollar than the subsequent investors.

However, now we must become a bit nerdy because there are two problems here to explain. First, a 20% discount is a low compensation for the high risk. Second, this structure motivates the angel to seek a *low* valuation at the next round, so that he can convert the loan to cheap shares, whereas the founders and the company overall may benefit from a *high* valuation. This is addressed by adding a 'cap' on the market valuation at which the angel converts. In fact, approximately 80–85% of cases have such a cap, and for seed-stage angel investments, it is typically set at $3.5–7.5 million, with $5 million being a very common number. This means that if the next fundraising happens above the capped enterprise value, the angel investor gets the shares at whatever is lowest – the discounted price or the cap. Let's say that the angel has a 20% discount and a $5 million cap. If the next funding happens at $6 million, then the 20% discounted value is $4.8 million. This will be the rate at which the angel converts. However, if the funding happens at $7 million, the 20% discounted value is 5.6 million, which is higher than $5 million, so the angel converts at $5 million.

Funding via initial coin offering

As previously mentioned, a new concept for funding has become popular in recent years: ICOs. An ICO is an Initial Coin Offering, also sometimes called a 'token sale'. It is a public offering of a new token or cryptocurrency, where investors typically, but not always, pay with a cryptocurrency. Most ICOs are paid with ERC20 tokens, which are implemented by Ethereum tokens. So far, ICOs have come in four basic forms:

1. Pure currency such as Bitcoin or Ethereum.

2. Utility token/user token, which gives buyers access to a service.

3. Equity token, which gives buyers shares in an asset such as a commodity or an operating company. This may be associated with distribution of dividends.

4. Debt token, which gives access to a return.

You can think of them as programmable, blockchain-based equivalents to:

1. Money

2. Gift certificates

3. Shares or exchange-traded funds (ETFs)

4. Bonds

But as they are programmable, there are countless ways to make them smart. For instance, companies can issue the equivalent of gift cards, bonus points, membership certificates, etc., which combine rules for what the tokens can give access to and for how long they will be valid, and so on.

The first token sale (ICO) was held by Mastercoin in July 2013. However, probably the most famous to date was made by the people behind Ethereum. Ethereum was initially described in a white paper by Vitalik Buterin, founder of Ethereum, in 2013.[12] Buterin had previously argued that Bitcoin needed a scripting language for application development. Since he couldn't get agreement in the community on how to do it, he decided with a core team to do it independently.

The development process began in early 2014 through a Swiss company, Ethereum Switzerland GmbH. Subsequently, a Swiss non-profit foundation, the Ethereum Foundation, was created. This development was funded by an ICO during July–August 2014, with the participants buying the Ethereum value token (ether) with bitcoin. The Ethereum ICO raised 3700 bitcoins within the first 12 hours, corresponding to approximately $2.3 million at the time. After that, the number of ICOs rose and by the summer of 2017, a total of $1.8 billion had been raised in startup venture funding globally via ICOs, which was more than through all traditional VC and angel investments combined – a stunning development.

Some established VCs have invested in ICOs. For example, Filecoin, an open-source, public cryptocurrency and digital payment system, was funded via an ICO with initial funding of $52 million from 150 investors, including Sequoia Capital, Andreessen Horowitz, Union Square Ventures, Winklevoss Capital and a number of highly-skilled Silicon Valley investors. Moreover, this ICO structure was symptomatic of how they often work:

> 'Ten percent of tokens allocated will go to advisors and ICO investors, with 15% going to Protocol Labs (the company creating Filecoin), 5% going to a new foundation and 70% being held for miners rewards. The ICO is capped in terms of Filecoin sold at 200 M, but the final price of Filecoin will depend on the total amount of USD raised, which is uncapped'.

In other words, some of the tokens are allocated to advisors, others for the company's operation, but most to future miners to run the network.

There is hardly any doubt that many ICOs have had a deficient foundation, and according to Buterin, perhaps some 90% of early ICOs will fail, some because they are pure fraud, others because most start-up companies generally fail. To quote:[13]

> 'This, basically, is tokens 1.0. There are some good ideas, there are a lot of very bad ideas, and there's a lot of very, very bad ideas, and quite a few scams as well. I expect that tokens 2.0 and the kinds of things that people will start building in 2018 and 2019 will generally be of substantially higher quality.'

What is often viewed as an attraction in ICOs from an investor's point of view is that you can invest in seed, if not pre-seed, and then have a publicly traded token, which will give you the same potential for huge profits as early-stage investors such as friends and family may get. Literally, this is true, but obviously, the ICO investors also participate in the risk that these investors take, and perhaps they are not equally good at it.

Use of crowdfunding

In recent years, crowdfunding has become very big and there are now more than 2000 crowdfunding platforms, including some that are very specialized and others that are more inclusive. Crowdfunding, like ICOs, can enable individual people to invest in companies or projects down to the stage where there is only an idea and nothing else. Crowdfunding platforms publish data about your business online and then users can invest in it within a certain period. You can typically raise capital on crowdfunding platforms in one of four ways:

1. People simply donate money to your project.

2. You pre-sell products but do not give equity (for example, Kickstarter and Indiegogo).

3. You give equity in the same way that you do to other investors.

4. People lend you money.

Some companies are very creative in their use of these options. For instance, Peecho, which operates as an intermediary between websites and print partners by using a global cloud print network, used crowdsourcing to find freelancers who did work for the company in return for shares. Many of these freelancers recruited their own subcontractors to get their part of the work done and therefore they passed on some of their equity allocation to those subcontractors.

Crowdfunding can be exciting, especially option 2 above, where you pre-sell the product. First of all, pre-sale via crowdfunding works as a very direct test of whether you have a market; second, it provides you with customers up front; and third, it gives you free exposure and marketing. Option 1 and 3 above may also be interesting, but with option 3, where you allocate shares, you must be aware that it may be impractical to have a lot of shareholders so early. After all, they have to be informed and involved in any subsequent public offering or a sale. One solution to this problem might be to have these retail investors invest via a feeder company so that combined they become a single shareholder in the operational firm.

Option 4 is relevant when the company has good traction but still needs cash – and cannot yet get it from banks.

Overall, we would say that option 1 is almost never available to start-ups, but the other three are and they become relevant in the sequence that we have listed: pre-ordering of products in the early pre-launch stage, equity funding when the product exists and lending when the business has clear traction and low risk of default.

FIRST OF ALL, PRE-SALE VIA CROWD-FUNDING WORKS AS A VERY DIRECT TEST OF WHETHER YOU HAVE A MARKET; SECOND, IT PROVIDES YOU WITH CUSTOMERS UP FRONT; AND THIRD, IT IS FREE EXPOSURE AND MARKETING.

Funding and support from incubators

Incubators (sometimes called seed accelerators) such as Idealab make small investments, typically in the discovery phase or when a company is about to enter the validation phase. In return, they receive small shareholdings. The employees in each of the involved start-up companies often work in an open office landscape, where they may inspire and help each other.

Many incubators are operated fully or partially by VC funds or receive funding from VC funds, charitable funds from the public or from private universities. Some incubators have the rule that they work only with companies and ideas that they encounter through certain trusted partners.

Funding from accelerators

Accelerators are somewhat reminiscent of incubators but they invest at a later stage than incubators and have different approaches. An accelerator is a kind of start-up factory. Its partners typically expect your company to be in at least the validation phase and maybe even moving towards the efficiency phase. Perhaps the best way to think of them is as similar to VC funds that specialize in early-stage investments and are very hands-on in their support.

The accelerator provides mentor networks for a period of typically 3–6 months and they typically invest around $10 000–$25 000, while elite programmes often invest as much as $100 000–$250 000 in exchange for 6–10% equity or convertible notes. They have a rather small core organization of employees, maybe only a handful, but at the same time they have large networks of perhaps 30, 50 or even more mentors who are serial entrepreneurs or in any another way highly experienced within the field of entrepreneurship.

Almost all accelerators host their start-ups physically, although the most famous of them all, Y Combinator, doesn't. They organize seminars and advise the businesses participating in their programmes. As compensation for the facilities, mentors and money, accelerators typically receive 3–8% equity.

To be admitted to an accelerator programme, you should have a brilliant idea, a battle-ready and 100% dedicated team, enough money to survive until an A-round VC investment, an early indication that the idea has clear market potential and a good understanding of the specific market.

If you have an idea but no team, your chances are almost non-existent, and if you are already ready for VC investment, your business is probably too mature for an accelerator programme.

A typical accelerator accepts roughly 1–2% of all applicants. A successful accelerator may use the following selection process per programme:

- Applications: 500–1000
- Initial Skype meeting: 100–150
- Follow-up meeting: ca. 50
- Two to three days' intensive selection process with participation from partners and mentors: 15–30
- Selected participants: 10

In other words, around 0.5–1% of the applicants will be selected. Of course, this suggests that companies completing an accelerator programme are of high calibre, and this was reflected in a study from 2015, which showed that more than one-third of US companies completing a series A-round had previously been through an accelerator programme.[14]

They know more than you think – and perhaps even more than you do

An experienced accelerator team may have received thousands of applications during its lifetime and therefore they may know a lot about what is going on in the markets – and perhaps also about what is happening within the specific market in which you operate. Therefore, if you tell them that you are the only one operating in your market, they might have seen several other businesses doing the same thing that you do, although you may not be familiar with those companies. If this happens, they will not take you seriously. Therefore, you should first study your market and second not try to impress an accelerator with something that is not entirely correct.

The accelerator programmes start periodically, with many companies joining the programme – almost like a freshman year at a business school. Contrary to incubators, accelerators have synchronous programmes for different companies and they also support them for a shorter time but in more intense ways.

Towards the end of each programme, the accelerator arranges pitch days or 'demo days', where their start-ups present their projects to different VC funds, angels and other potential investors. Many accelerators have also founded their own VC funds, so they can participate in some of the subsequent investment rounds. These pitch days can be popular because whoever made it through the needle's eye to join an accelerator programme is probably on to something.

For the entrepreneurial companies, the money from an accelerator is the least important factor. What matters much more is what they learn during the accelerator period. Furthermore, by being selected for an accelerator programme, they become more visible to other potential investors. Pitch days give access to real investors – investors who could have been very difficult to get in touch with. Some entrepreneurs also use participation in an accelerator programme as an opportunity to move their headquarters closer to a major VC centre, such as Silicon Valley.

This being said, it should be mentioned that not all accelerators are equally competent (or competent at all), so you must check how well things have gone for previous participating companies before you apply to their programme. Additionally, you should be aware that some accelerators specialize in specific industries.

The most famous (and very successful) accelerator in the world is Y Combinator, located in Silicon Valley, which graduates about 200 start-ups per year. There are two other very large accelerators in the US: 500 Startups and Techstars, each of which graduates approximately 150 start-ups annually. You can track the performance of the best accelerators worldwide over the world via the website seed-DB.com, which the last time we checked listed more than 170 of these. In the US alone, there are approximately 1000 accelerators and in Europe roughly the same number. The number in Asia is growing rapidly but is difficult to measure.

Funding from venture capitalists

VC funds are typically the first top professional or institutional sources of capital that a successful start-up encounters, unless they have participated in a top-notch accelerator programme. VC funds mainly receive their money from pension funds (especially in the US), state funds (mainly in Europe), university funds (mainly in the US), banks, very wealthy families and other investors. The minimum investment from a given investor is usually $1–5 million and in some cases even much more. However, they frequently have 'entrepreneurs' funds' or 'sidecars' for people who add a strategic value to them. These private investors may be angels, former entrepreneurs, very successful business people, etc., who via these funds sometimes can invest as little as a few thousand dollars. Furthermore, it is normal that a VC fund's leaders have invested a minimum of 1% of the capital in their respective funds, and often far more.

While many start-ups can skip seed investors because they are self-financed, at least for a while, many of the most successful growth companies do receive VC funding. Typically, VC funds achieve at each round about 20–30% of the company's capital via capital increases, and as there often are several rounds, a process where, for example, they take 25% each time means that the former investors' shareholding falls from 100% to 75% in a first round, then to 56% in the second, to 42% in the third, and so forth.

However, to receive VC investment in the first place, one must usually deliver high and quick returns. Driving a VC business is a tough game in which investors expect good results in one fund before they will invest in the next. In addition, they also have a 'hurdle' of typically 8–10% annual return and unless they can provide more than this, their partners receive no 'carry' of usually 20%, i.e. a share in the passive investors' profits – and it's not a fixed salary that motivates them financially but instead a carry, which can be far greater. Therefore, they typically aim for a threefold to fourfold increase (3–4×) of the total capital invested over a 10-year period.

However, as we have already seen, US-based VCs have historically been far better at generating good returns than have European funds.

Founder friendliness

Some VCs are very founder-friendly and offer some of the same services as a typical accelerator, including, for instance:

- access to standard legal templates for stock option plans, employment contracts, etc., to save time and legal costs for their portfolio companies
- hands-on assistance with key management recruitment.

One of the most founder-friendly VCs is probably Andreessen Horowitz, which has more than 100 team members dedicated to helping its portfolio companies with anything from legal challenges to executive recruitment and numerous other aspects of running a start-up. In fact, this company has modelled itself on a combination of the talent agency Creative Artists Agency (CAA) and the financial companies Allen & Company and JPMorgan. CAA is brilliant at attracting the best talent, which is what a top VC must also do, and once an artist is in the CAA stable, the company seeks to service them in countless ways. Allen & Company has stayed true to its strong values for a century and hosts events that attract the best of the best – again something a top VC likes to do. JPMorgan – especially the man himself – has been excellent at orchestrating the structuring of businesses for large-scale success.

VCs that provide a broad spectrum of services to their portfolio companies are sometimes referred to as 'platform companies' or 'platform VCs'.

As an entrepreneur, you can check how founder-friendly different VCs are through the site thefunded.com, which has more than 20 000 members, of which approximately 95% are start-up CEOs. Combined, these have rated approximately 7000 VC funds plus many of their partners. The site also contains a discussion board about fundraising.

The favourite children

Since VCs know that only a few of their investments in each fund are likely to provide the bulk of their total returns, they often begin to dedicate the focus largely to those lucky few. As David Cowan from Bessemer Venture Partners once said: 'Just focus on the top five – the rest is distraction.'[15]

About VC funds' returns

When people invest in VC funds, they typically make commitments but initially without paying anything in. However, each time the fund makes an investment, it 'calls' the necessary funds from the investors, and when it makes an exit, it 'distributes' the net proceeds. Their returns are measured and compared by multiples (such as 1.8×) or their aforementioned IRR (the average annual return of the actual invested funds). Their return also varies greatly, from loss of most of the investments to, for example, Kleiner Perkins VII from 1994, which gave 32.5×, Benchmark Fund I from 1995, which yielded 92×, and the Lowercase Ventures Fund I from 2007, which at the time of writing is rumoured up by over 200× after its investments in Uber, Instagram and Twitter.

Let us do some simplified maths. A VC fund of $100 million is being raised. It has 15% annual return, which is equivalent to 3.5× over 10 years. There is a hurdle of 8%, so the fund's partners receive a 20% profit of 7% annually (15–8%), i.e. 1.4% of the fund annually. In 10 years, this grows to $14 million in profit sharing. We can then further assume that the VC firm starts a new fund every five years and therefore on average has two active funds in parallel. Now we are talking about $28 million in profit sharing to partners in a period of 10 years – or $2.8 million per year. This is real money. And if a VC firm has real success, its combined funds might not be $100 million but up to several billion dollars. This is where some fund partners get their mega-yachts from.

What do these conditions mean for their potential investment in your company? As we saw earlier, their return expectations are often 3–4 times

(3–4×) the committed capital after about 10 years, but for *each investment* they expect perhaps 10× as they include the risk that something goes wrong in many of the investments.

Furthermore, they do not want to spend too much of their personal time on small businesses, so unless they are focused on early stage, they might have another key rule stating that a given investment must be expected to give the fund an exit value of approximately half of its original capital. In other words, if they have raised $100 million in a given fund to invest in your company, they may expect that they can make an exit of your company of at least $50 million – for them. And if through their investment they acquire 25% of your company, your company's total exit value should be around $200 million before it becomes interesting to them. So can you deliver that?

Two rules of thumb regarding VC investments

None of the following rules is applicable in every scenario – certainly not – but they are great to remember if you pitch for a VC fund:

- When investing around series A, the fund may expect a return of investment in your company of around 1000% (10×) over a period of maximum five years.
- It may also expect that its investment in your company should give it an exit of around half of the fund's total amount, i.e. half of the investment that the investors together have promised to invest.

Let's walk through this example again, but this time in another way (simplified because we ignore liquidation preference and sometimes participation with liquidation):

- The VC firm invests maybe $10 million in your company.
- This gives it 25% of the shares, which means that the company was valued at $30 million before it went in and $40 million after.

- Within 4–6 years, your company may have a total exit value for the existing shareholders of $400 million, which means that the 25% owned by the VC is now worth $100 million – it made its 10×.

It is your job to deliver this return; if you cannot convince your VC that it will happen, it will be difficult to get it to invest.

Oh, by the way, there is an exception to these rules of thumb. Since VC funds are mainly measured on IRR, they actually do like smaller returns, if they are *quick*. For instance, if they invest in your company and can exit after one year with a 100% return (2×), their IRR on that investment was 100%, which contributes to a good overall IRR.

Most VC funds focus on specific stages, such as series A, B, C and so on, but some are 'balanced' and invest across several stages. Funds specializing in series A and B usually focus on getting the product and marketing fully in place and ensuring that the concept works 100% before any scaling is done. In addition, they ensure – particularly in series B – that the economic structure becomes streamlined and that the company earns money from its clients (it does not mean that the company overall is profitable).

Series A and B funding rounds usually include significantly larger amounts than investment rounds made earlier in the company's progress, and it is among such funding rounds that you will find so-called unicorn hunters – funds that aim to invest in companies that they believe can have an exit value of more than $1 billion.

The reported average size of A-rounds is summarized in the table below.

Average series A-round in the world's top 20 business incubators ($ million).[16]

• Silicon Valley: 6.5–7.0	• Austin: 6.0–6.5	• Seattle: 5.5–6.0
• Paris: 4.0–4.5	• Tel Aviv: 4.5–5.0	• Vancouver: 4.5–5.0
• New York City: 7.5–8	• Bangalore: 4.0–4.5	• Berlin: 5.5–6.0
• Sao Paulo: 6.0–6.5	• London: 7.0–7.5	• Amsterdam: 5.5–6.0
• Los Angeles: 6.0–6.5	• Sydney: 2.8–3.0	• Singapore: 4.0–4.5
• Moscow: 3.5–4.0	• Chicago: 5.5–6.0	• Montreal: 8.0–8.5
• Boston: 10.0–10.5	• Toronto: 6.0–6.5	

Series C, D and so on are typically close to what you would say is growth capital. This means that the investment happens at a growth stage where the company usually could survive without further capital if it prioritized profits over growth. For many businesses, series C is the final round before they turn cashflow-positive.

Start-up investors are an ecosystem where many help each other

There is great cooperation between many institutional venture investors. Studies indicate that business angels in about 10% of the cases have good relations with VC firms and can help with introductions to these. Furthermore, early-stage VC investors manage to arrange contact with late-stage VC investors in 31% of cases, and 5% of angel investors cooperate with corporate investors, just as 14% of VC investors do.[17]

Funding from growth funds and private equity funds

Growth funds are a newer class of funds that invests in companies that have already proven their commercial justification and typically are profitable or could become so, if they slowed down, but now seek capital to scale further. Some growth funds invest in profitable businesses only, while others also invest in unprofitable companies with proven business platforms. A growth fund usually invests approximately $5–30 million in each company.

Private equity funds are funds that invest in companies that are not publicly listed. They may invest to finance a generational change or redemption of investors who want out of a business. It may also be to save and turn around ailing companies, to make consolidation plays or for other purposes, but it can also be to help – and profit from – a growth company that is expected to be sold or go public within a few years.

Unlike VC funds, private equity funds predominantly invest on the condition of being able to get most shares and thus full control. However, some private equity funds have begun to make non-controlling growth and minority investments. They typically invest when the companies have reached a value of approximately $15 million and up to several billion dollars.

Funny fact, by the way: people working in private equity typically wear a suit and often a tie. In VCs, they more often opt for jeans and some cool stuff. Why? Because those in private equity call up management/owners of older companies and propose a deal. VCs, meanwhile, are bombarded by proposals from younger people. Different tasks and different cultures.

Pre-IPO financing

An IPO, as mentioned, is a listing on a stock exchange, and a pre-IPO is intended as the last capital injection before the company is listed on a stock exchange. While there are virtually no focused pre-IPO funds, the very large asset management firms in particular frequently invest before an IPO as well as in companies already listed. Recently some of them have begun to invest in earlier stages than before, thus blurring the lines between VC and private equity.

Companies typically do pre-IPO rounds as a back-up in case – contrary to expectations – they cannot raise money through an IPO and to make acquisitions of other companies, such as retailers of their products. The latter can be good preparation for a better IPO. However, they can also make a pre-IPO round to get rid of shareholders they believe would not fit the IPO for image-related reasons, or who would like to get out partially or fully for personal reasons.

Typically, a pre-IPO round is structured so that the investor receives a discount of the expected IPO price. Pre-IPO rounds are typically from tens of millions of dollars and up to billions.

Funding from companies, strategic investors and corporate VC funds

Larger commercial companies such as IT and pharma companies have become very relevant as investors, especially in recent years, as they often have substantial liquidity and are looking for innovation. Investment typically comes from three places in a company: (i) the chief financial officer (CFO), mergers and acquisitions (M&A) or strategy team, (ii) business lines and (iii) internal innovation or corporate VC funds.

In particular, internal corporate VC funds have become increasingly common, as they act as eyes and ears, which serve to prevent them from being run over by innovative quantum leaps in start-ups. Usually, the companies invest only in business models that are strategically relevant to them, either because the start-ups they invest in could become competitors ('if you cannot beat them, join them') or to help them become more profitable. They may also invest in companies before they submit a big order to them – that way, they earn financially by helping the start-up company commercially. Investments from commercial companies can be everything from a few hundred thousand dollars to hundreds of millions.

Lars on how to raise money from commercial companies versus venture capital funds

I have raised money from both VC funds and strategic investors, and my personal experience with the latter, which included Intel, Deutsche Telekom, BT, Lucent, Reuters, Loral Space & Communications, KirchGroup and Singapore Press Holdings, was far better. The problem with some VC funds is that they sometimes say 'almost yes' while staying on the fence and perhaps even waiting for you to become desperate. Once you are quite desperate, they may seek to impose unreasonable conditions.

> Strategic investors, on the other hand, have a self-interest in your business success that goes beyond investment returns, and therefore, in my experience, they can be both more reasonable in negotiations and more patient and helpful afterwards.

Funding/investment through venture debt

In recent years, a phenomenon called venture debt has emerged. This is a mixture of loans and options or warrants to purchase shares in the company. Silicon Valley Bank was a pioneer and it now offers venture debt worldwide to companies with a revenue of about $10 million and more. In addition to the loan and the interest rate, venture debt providers typically ask for an option of 1–2% of the company, so that they can enjoy both interest payments and capital appreciation.

The reason loans can sometimes be a cheaper form of capital than, say, selling shares to a VC is that banks have access to much cheaper capital than VC funds do, and in the event of bankruptcy, lenders get their money back before shareholders – in cases where lenders cannot get their money back, they take over the shares and therefore the entire project.

Financing via initial public offerings

IPOs can occur at all stages, from early in a company's development until after receiving private equity investments, but an IPO typically happens when the company has proven its business model and achieved a growing customer base.

In principle, an IPO could be focused only on offering existing shares in the public market, but in practice it almost always involves the sale of new shares whereby it raises capital. This is because the company can not only use this capital but also get some shares out in the market instantly, so that you get a reasonable liquidity for them.

Interestingly, a study of 69 venture-backed companies that went public between 2000 and 2015 showed a peculiar correlation between the age of the company and how it performed after its IPO: companies that went public when they were 6–10 years old typically made great post-IPO returns, whereas those that were older or (in particular) younger did far worse.[18]

Change in company performance after an IPO.

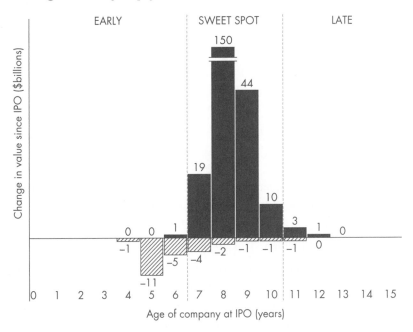

Pros and cons of external financing

What are the main advantages and disadvantages of external financing? The most obvious advantage is, of course, money. Another may be that the exercise whereby you over and over must discuss your company with clever and critical investors can strengthen your analysis of your business considerably. A third reason may be that the new investors can help you in many concrete ways – this may apply especially to incubators, accelerators, VC funds and strategic investors.

But there may also be disadvantages. One, of course, is that your influence and your ownership are diluted and oftentimes the founder team ends up with a total of just 10–15% of the company through a final 'liquidity event', as it is called (an event such as the sale of the company or an IPO, whereby shares become sold or sellable).

Average dilution by series A-round in the world's 20 largest incubators.[19]

1.	Silicon Valley:	19%	8.	Austin:	30%	15.	Seattle:	22%
2.	Paris:	34%	9.	Tel Aviv:	21%	16.	Vancouver:	17%
3.	New York City:	16%	10.	Bangalore:	18%	17.	Berlin:	10%
4.	Sao Paulo:	25%	11.	London:	19%	18.	Amsterdam:	38%
5.	Los Angeles:	18%	12.	Sydney:	13%	19.	Singapore:	22%
6.	Moscow:	16%	13.	Chicago:	24%	20.	Montreal:	19%
7.	Boston:	15%	14.	Toronto:	19%			

Here is another consideration: usually, more capital equals more safety. However, many VC fund managers look for the opportunity to build companies with a market value in the hundreds of millions of dollars, if not north of a billion. This means that when you may be faced with an opportunity to exit your company for, say, $100 million, which would provide financial security for the founder team for life, the VCs may be pushing to continue with an aggressive growth strategy, so that the company might reach their far more ambitious targets. This might work, but it can also increase your risk level substantially. For you, your business may be everything, but for them it may be 5% of a portfolio, which they want to gamble to reach 20×, even if it increases the risk of bankruptcy.

You can, however, try to secure yourself in your shareholders' agreement (i.e. the contract between the shareholders) so that it is you who decides when decisions for aggressive growth are made – for example, through individual shareholder agreements or by the use of different share classes. Or you can try to sell a bit of your shares along the way to calm the nerves and obtain at least some financial security. Whether you succeed with this is another matter.

And then there's the dilution of shareholdings and loss of control. Studies show that founders on average have 41% of the shares after an A-round and 18% after an E-round. Similarly, they lose influence on the board. Already after an A-round, they occupy on average only 34% of the board seats. Additionally, after an A-round, 19% have changed the CEO; by a D-round 38% have changed their first CEO and 23% have even changed their third (or more).[20]

STUDIES SHOW THAT FOUNDERS ON AVERAGE HAVE 41% OF THE SHARES AFTER AN A-ROUND AND 18% AFTER AN E-ROUND.

As explained above, external investors can be both a gift and a curse. We have heard of people who would have been better off without their outside investors. Many of these issues could have been avoided if the company had (i) had a good shareholders' agreement, (ii) ensured that the new investors shared strategic vision with the founders and (iii) done background checks on the investors in the same way as you would do with new employees, i.e. in particular, speaking with other companies they had invested in or checking them out on thefunded.com.

While considering an investor, in our view you should therefore consider the following questions:

- Is the investor 100% aligned with your strategy or if not, are you willing to change your strategy?
- Does the investor have the same goal as you regarding growth and overall strategy, etc.?
- Does the investor's intended exit align with your own plans?
- Do you want the investor to be active or passive?
- If you want the investor to be active and help, where do you really require assistance – functional assistance in marketing, IT, sales, etc., industry knowledge, coaching through the growth phases, geographic knowledge, social network or something else?

Mads about how time-consuming fundraising can be

If you have a young company with a marketable product and sound finances, you might, as a founder/CEO, perhaps use half your time and money on sales and marketing, 30% on the product and 20% on administration. However, if you must raise capital, the distribution will probably change to perhaps 40% spent on capital raising, 20% on administration, 20% on the product and 20% on sales and marketing. It is not unusual for an entrepreneur to use 50–90% of his time on fundraising for 4–6 months each time a new round must be raised. What suffers because of this is often sales and marketing.

I have received investments from everything from family and friends to billion-dollar funds, and during that process I have used about 30% of my time talking, meeting, building relationships and negotiating with new investors. Although I have raised more than $150 million, I have actually received a rejection 50–100 times for each funding commitment. The trick here is to avoid being depressed over the many refusals and instead to learn from them.

The importance of vintage in the venture industry

Returns on VC fluctuate a lot over time where, as with wine, there are some vintage years that produce great outcomes for most players and others that don't.

A pan-European study showed superior performance for VC funds founded in 1990–1994, which as a group reached a pooled net IRR (annual return of the invested money) of 12.87% – hardly surprising since they were well positioned to exit during the subsequent internet frenzy leading up to the crash in 2000.[21] However, other vintage intervals gave negative returns:

	1980–1984	1985–1989	1990–1994	1995–1999	2000–2004	2005–2009	2010–2013
Pooled IRR	6.21%	6.97%	12.87%	0.52%	–2.21%	2.75%	–8.53%

Simply put, the sector had a golden period for funds initiated between 1980 and 1994, obviously because these funds could invest in reasonably priced if not depressed markets and exit during good times.

9.
MY FUNDING PROCESSES

In the last chapter, we discussed the different sources of start-up funding. However, it is one thing to know about funding sources, an entirely different thing to know how to actually get the money. In this chapter, we review how to behave in your quest for funding. What support material should you prepare? How do you find investors and get meetings set up? How do you behave during those meetings? And what happens afterwards, if investors are interested?

Unless you do crowdfunding or an Initial Coin Offering, it normally takes a lot of investor meetings to raise money for a round. Indeed, a study by DocSend showed that for a single round of fundraising (seed or series A), a start-up company on average contacted 58 different investors and had 41 investor meetings. This generated on average $1.3 million and typically took approximately three months.[1]

FOR A SINGLE ROUND OF FUNDRAISING (SEED OR SERIES A), A COMPANY ON AVERAGE CONTACTED 58 DIFFERENT INVESTORS AND HAD 41 INVESTOR MEETINGS.

So it's not particularly easy. Let us jump into the investment process head-on, namely with the following 10-step fundraising guide. First, it's important to know that you actually start preparations long before the real hunt for the money.

1. *Visibility.* Before you plan to seek capital, you must make yourself visible to potential investors. Arrange meetings with them, if possible, and sign up for any sessions where many companies can pitch. Thus, you can learn from seeing how others do it at these events, but at the same time you are already meeting some investors. Bear in mind that investors would like to follow you over a period to see how your thoughts and your company develop. As former entrepreneur and later venture capitalist Mark Suster from Upfront Ventures says: 'I don't invest in a dot, I invest in a line.' In other words, he invests not based on experiences and impressions gained at a single time but after having followed

a company over a timeline. This process of following a company over a long time is called 'live due diligence' in the industry (a due diligence (DD) is a thorough analysis and check of the company).

Now let us assume that it has become clear to you that you will need capital from investors. The next step is:

2. *Set goals.* You determine how much you want to raise and what you want to spend the money on.

3. *Timing.* For how long do you need to be funded in this round, and what should you do if the funding round goes wrong?

4. *Choice of investor/type of lender.* You should find out which types of investors might be interested in investing in a company at your stage, with your location and your business focus. It is important here to focus on investors who are both located in the right place and have experience with exactly the business area you are working with.

5. *Spring cleaning.* Now you need to make your business presentation ready and before that you need to do a clean-up on all fronts. Organize your sales reporting, accounting, cash management, financial procedures and tax structure. Perform a legal audit. In other words, conduct internal due diligence.

Now you are ready to hunt for money:

6. *Check who has money.* You should check for each potential investor and determine whether they have funds to invest right now. You can often find this information via Pitchbook.com or Crunchbase.com, or you can explore on the investors' websites.

7. *Check out their ticket size.* You should check the amounts, or so-called 'ticket size', they usually invest. If what you are looking for is far outside their norm, you can forget them.

8. *Identify the most relevant partner.* If you are interested in a fund with multiple partners, you should try to find out which partner is most relevant to your business. Please beware that the typical hierarchy in a VC firm is as follows:

   A. General partners or managing directors

   B. Vice president or partners

   C. Principals or vice principals

   D. Senior associates

   E. Associates or analyst.

   Other titles you will sometimes encounter include 'entrepreneur in residence', or EIR, which applies to former entrepreneurs standing by to lead start-ups in which the VCs invest. These are normally smart and experienced people. By the way, you should be aware that 'associates' come in two forms. The first is the associate employed by the VC; the other may be a former star investor or entrepreneur with a loose affiliation with a VC as a talent and deal scout. The latter may be far more senior than the former but not employed full-time.

   Anyway, now you have made a preliminary list of potential investors, so you can start refining your presentation material:

9. *Make an executive summary/data sheet/PowerPoint presentation and a financial plan in Excel.* This is typically a 1–2-page summary of your business and an 8–15-page PowerPoint presentation (later in this chapter we touch upon what they should include) plus a simple financial model.

10. *Perfect your email presentation.* If you need an introductory email, it should be short, direct and able to generate interest, and it must initially state clearly what you seek and why you are a competent person with a great team. Before you send it, you must print it out and read it to yourself many times. It must be perfect!

11. *Make a Q&A (questions and answers).* **Make a list of the obvious** questions investors probably will ask and learn and rehearse the answers to perfection. Remember that many VC funds appoint a so-called 'red team' for grilling partners who recommend investing in a business such as yours. Red team members will point out all the reasons *not* to invest in your company. So, in the preparation of your Q&A, you must try to think as if you were on the red team in a VC fund. Which questions would you ask?

With these documents and presentations in place, you are ready to meet the investors. But how do you set up the meetings?

12. *Seek a privileged introduction.* The chances of getting a meeting are by far the greatest if you get a privileged introduction. This can be achieved if you know someone who knows the investors personally, or via the management of one of their portfolio companies (which you can often find via Pitchbook.com or Crunchbase.com). You can also use LinkedIn to find out who they know and thereby to identify a potential mutual acquaintance. Moreover, remember this key rule: it is more important that the person who introduces you knows the investor very well than that they know you very well.

13. *Alternatively, find their contact information for cold contact.* Cold contact, i.e. a contact without a privileged introduction, is your back-up solution and much harder. If you try this, use the internet, Email Hunter or similar sites and apps to find their contact information, and try to add them on LinkedIn to get LinkedIn message access. Alternatively, you can simply try to guess their email (hint: look at others from the company and use the Rapportive application).

14. *Send emails.* If you have not been able to get a meeting in place via privileged contacts, send emails. If they do not reply to these, you should simply try again and again. If they still don't reply, then call them. Remember that your goal with the email and phone call is just to get the first contact, which hopefully leads to a meeting. So, do not say any more than what is needed for this. If you have them on the phone, get them to talk also – otherwise they might very well be answering emails while talking with you without really listening. Therefore, ask 'why' questions and speak clearly and not too fast or too slow.

15. *Get the first interactive contact.* Your first contact may very well be a video conference (for instance, Skype). Seen through the investor's eyes, this is a pre-screening. At this stage, you should try to avoid contact with a junior person in an investment fund, since such a person rarely has any decision-making power other than the ability to eliminate you from their funnel, and therefore you just give investors another chance to say no without having met you first.

Finally, let's assume that you survived the first interview and now there is someone who is ready to meet you and your team in person. What do you do then?

16. *Personal presentation.* If the first interactive contact led to a personal follow-up meeting, you should at this meeting explain your business orally to the investors and explain how you expect to develop it while using the presentation to guide the conversation. Always bring one or more copies of the presentation to the meeting and leave them there. Assume that they will be circulated to people you have not met. Some people are afraid to talk about their business model, but you should generally not worry about this. So save confidentiality agreements (NDAs) for later. They are relevant only much later in the process when you share internal, confidential documents.

You have found someone who is interested. Yippee! But what will happen then?

17. *Term sheet.* A term sheet is often the first thing you will receive from an investor if they are interested. This means that, very often, it will come before the due diligence is completed, or even begun. As a consequence, it doesn't mean that they will invest, only that you have reached the second-last hurdle in their investment funnel. Term sheet is just an abbreviation of the shareholders' agreement and you use it to negotiate based on a manageable, short document rather than a 50-page contract. But beware. Whereas some VCs issue 2–3-page term sheets, others might provide some with 15–30 pages or even more.

18. *Due diligence.* After you and the investor have signed the term sheet, the investor will begin on the previously mentioned due diligence. Here they try to learn about the key people, the company, its competitors and even the industry to make sure that everything is correct, lawful, sober and commercially promising. During this due diligence, there will often be a need for a so-called data room, which is simply a password-protected, specialized version of Google Docs or Dropbox, for example, where you store all the key documents for the company. At this stage, you can ask for a signature on the NDA. Note, there are many great checklists for start-up due diligence on the web – just type in the words and they will pop up.

19. *Shareholders' agreement, subscription form and cap table.* Sometimes, in parallel with the due diligence, you will draft the revised shareholders' agreement and the subscription document, which eventually must be signed. Enclosed with this there can also be a so-called cap table (capitalization table) showing the specific shareholding structure before and after the intended capital increase, including the allocation of share options before the investors transfer the money. This is based on the former term sheet, but do not expect that a smart investor will not try to negotiate some of the things again. Perhaps they won't. But perhaps they will. Please note, the agreement must have an escape clause which makes you free if the money is not paid within an agreed date. You should also note, by the way, that some VCs, especially in the US, like contingent financing schemes, which means that your funding will be released in stages as you meet predetermined milestones. Or else . . .

20. *Signature.* The last part of the process is that you, other shareholders and the investor sign, after which your company receives the money.

With the exception of crowdfunding and ICO token sales, the 20-step process above is how start-up-funding normally works. However, within these 20 steps, there are also 20 processes that can go wrong. In general, finding investors makes us think of shooting precision shots with a machine gun – each shot in the gun must be perfect and adapted to the individual investor, but you probably need to fire a lot of shots to get the money in the box. Since the typical VC declines perhaps 200 proposals each time it invests in one, you should take a 'no' with a smile and learn from every interaction – ask yourself and the investor every time *why* the answer was a no and not a yes.

However, it must be said that one can also experience the opposite, namely that VC funds are queuing up to invest in your company. Such situations may evolve into 'term sheet battles' and some start-ups in this situation will do a tender, which is kind of a beauty contest in which each VC fund can give its investment proposal on a given date. Expect nice and simple term sheets in such a situation.

Legal audit is important

In a legal audit, lawyers examine whether your company has appropriate and well-executed contracts in place with employees, suppliers, customers, financial partners, etc. Here they are looking for red flags such as 'poison pill' clauses on termination of cooperation if the ownership structure in your business changes radically, and so on.

Tools you need from the start

Now we want to elaborate a bit on point 9 in our 20-point funding plan above. Point 9 now is about preparing your tools for the funding process and here is what we think you need:

- Two rehearsed, oral elevator pitches of 20 seconds and two minutes, respectively. Write them down, then learn them by heart.
- Half-page summary of your investment case.
- Fantastic template for pitch email.
- Excel with financials.
- Demo reel or video on YouTube or Vimeo, and if relevant, physical working demo.
- Pitch deck – various-length PowerPoint shows for 10-, 20- and 30-minute presentations.
- Investor control schedule (like a sales planning tool).

The pitch and the summary

The purpose of the elevator pitch is to provide a simple explanation of what the company wants to achieve, which is articulated in such a short and simple way that it can be told to someone in an elevator from the ground floor to about the 10th floor, depending on the elevator speed. Such an elevator pitch should last 20–60 seconds. The pitch typically describes a market segment that the company wants to dominate, such as the combination of:

• fulfilment of some needs	• a price segment
• a customer segment	• a service level
• a product segment	• an image
• a geographical area	• special user benefits or features
• a demographic segment	• a quality level.

For example, in the elevator pitch you can explain that you are to be/become:

'The very best supplier of X, to meet the need for Y, in the are Z, by making Q'.

It should be possible to say this within 20 seconds or a couple of meetings. And it shouldn't be too complex. Companies that want to do too much are called 'Swiss knives' by professional venture investors, and that isn't meant as praise. If you are really good at it, you can say it instantly and fluently, even if someone wakes you up in the middle of the night, continuously slaps you in the face or hoses you with cold water.

Sometimes you will see corporate missions described as how much the company should earn, or how big a market share it is aiming for. This may be relevant at the operational level, for a department or a sales person and for an investor, but it does not communicate the strategic message since it does not mention anything about *how* you will achieve these attractive results. The sentence above actually did (in a brief way) because it said that you would be the best supplier of a specific product within a specific area by doing something specific. However, as we mentioned in explaining why you do something, here is a better generic template:

'You are probably familiar with the problem A, right? In 20xx, I and some of my friends thought about this and decided to solve this problem because it is a big problem, and it could be a really funny project. So we came up with a fantastic solution. We do it by B, which means that we achieve C. Now our aim is to become the very best supplier of X, to meet the need for Y, in the area of Z, by making Q'.

This is could be your 60-second pitch. But please do not take this template too literally – just note that it does tick some boxes: what motivates you, which problem you solve and how you do it.

Often, you see parts of the mission statement being too product-specific. Here, it is much better to think of the *needs* you solve for the customers in the relevant market segment instead. Keep in mind that the market segment in which the company operates may well be served in new ways in the future. Taxi companies perhaps thought their mission was to drive a taxi, but Uber reminded them that it was to move people, which could be done in a completely different way, i.e. in private people's own cars (and incidentally also soon in a third way, which is via robotic cars).

The written summary

Your next tool is the written summary, which should be derived from your pitch and should have headlines that match those in your PowerPoint presentation. It should typically, as a minimum, give a simple summary of what your company does, how far along it is with investments, who is involved in management or as investors, and perhaps how much additional investment is needed until exit (what is the maximum drawdown).

Oh, about the market: skilled investors are really, really focused on how big the market opportunity is. The San Francisco investment firm Ironstone uses quantitative analysis to predict which start-ups are most likely to succeed, and its historical findings have shown that 80% of the success driver comes from addressing the right market versus only 12% from being the right team and 8% from other internal factors.[2] So . . . is your market opportunity enormous? Just asking.

The pitch emails

As mentioned, the best case for you is that you don't need to send any pitch emails, since a friend of yours already knows how cool your project is and will whisper it into the ears of people in high places, such as those of VC partners.

OK, this is not happening so often, so let's discuss the damned email. Here is what *not* to do: write an email from a Gmail account saying something to the tune of 'Hi Michael, I have some very interesting ideas for a start-up, I wonder if we could meet for a beer and discuss them.'

No, you can't – the VC executive is very busy looking pitch decks.

Another mistake would be to write emails to several partn same VC company. Yes, they actually do talk to each other and no, i not cool if you write to several of them. Instead send an email that inforn the recipient about the size of the market, what has been raised to date from whom, revenues, stage of business roll-out, and any reputable key people in management and among previous investors.

Mads on writing a pitch e-mail

Here is an example of a pitch email I have used for investors who already knew a bit about my project (sensitive data is removed). However, it is two to three times longer than we would suggest for an email to new investors.

Hi Michael,

Hope you are well. As you know, over the last two years we have built CompareAsiaGroup into the leading Asian financial comparison platform across seven markets with a population of 500 million.

Since the $40 million round last year (led by Goldman Sachs, which included Jardines, Mark Pincus, ACE & Company, DST, etc.), the business has grown 12x revenue, helped 20 million people compare and select financial products, distributed a lot of financial products in the process (e.g. $3.5 billion in personal loans) and reached profitability in the first market.
As you also know, Credit Karma has proven itself in the US, Check24 in Germany and MoneySuperMarket in the UK (active only in the UK with $3 billion market cap). In fact, financial comparison is one of the biggest internet models and CompareA-siaGroup is the leader of this in Asia.

is top-notch, led by Sam Allen (previously
director based in Asia, prior to this with
Sachs), and includes the former MD of
CMO of Comparis (the oldest financial
world), the head of commercial products
lly impressive guys.

off a $50–100 million round to expand
broaden our geographical footprint and
invest more in our brand. While the round will largely be
taken up by the existing investors, depending on what size
round we end up going for, there may be an opportunity now
to come in alongside existing investors (minimum $5 million +
ticket size). This round will see the business through to a $3–5
billion IPO within three years (the opportunity is $53 billion
spend in Asia).

I will be in Silicon Valley next week Wednesday to Friday
(11–13 May) and would love to discuss with your team in more
detail then. This also provides an opportunity to meet Sam
(CEO) and Prashant (CCO), who are joining me. With whom
in your team should I connect? There is a chance that I'll be in
Boston mid-June and would love to meet you then as well, but
would like to get the dialogue started early. I hope you agree
with that approach?

Yours, Mads

Email: xxx

Mobile phone: xxx

Excel with financials

You need an Excel spreadsheet with your financials. Of course, no VC is
going to take a meeting because of an Excel, but it would be wise to have a

well-structured Excel with you for the first meeting – just in case. You probably won't need it the first time, but if they ask, you should have it. And later, if there is a later, you *will* need it.

What should it contain? First, a simple overview over your past and predicted P&L (profit and loss) and liquidity status, the latter including a countdown to the maximum drawdown, so that the investors can see the size of the financial hole that needs to be filled before you turn cash positive. There should be lots of explanatory footnotes. If you have recurring revenues from clients, it also becomes useful to specify customer acquisition cost (CAC), which is what the marginal cost of generating a new client is, plus customer lifetime value (CLV), which is the lifetime operating profit from the average client. This will enlighten the investor about how meaningful it is to invest in expanded sales and marketing activities. For instance, they might want to know the return and payback time if you triple the sales force versus what you have planned.

Since you are now pitching to a VC, it should also calculate exit value and, derived from that, IRR and multiple for the investors in the planned round. The exit value should typically be calculated based on multiples of revenues and potential profits, plus on growth rate at the time of exit.

A very important point here is that the VCs probably don't believe in your forecast and your exit multiple assumptions, so they want to be able to calculate what will happen if it goes worse or much worse, or perhaps better, or if the business is structured differently. For this reason, you should indicate all the input variables in a different colour so that the VC can see where they can change assumptions. Also, you should separate investments from ongoing business. Beware that the moment the VC analyst or partner actually starts playing with your model in Excel, they are probably well on their way to getting mentally hooked. So once you get beyond the first meetings, let them play with your model and see what they come up with.

Demo reel or physical working demo

Nothing can have greater effect on an investor within a very short time than seeing an actual cool product. If you can make a quick demo reel or online demonstration – 30 seconds to max (max!) 7 minutes, that will be helpful. Less than one minute is perhaps best, and if you make one that is longer than that, make another one that is less than one minute. Of course, if your product is physical in any way (even as a screen interaction), if possible bring it with you for the meeting. If it's a nuclear reactor, bring a model.

The pitch deck

In the old days, there were two formats of material that an investor could receive, namely Word and PowerPoint or derived PDF. Today, PowerPoint (and PDF) has won and investors have become so used to this format that most do not even want to read it if you send a Word document.

TODAY, THE POWERPOINT HAS WON AND INVESTORS HAVE BECOME SO USED TO THIS FORMAT THAT MOST DO NOT EVEN WANT TO READ IT IF YOU SEND A WORD DOCUMENT.

When you create your presentation, you should again pay close attention to the mindsets of professional investors. First, a VC is not a social institution. It's fine if you want to save the world, but VCs need to make good money for their investors or they are out of business soon. What the investors then do with their profits, such as saving the world, is another matter.

Second, you should expect that they probably know everything in this book, and a lot more too. They know, for example, that the market opportunity should be huge, that the team is also key, that several founders are better than one, that network effects are amazing, etc. But they also know that most venture fund returns come from only a few of their investments. Here is what the Danish Growth Fund wrote after examining 445 Danish investments by 32 venture funds managed by 15 managers in the period 1998–2013:

> 'Often it is a single investment that ensures a great return for funds and a multiple above 1. This is especially true when we look at the four most promising funds in Denmark, where a single investment represents from 45% up to 86% of the funds' (expected) return. Without that investment, the funds would have a multiple lower than 1. So, it is crucial that the funds manage to hit those "home-runs"'.[3]

Because of this knowledge, professional investors – and especially skilled VCs – chase exceptional winners. If they spot such a potential huge opportunity in a portfolio company, they will often invest heavily and eagerly in each of that company's later investment rounds, while on the opposite site they tend to refuse to invest further in companies that are not going well. Two good rules describing their behaviour are (i) success breeds success and (ii) VC funds are not welfare organizations.

One aspect of this is important to know: until the dotcom bubble and its crash in 2000, some (though not all) VC funds would invest rather indiscriminately in a space they deemed hot. For instance, in the web search space during the 1990s, money was sprinkled generously on companies such as OpenText, Magellan, Infoseek, FAST, Teoma, Inktomi,

Lycos, and AltaVista – much of it in the hope that if the overall cake became big enough, everyone with a piece of it would become rich. However, as we now know, while the space did grow as expected, virtually all these companies ceased to exist, while Google became dominant. Today there seems to be much better understanding that each category in tech markets tends to end with a 'category king', which will often make 70–80% of total profits, if not more, while most early players will go bankrupt.

How should my pitch deck look?

When we discussed sales meetings, we pointed out that you should avoid sending your presentation beforehand, or if you must, make it very short. First, if they have already had your presentation, they might sit and read your slides while you present, which will destroy the focus. Anyway, here are the typical slides you want in your pitch deck – and in this order:

1. Front page – preferably with contact information.

2. Your amazing team and their experience and, if relevant, their previous collaborations.

3. The major problem you solve.

4. How you solve the problem.

5. Which competitive advantage you hopefully have that can make it very difficult for others to compete with you.

6. More in-depth information on how to solve the problem/ your product.

7. Why just now?

8. Why the market is – or will become – huge, how much of it you can get and whether you are poised for the role as a category leader.

9. Your go-to-market strategy and how to earn money.

10. How you get customers and how far you have come technologically and commercially (so-called 'traction').

11. Predictable milestones. When will you achieve what?

12. Your realistic financial projections. Preferably in round numbers, and perhaps with high case, low case and base case. Keep track of the assumptions behind these numbers and remember that investors are particularly interested in (i) your company's likely exit value, (ii) when the exit can be expected and (iii) how much additional capital there is to be invested in this exit (max drawdown).

13. How much capital you will raise now and what you do with the money. And then of course: How far will you go with it? To break even, or just to meet some milestones before the next round? Here you should, however, not specify a valuation in writing; you should rather explain that orally.

14. Summary: what you just said, repeated briefly.

A study of 200 pitch decks showed that the average size was 19 pages.[4] However, we would argue that the best investor presentations have fewer than 15 slides; typically, 8–12. Should there be a few more, it should be because there is less content on each slide. If you have 25 slides, for example, there should be very little on some of them. And you must have a version which you can present within 10, 20 and 30 minutes.

Why a short pitch deck for the first pitch? After all, this is your *huge* idea? Partly because you may have only 15–20 minutes to present it. But also for another reason: even though you will leave print copies of your presentation after (after!) the pitch meeting, if there is any interest at all they will typically ask you to email it in electronic form after the meeting (if not, they probably aren't interested). The PowerPoint or PDF that you email them might be passed on to various partners, analysts, investment committee members and/or advisory board members in the VC firm, and these are typically extremely busy people with very little time and patience. Therefore, your slides must be completely self-explanatory. And never forget to include contact information on the first and last slide: name, email address, LinkedIn, website and telephone. Always!

So again: short, sharp, simple and self-explanatory. If in doubt, read the following. The company DocSend provides software which enables you as the sender to see when a recipient opens a document and how long the recipient looks at each page. In the study of 200 pitch decks above, DocSend and a Harvard professor analyzed what happened with these 200 decks as they were emailed from start-up companies to investors. On average, investors spent (hold on!) just 3 minutes and 44 seconds studying a forwarded pitch deck. This is 12 seconds per page, if indeed they read it at all.

INVESTORS SPENT 3 MINUTES AND 44 SECONDS STUDYING A FORWARDED PITCH DECK, WHICH WAS ON AVERAGE JUST OVER 19 PAGES. THIS IS 12 SECONDS PER PAGE, IF INDEED THEY READ IT AT ALL.

Lars on scepticism about the value of commercial partners in pitch decks

A typical problem in start-ups with indirect sales through other companies is that they think that their impressive sales partner network will do the work by launching the product to business customers. I have tried that strategy many times myself, where some companies had to sell my software to other companies. My own harsh experience is that large companies are often incredibly poor at launching new and innovative products if they were not developed in-house and thus are supported by insiders. You typically need to have the products and the market started even before your partners can help you properly.

However, if you instead sell products targeted at consumers, it may be different – for example, if you secure shelf space for a consumer product in supermarkets, you probably have a promising company. I experienced this myself when we as students imported containers with cakes and sold them through supermarkets. But generally, if you have products for companies, you should not count on big sales partners automatically lifting your company. Experienced investors know this and therefore they will not necessarily be won over by a great partner list in your pitch deck.

The pitch meeting: what's on investors' minds?

When you do the pitch, you cannot know what goes on in the investors' minds. In Appendix B, we list 46 investment criteria that we think most experienced investors will consider. Some of these are obvious, such as the clearly scalable business model, perhaps the presence of network effects or strong intellectual property rights. However, professional investors may also focus on issues relating to your funding history. Here are some signs they will find promising:

- Your company has participated in prominent incubator/accelerator programmes.
- It has already received funding from reputable investors such as some of the most successful VCs – preferably at an early stage in its development.
- The early investors have participated in the subsequent rounds (especially important if these are high-performing, prominent VCs).
- Their funding has taken place at short intervals, preferably with a maximum of nine months between each round (this also means that they raised many rounds if they are no longer at the seed stage).

In other words, they like it if very smart people have already chosen to invest in your company and repeatedly have been willing to pony up more money without much hesitation when you've needed it.

The trend is your friend

Another factor they might consider is whether you have accelerating momentum, not only in your revenues, etc. but also in the public mindset. For instance, it doesn't inspire confidence if your company had lots of press coverage when it was founded but then less and less afterwards. Or if it made great hires early on but not lately.

A smart VC might use Google Trends to check momentum in search queries on your company and products and use LinkedIn to check the trend and quality of your new hires. However, interestingly, some players in the sector have also begun to apply artificial intelligence screening procedures when searching for the best investments and to assist them in their due diligence processes. In 2009, Businessweek magazine asked the CEO of AI company Quid, Bob Goodson, to use his software to pick 50 unheard-of companies with particularly great prospects.[5] He did it, and it turned out later that if a VC fund had created a portfolio with investments in only those 50 companies, it would have had the second-best performance of all VC funds ever.

Yes, ever. In 2017 he repeated the task, this time beginning with a database of 50 000 non-listed start-up companies, which he subsequently narrowed down to 5000 by screening for:[6]

- young, low-valuation start-ups that had raised money quickly from a set of top-performing VC firms
- higher-valuation companies that already showed clear commercial traction
- companies operating in the most promising business segments, which he identified by studying what types of business the most successful VC companies had invested most money in recently.

He then narrowed the list further to 200 companies by ranking:

1. How much time it took between each round (shorter time and preferably less than nine months between each round was best).

2. How many rounds were raised (many was better).

3. Amount raised.

And then he took it down to 50 by looking at, among other things:

- whether the founders had worked together before (a positive)
- where the founders had gone to school (top universities were good).

Goodson doesn't disclose his exact formula, but from interviews it appears that his AI system doesn't like companies that have had extensive press coverage early on, but it does like great momentum in press coverage as they evolve. It also looks at trends in hiring as well as the quality of the management a company can attract (LinkedIn is the obvious source). And it looks at whether prominent VCs that invested early on participate in follow-up investments. Proportional reinvestment from top-notch investors is a clear plus.

Among venture funds, SignalFire and Correlation Ventures are both examples of Silicon Valley VCs that have used big-data analytics to monitor millions of sources and predictive modelling to spot potential investment opportunities.[7] According to them, much is still left to human talent, but the AI analytics help crunch the numbers and focus on people who have enjoyed successful endeavours in the past. Another company, Growth Science, has determined that up to 80% of predictors of future performance come from outside factors (such as market conditions) and its software analyzes these factors alongside internal growth predictors to give you a report on the likelihood of that company's success.

What do investors think about presenters at pitch meetings?

What works when you present to an angel investor or a VC? What will impress them? Perhaps the best expert in the world on this subject is Lakshmi Balachandra. Lakshmi worked for two VC funds where she noticed how the analysts and partners often were very excited about specific start-ups – until they actually met the entrepreneurs face to face. Then they often lost all interest.[8]

Evidently, something went wrong during the presentation meetings, so Lakshmi spent many years studying videos of hundreds of start-up pitch meetings to VCs and angel investors to find out what that could be. Why did some presentations generate no interest among the investors, while other sessions got the founders to the next step in a fundraising process?

Her findings were perhaps surprising. What *didn't* work very well at all was to come blazing in and give an over-energetic, alpha-male 'here we are and we are driven and passionate and confident' presentation. Neither did it work well to base a pitch on traditionally female traits such as warmth, sensitivity, expressiveness or emotionality. So what *did* work?

Laughing, for one. Entrepreneurs who laughed during the meetings did better than average. It was also helpful to discuss mutual friends or acquaintances. 'Ah, you know John from XYZ? I studied with him; we had a lot of fun.' However, on a broader scale, these were the three main findings:

- Being calm and considerate was better than being excited and passionate.

- Exhibiting character and trustworthiness was more important than demonstrating professional competence.

- Being receptive to feedback was important. The most successful fundraisers didn't react defensively to critical questions but listened carefully and gave thoughtful answers.

There have been other interesting studies. Two MIT researchers, Sandy Pentland and Daniel Olguín, fitted executives at a party with devices that recorded data on their social signals, including tone of voice, gesticulation and proximity to others.[9] Then, as the study said, 'five days later the same executives presented business plans to a panel of judges in a contest. Without reading or hearing the pitches, Pentland correctly forecast the winners, using only data collected at the party'. In fact, he predicted the winner correctly in 87% of the cases without having read their plans or seen their pitches. How? By observing how they behaved at a cocktail party, where he looked for the ones who talked more, listened more and were more energetic – these, it turned out, were the most successful pitchers.

Don't get this wrong. We are not suggesting that you should focus on giving a good act during a pitch meeting – that you should try to be something you are not. The key lesson is something else: be the energetic version of yourself, but not over the top. Try to be thoughtful in general. Try to earn people's trust in general. And try to listen and learn a lot – in general. Be that person in general and then come as you are for your pitch meeting.

How do I run my pitch meeting?

Now let's look at your pitch meeting as it might play out. You and your partners are heading for the offices of angels, incubators, accelerators or VCs. First question: how do you dress? We recommend that you appear quite formal but not flashy. Don't dress like the person you are now but like the person you want to become. Dress as you imagine yourself as the future head of the medium to large business you hope to create. Then practise the pitch on some investors or other people who are not important to you commercially before you go to those who really count – think of the first as test investors.

Next: don't be even remotely late; instead, be early. Show up in really good time for the meeting and have printed versions of your presentation with you. You cannot know how many people from the investors' company will be present, so you need to print more than enough copies, just in case. But don't pull out five presentations if there are only two investors present at the meeting – that would make you appear like a disappointed loser. No, open your bag and pull out the appropriate number of presentations only. Two investors, two decks; five investors, five decks.

If you want to show PowerPoints, you should, well in advance of the meeting, ask in the reception whether there is an overhead projector in the meeting room so you can set it up. If you have a 20-minute meeting, you would obviously not want to spend the first five of those minutes fumbling with technical equipment.

In the dialogue at the meeting, you should not be thinking of closing a deal as you will not reach any agreement either in this or the many future times you may see this investment fund – not at all! Your first meeting is not about getting the money – it is about getting to the second meeting. Create an intimate atmosphere. Create dialogues. Listen to them, as they listen to you. Remember, it's conceivable that they think they are smarter than you, and they probably think of how they could shape your business better than you have realized that it can be shaped. Therefore show that you are willing to listen and learn. Be self-confident but not close-minded, overconfident and stubborn.

Famous first words

How do you begin the meeting? First, ask how long they have allocated to see you. They might, for example, say 20 or 30 minutes but without revealing that they may allocate more perhaps if they like the story. Then use a few minutes to ask about the status of their funds and specifically whether they have money to invest now, if you have not already found this out. Unless it's a top fund, you might be surprised that they have spent all their money in their last fund but have not yet raised enough to start the next one. In such cases, the fund can therefore actually not invest and they are just trying to build relationships for later. Yes, you should search for this information before the meeting, but you sometimes first find the whole truth when the meeting takes place – and it leaves a professional impression to ask. If they have no money right now, change your tactics a bit. Tell them that there will be more rounds later and that you would like to build a relationship so that they can follow you.

Also ask about what kinds of investments they are excited about right now. This is a sales meeting, so remember the sales compass – even though you have only a short time, you need to ask questions and qualify the investor apart from the issue of whether they have money. If they told you that you have 20 minutes and they spend the first 10 talking about themselves, you can be pretty sure that they in fact have more than 20 minutes. So yes, get them to talk. Show an interest in them – then they are more likely to show interest in you.

Then you pitch, but do not hand out your printed material until the end of the meeting – otherwise you run the risk that they read it instead of listening to you. Remember what we said about speeches – the audience must never be diverted from attention to what you say.

You should now reveal everything in your presentation that can convince the investor to spend more time on your company. You must also assume that your competitors might get to see your presentation material. This is not supposed to happen, but it might.

Preferably, eventually also ask whether they have suggestions for other VC funds that might be interested since you can assume that many funds discuss you and your company with each other and may co-invest in you or others. For the same reason, it can be dangerous to get too many rejections in the same circles as you will be known as the one nobody will invest in. Therefore, you should ideally do your initial practice in circles that are distant from those you really want to make interested.

Should you introduce the terms during the first meeting? No – we suggest being pretty vague about that, at least until you have a BATNA from one investor, perhaps in the form of a term sheet for some of the round. The best course of action is often either that the VC comes up with a proposal or that a neutral middle man takes the discussion. Of course, earlier on we discussed the advantage of being first mover in a price negotiation, but, well, this is different. You are *not* in a negotiation in the first or second or perhaps third and fourth meeting. You are most likely still selling.

Finally, how does the pitch meeting end? One outcome is a flat rejection, which is obviously bad but at least clear. Another is a request for more information or a follow-up meeting, which is great but perhaps the beginning of a protracted live due diligence. However, many pitch meetings end with something like 'Very interesting, let's stay in touch'. Sounds great, doesn't it, but it probably means 'No', or perhaps just 'No, not for now'. In the latter case, you may be able to come back later if things go well for you. Indeed, again it might be the beginning of a 'live due diligence' where the investors follow you for a longer period to see how your company evolves. If you think the VC may be doing a live due diligence on you, then by all means consider them a warm contact: inform them continuously without being pushy, perhaps directly, or perhaps – and potentially far smarter – by informing people you know that they know. This is one of the reasons we think it is great to introduce a monthly newsletter or update stream on social media even from day one of your project.

WE THINK IT IS GREAT TO INTRODUCE A MONTHLY NEWSLETTER OR UPDATE STREAM ON SOCIAL MEDIA EVEN FROM DAY ONE OF YOUR PROJECT.

How do investors determine my company valuation?

There are countless ways to value a company. To a large extent, which ones are most relevant depends on what you are selling to the investors. Here are five scenarios in case of a trade sale:

1. The investors just want parts of your team for a temporary task.

2. The investors want the entire team, indefinitely.

3. The investors want to use your technology and/or IP rights in their own organization.

4. The investors want your business, which they can leverage better than you can.

5. The investors need to get your business partly to leverage their own and partly to avoid competition getting it instead, which would be problematic for the potential buyer.

Obviously, the two first command very low valuations. Motive #3 is better because the buyer can leverage your products, patents, etc. within its own organization. Motive #4 adds further value through the revenue flow you already generate. Finally, #5 can sometimes generate valuations that can look insane unless you know the context – such as Facebook buying Instagram, which had 13 employees and no revenues, for one cool billion dollars.

In the following, we will focus on valuation methods relating to scenario #4, where the buyer buys a business for its expected future cash flow, which is also what investors in crowdfunding, ICOs and IPOs should look for.

Two essential approaches are particularly common here. Either you take all expected future dividends until a selected end date and estimate their present value by 'discounting' each annual dividend with an annual factor such as 10%. The result is called DCF for discounted cash flows. For example, perhaps expected $100 profit in year 2 is considered worth $90 today, $100 profit year three is worth approximately $80 today, etc. Or else you use multiples of revenue or earnings from listed companies from other trades, i.e. the so-called 'comparables', or 'comps', or 'peers'. These can be found in the news flows and databases from CBInsights, CrunchBase, Fortune Magazine Term Sheet, Strictly VC, etc. However, when considering these, please note that in the early stage, the valuations can be influenced by the founders' experience. One early-stage company may have far higher valuations than another with a very similar model simply because the former is run by people with huge experience and star power and the latter isn't.

There are lots of long books on both core models. But they are not the only ones – other methods include a multiple of the last or next year's projected revenue, cash flow, profits or other methods. In any case, a professional investor will also give plenty of consideration to the following four elements:

- How big is the risk that it all goes wrong?
- What exit value of the company do you expect?

- Maximum drawdown to exit – how much capital should be further invested before break-even and at what valuations might it occur?

- Time to exit – how much time is expected to pass before there will be an exit option?

Now, let's add some detail and a few technical terms. First, we have the Venture Capital Method or VC Method, which derives from work by Professor William Sahlman from Harvard. According to this, you can estimate likely exit value and then discount it by a derived return on investment such as 30× or 10×. Say what? Well, for instance, if you think the company can exit at $100 million in due course, and if your threshold for wanting to invest is a 10× return, then you are willing to invest at a pre-money valuation of $100 million/10 = $10 million. Of course, when doing this calculation, you need to take likely dilution by subsequent capital increases into consideration.

Here is another method for seed: the Rule of Thirds. It means that when the company gets its first funding, one-third of the equity goes to investors, one-third to the founders and one-third is reserved for stock options for future management. Of course, this is not a calculation method, but rather a screening method. If founders won't accept something along those lines and have no good reasons for rejecting it, some investors will balk.

Another core model is the Berkus method, named after angel/VC investor Dave Berkus. It goes like this. The seed value of a start-up can be split into five elements:

Sound business idea/great market opportunity	$500 000
Existing prototype	$500 000
Good management team in place	$500 000
Strategic business relationships in place	$500 000
Product roll-out has begun and seems to work	$500 000

Of course, many investors have a much more detailed list of success drivers, such as the 46 we list in Appendix B. Such an approach is often called the Scorecard Method. Evidently, the higher granularity you use, the lower amount you assign for each, so that if all are met, you reach approximately $2.5 million. One of the better-known detailed scorecard methods was developed by Cayenne Consulting and can easily be found on the net.

Of course, in addition to such rules of thumb, the wise investor will add what comes from a gut feeling, which may add or subtract a lot from what his standard valuation model comes up with. But what is important to know is that on average, the seed pre-money valuations paid by angels and seed-focused VCs is $1.5–2 million, depending on vintage.[10]

The last approach we would like to mention is the Risk Factor Summation Method. Here you list the following 12 risk factors:

1. Management

2. Stage of the business

3. Legislation/political risk

4. Manufacturing risk

5. Sales and marketing risk

6. Funding/capital-raising risk

7. Competition risk

8. Technology risk

9. Litigation risk

10. International risk

11. Reputation risk

12. Potential lucrative exit

Then you assign to each of these one of these ratings: −2, −1, 0, +1 or +2. When done, you add the ratings together and multiply the result by $250 000. If you gave +2 to each risk factor, the valuation becomes $6 million, and if they were all valued −2, the valuation is −$6 million. Obviously, no one would invest in a company they think has negative net valuation.

Some mechanics of valuation calculations you need to know

The amount of shares an investor will receive for an investment depends mechanically on so-called pre-money valuation of your company and its shares and on the amount invested. While pre-money valuation is up to negotiation, post-money is simply pre-money valuation plus the money that just came in: post-money = pre-money + investment.

That was simple, but let's play with it a bit. Let us imagine that your company is $9 million worth pre-money and an investor invests $3 million, then post-money valuation is 9 + 3 = $12 million. Thus, the new investor will own 3/12 = 25% of your company. It is important that you understand the pre-money, post-money and what ownership the investor gets, since confusion here can be expensive. Among other things, you should therefore make sure to have the previously mentioned cap table created early in the process.

Here comes a snag: when determining valuation before the investment, you should also pay close attention to the concepts of undiluted and diluted shares or valuations. Undiluted is the existing shareholder's valuation here and now. If this amount is $12 million, the value per share is the $12 million divided by the number of shares. That is obvious, but a professional investor such as a VC will also consider the new shares that will be issued as employee stock options and perhaps for other purposes that will dilute the investor's shares. The VC will estimate this and therefore downgrade the value of each outstanding share already issued today by expected future dilution. In some cases, a VC would only calculate based on the number of shares outstanding after the existing stock options are effectuated, but they might also include the additional stock options expected to be issued in the years to come – which makes sense. This makes diluted value even lower.

Does it mean that you have miscalculated if the investor makes tons of money on your company?

You sometimes hear about reluctance towards an investor who earns too much. You should not think in that way, in our opinion, since if an investor makes money on your company, you probably also do. Furthermore, investors who have made money by investing in you tend to also invest in your next start-up – and typically at a much higher valuation.

What should I be aware of in the shareholders' agreement when dealing with investors?

Before we walk you through some of the most important elements of the shareholders' agreement, we will first suggest that you get a lawyer to look through the papers and advise you in your negotiations as early on as from the term sheet stage. However, it is very important that this lawyer has conducted these types of transactions before. Similarly, you can prepare yourself for the process by reading examples of term sheets, which can be found on, among others, the National Venture Capital Association or the British Private Equity & Venture Capital Association websites.

Reason? Forewarned is forearmed, and while the valuation is obviously one of the most important parts of the deal, you may, as an entrepreneur, easily get the world's best valuation while still receiving a very poor deal if the rest of the contract terms are adverse. So grab a cup of coffee because now we shall dig a bit into what these terms might include. It's pretty dry, but it's also pretty important.

The term sheet

Most VC companies have a standard term sheet, which they use as the benchmark in every negotiation. We will now review the typical major aspects of the term sheet and the shareholders' agreement, so you know what you are signing.

About the VC Leading a Syndicate

- *Exclusivity clause.* If the investor offers himself as the head of an investment syndicate, he will almost always demand, and should also receive, exclusivity so you do not negotiate in parallel with others. This should usually be accepted.

About the VC Securing Your Commitment

- *Vesting and lock-up clauses.* Investors are usually afraid that you will leave the company shortly after they have invested, potentially leaving them with a ship without a captain. They will therefore often try to protect themselves from this by asking you to 'vest your shares', i.e. that while you owned your shares yesterday, you will now return them all to the company but get them back over the following period (typically four years). This is to ensure that you stay at least that long. Alternatively, you get a lock-up on your stocks so that you cannot sell them within a few years after their investment. These are two typical examples of protection against you leaving the company, but there are many other forms. Moreover, the investors can also insist on a redistribution of the existing shares if they do not think the split reflects the future importance. Your view on this depends on your perspective on the management.

We suggest that you agree to vest your shares only if you retain all of them, in case they fire you. This will avoid a situation where they not only can fire you and take your shares but in a sense have a financial incentive to do so.

About Securing Influence for Either You or the VC

- *Founder board member clause.* A founder, who is the CEO and on the board, can ask to become a 'founder board member' instead of a 'CEO board member'. This is in order to maintain a board position, even if another CEO is hired. This can be reasonable if the founder has an important role in the future, but an investor would probably not be so happy with such a board member that can never be repealed. You should expect strong push-back on this.

- *Voting preference clause.* VCs can ask for preferential voting rights, which means that their votes count extra (to the extent that it is legal), or they may require veto rights regarding budgets, sales, employments, etc. Whether this is reasonable depends on the specific circumstances.

- *Number of board meetings.* Many term sheets demand monthly board meetings. This is probably more than you will want, but it is also more than the investors want if the company is reasonably on track. We recommend accepting this and then later suggesting the number of meetings that actually makes sense.

About Protection of the VC in Case the Company Disappoints

- *Anti-dilution clause.* VC contracts very often contain clauses that protect them if a subsequent capital increase takes place at a valuation lower than the one at which they invested. On average, about 7% of the investment rounds are such down rounds. This depends not only on the company but also on vintage. In 2002 and 2009, which were crisis years, down rounds in the United States were respectively 13% and 12%.

In case such a down round occurs, investors would like to be compensated for having previously invested at too high an evaluation. The compensation typically comes in the form of free shares, whereby other shareholders in the company, but not the VC fund, will be punished. Such anti-dilution clauses are difficult to avoid, but please note that they come in three versions. 'Full ratchet' means that all the investors' shares are adjusted down to the price of the subsequent down round. 'Narrow-based weighted average anti-dilution' means that it is adjusted only partly down to the new round according to a specified equation. Finally, 'broad-based weighted average anti-dilution' adjusts it even slightly less. We suggest that you do not agree to a full ratchet, but the narrow- and broad-based models can be reasonable, and indeed approximately 90% of all term sheets use one of these two weighted measures.[11]

- *Liquidation preference clause.* VCs will often insist on a so-called liquidation preference, which means that their capital will be rewarded first when an exit occurs. A 1× liquidation preference means that nobody gets anything before the VC has received their money back. This is used in approximately 90% of all term sheets, so you probably shouldn't make a big fuss about that.

It should be noted that investors in subsequent rounds surely will do the same, so that they will stack their preference above the preference of previous investors, and so forth. If the company is sold for the same valuation as they invested or more, this has no effect, but if it is sold at a lower valuation than the last capital increase, the other shareholders will feel the effect of the clause – and at very low valuations, the other shareholders might not receive anything at all.

These clauses are very common and jointly referred to as 'non-participating preferred'. Sometimes VCs try to get up to 2× or 3× liquidation preference. This preference should be compared to other conditions, including the pre-money valuation. A few investors try to be tougher by asking for 'participating preferred', i.e. the investor is both the one to get their full amount back plus the remaining money will have their original share. But this is unusual and we would usually advise you not to say yes to anything beyond 1× non-participating liquidation preference. By giving an investor 2× or higher preference, you also create potential conflicts of interest.

- *Accruing dividends clause.* VCs can ask for 'accruing dividends', which means that they must have x% dividend before others can get a dividend. This is simply part of the price negotiation and the higher the valuation, the more likely it is that VCs will try to compensate with this kind of clause. Frequently, they will ask to be the first to receive dividends each year, and in case these cannot be paid, their right will be accumulated as profits accumulate.

- *Buy-back rights clause.* Investors often require that the company must buy their shares back at the invested price as well as accruing dividends that are not paid if the company does not meet certain requirements, such as an exit on a given date. Since you probably cannot afford to do this, what it really means is that you are obliged to find another buyer for their shares. Here you should be careful with creating a condition where a realistic change or delay automatically can result in a threat of bankruptcy.

- *Contingent investments clause.* Especially in the US, it has been quite common for many years that an investment offer is contingent on future performance and divided into portions, or tranches, that are released one at a time as milestones are (potentially) reached. Many VC companies *only* invest in tranches. This model has significant benefits to the investor. First, it limits their risk, and second, it gives them a higher IRR. A multiple of 3× on a #10 million investment, for example, gives a higher IRR if 2.5 million is invested yearly over a period of four years than if all $5 million were invested the first year. In principle, such agreements should justify a higher valuation and can make sense for both parties. However, an alternative is that everything is paid up front, but then is adjusted for the buyer's price and thus the number of shares is dependent on how well or whether the milestones are achieved.

About Securing Flexibility and Shareholder Protection in Case of Sale of Shares or the Whole Company

- *Drag-along rights.* Drag-along rights means that if, for example, someone offers $100 million for the whole company and you own only, say, 50%, then you can force the remaining shareholders to exit the company with you. Drag-along is typically a practical necessity to prevent minority shareholders from holding up a good business deal or taking other shareholders hostage by demanding a higher price for their own shares to accept the deal.

  Drag-along rights will typically come with a minimum price, which is higher than what the shares were valued at when the clause was made. In addition, there will typically be a certain percentage of shares that is required to use the drag-along rights – we propose you request that this minimum is about 50%, although 75% is not unusual.

- *Tag-along rights.* These rights mean that if you sell your shares, another shareholder can sell their shares as well. The fewer shares a given shareholder has, the more important tag-along rights are; otherwise they may fear that you will sell your shares, after which they are left with a new owner, who controls the company and whom they do not trust.

- *Pre-emption/first right of refusal.* VCs typically require veto regarding future capital increases as well as the right to buy any new shares on the same terms as they are offered to others. This is rather standard and should often be accepted.

The clauses above are those we consider to be the most important, but there may well be more. However, these clauses alone should make clear why you need a lawyer *experienced in such deals* on your side during the negotiations.

In addition to this, you should be aware of who controls the company after you have received funding. A company works in a way that the shareholders select the board, the board selects the CEO and usually the CEO chooses the other employees. The board's choice of a CEO is typically done by a majority vote, and how the board is elected is usually defined by the shareholders' agreement. However, many investors will try to define some circumstances where they alone can decide on, for example, your salary as a director, so that you cannot give yourself a sky-high salary after they have made an investment. This is not uncommon, but you still need to be aware of how much power they have and that you do not lose your flexibility.

Please note that each part of a negotiation about capital increase, trade sale or similar will typically have advisors, and it is always important to ask these a simple question: 'Do you see anything unusual in these terms?'

51% of the shares rarely mean full control

Many novice entrepreneurs believe they can keep control of their company if they retain 51% of the shares. When VC funds invest, however, their different clauses will largely limit the original investors' power, even if these have most of the shares.

Mads on preferential voting

I have in one of my companies less than 50% of the shares but appoint four out of seven board members, and thus I decide who will be the CEO of the company. In other words, it is possible to maintain control over who will be the CEO, even if you own less than 50% of the shares. Some investors in your company would

What should I think about the term sheet they gave me?

The investors may give you a standard term sheet, a founder-friendly one, or one that rather could be called investor-friendly. So, when you look at what they gave you, which one is it?

Let's start with what is standard. Such a term sheet will probably have a 1× participating preference share (the investors get their money back before previous investors and founders), weighted average anti-dilution clause (only partial adjustment of share price in case of down round) and standard governance and consent rights (about appointment of board directors and what the investors can veto). This can indicate that the investors are excited about you but are not expecting problematic competition for the deal. If they start to ask for more, such as 2× preference, they may think you have your back against the wall. And if they ask for less, they might be afraid to lose the deal.

How does the share subscription work?

A subscription of shares typically has a couple of steps. First, the lawyer has the share certificates and subscription contracts. The investors will then transmit the money to the lawyer's client bank account, where they are in 'escrow' – on standby to be paid out upon signature. This also provides 'proof of funds', showing that the investor actually had the money. Once the documents are signed, the lawyer releases the money to your company.

How can I raise loan capital?

Now we have looked a lot at funding via issuance (selling) of stocks, but as mentioned above, there are also other forms of capital. Ordinary bank loans for start-ups are almost impossible to receive – unless you pledge your house or the like as collateral. However, the banks still lend to companies in later stages of development. This can be for both profitable companies with good cash flow and for less profitable or unprofitable companies that can provide security.

Some banks and a lot of credit companies offer so-called 'factoring' products. Factoring can mean, for instance, that if one customer will pay you in 60 days from now, then the factoring company gives you the money immediately against taking over the claim against your customer. Such a solution may sound cheap with, for example, 2% for 30 days. However, this actually corresponds to 26.7% per annum in compound interest and this huge cost may mean that your business is no longer profitable, which oddly enough can make it dependent on continued factoring for its survival. Thus, pay close attention to all types of loans and their costs.

Can I avoid raising capital by streamlining my working capital?

Many companies that consider raising capital could avoid it by streamlining their working capital. For instance, if your business (i) needs $1 million to grow and (ii) has annual revenues of $12 million and (iii) has customers who pay after two months, it may help if the customers were paying after one month instead of two, as the company then would have an extra million available for growth funding.

There are many other methods to streamline your company's working capital, but the four most frequent forms of this working capital optimization are:

- Reduce your costs
- Pay your suppliers later
- Lease hardware, software and equipment instead of buying it
- Get your money earlier from your customers.

Regarding the last method, it should be mentioned that the collectibles from customers are the opposite of a good bottle of wine because their value deteriorates over time. The longer you wait to charge and collect money from your customers, the lower is the likelihood of them ever paying you. Therefore, your business should have a clear structure for billing and collecting, which must be strictly followed. In addition, you should receive an overview from your finance people every week on who has not paid you and what is being done about it – then your business must follow up immediately and relentlessly. Being sloppy with unpaid bills can kill a start-up.

How do I get grants for my business?

In addition to selling shares, borrowing money and streamlining your business, there is another way to receive funding – grants. Most grants have some requirements as to how you need to spend the capital, but there is no claim for repayment and grants can therefore be the cheapest form of capital alongside streamlining your business.

How much can you get from grants? We know people who have raised more than $10 million in grants for their business.

Most grants have quite clear purposes, which means that your strategy must fit their purposes, so you must either change your strategy or do a project matching that purpose. Whether it makes sense to change strategy depends on the specific situation. However, be aware that getting grants is rare and can be time consuming.

Are you overoptimistic?

Most entrepreneurs are exceptionally optimistic by nature – this has been proven in many studies. Experienced VCs know this and take overoptimistic forecasts into account. Well-known venture capitalist Guy Kawasaki says that he divides entrepreneurs' expected revenue by 10 and adds a year to their roll-out timing.[12]

About investors and their board positions

External investors, and at least angels, strategic investors and VCs, require a formal board where they typically demand board seats. Angels, however, usually leave the board once VCs enter. Typically, the board grows from around three to six people as the company goes through its different funding rounds. If you receive an investment from a competent VC, you should note whether the board member they nominate is a senior or a junior partner. An experienced and thus senior VC partner typically sits on between 8 and 12 boards, and a very experienced senior VC partner may have been in 40–50 boards throughout their career. This provides a high level of pattern recognition, which can be of great value to your business.

Typical poor investments

Investigations have shown that many investors invest 2–3 times more capital than justified in start-ups which have not yet achieved a product/market fit. They also invest in soloists and founding teams lacking technical skills, although indicators show that these companies have a much lower probability of achieving success.[13]

11 tips about presenting to investors

- Practise before taking the first important investor meetings for your start-up. The best way is to pitch for some investors that are less important.
- At an important investor meeting, do not dress like the person you are now (perhaps a poor student) but like the person you hope to become (such as the CEO in a growth business).
- Show up early for the meeting and request access to the meeting room before it starts so that you can set up your presentation.
- Bring the printed version of the presentation, but do not distribute it until the end of the meeting and once you do, don't leave spare copies.
- Ask from the start how much time the investors have for the meeting but assume that they may have more time in reserve if they are interested.
- Your behaviour should be neither too alpha-manly and over-energetic, nor too sensitive and soft. Investors prefer calm and thoughtful.
- Radiating character and credibility is more important than the radiance of professional competence.

- Be sensitive to feedback and give thoughtful answers.
- End the meeting by asking what they thought about the presentation and what the next step is.
- Also ask whether they can recommend other investors for your case. And possibly if they can introduce you.
- Whatever you do, never waste a professional investor's time.

PART 3.

ABOUT MY TEAM AND MY CORPORATE CULTURE

So far, we have studied your personal role and challenges as an entrepreneur, as well as your company's core idea, structure, business models and financing.

However, now we come to some of the aspects of building up a company that can give you the greatest joys but also the biggest challenges, namely the people around your project. We will discuss both your core team, with whom you can discuss anything, and your entire staff, including freelancers. How do you choose your team? How do you hire and fire people? When do you need freelancers? And how do you manage effectively? We will review these and many other organizational issues in this section.

And then we study something else that is both fun and cumbersome in building a winning business: the culture.

10.
MY CORE TEAM

You can have the greatest business idea in the world, but if your team is not great, the project will surely fail – unless management is successfully replaced. Thus, throughout this chapter we will comprehensively review thoughts concerning your core team, including how you put together a great founder team, how you govern your mutual relationship (for example, the share allocation) and how you work with board members, mentors, coaches and advisory boards.

People who have not tried to build companies might think that first and foremost it is about getting the good idea and that the work effort comes in secondary position. To some degree, they have a point, because as previously mentioned, a study has shown that 80% of the success driver comes from addressing the right market, which is certainly part of the idea, whereas only 12% accrues from having the right team (and 8% from other factors).[1]

But wait a minute. The inventor genius and serial entrepreneur Thomas Edison once noted (in fact, several times) that in his view 'genius' was the result of 2% inspiration and 98% perspiration, i.e. 2% is the good idea and 98% is perspiration – competent work.

Here is how we see it:

- A great team with a so-so idea will know how to pivot until the idea has become great.
- Great investors will be able to change the team if they like the idea.
- In either case, Edison was right: entrepreneurship is mainly perspiration.

The reality is that most of us get plenty of ideas throughout our life, but very few of us implement them. Most people just don't have the kick-ass mentality. 'Ideas are a dime a dozen. People who implement them are priceless', as people often say. Many people have dreams, but few of these ideas are turned into personal goals and then commercial realities.

GENIUS IS THE RESULT OF 2% INSPIRATION AND 98% PERSPIRATION.

Implementation requires a well-functioning team. Researchers examined 96 unsuccessful investments by 49 VC firms to try to figure out what went wrong. Was it a lack of demand? Or maybe innovative technologies that blocked the way? No, this was rarely the problem. Actually, the answer was that companies in 65% of the cases failed due to *internal* problems – i.e. problems within the team.[2] Therefore, we will look at how to find, hire and build a super team that can increase the possibility of success for your business.

What does a start-up team consist of? We can divide it into two main groups: on the one hand is what we call the core team, consisting of co-founders, the board and a possible mentor, coach or advisory board. On the other hand, we have the employees and freelancers. In this chapter, we will discuss the former only – the core team – and in the next chapter we are going to talk about employees and freelancers. But let's start by looking at co-founders.

Should I have a co-founder?

You have a business idea. Should you found your business alone or should you do it with others? The typical motives for having a co-founder are:

- If you can convince others of the idea, it is more likely that it is viable.
- You can share the risk and/or you have collectively more capital to invest.
- You have complementary personalities and your different knowledge and capabilities can give you better results.
- You can share the victories.
- You can share the defeats and the tough days.
- You still have a management team if one of you is sick.
- You are at least two people who think and fight as owners.
- You have a much larger social network.
- You get more inspiration and see things from a new perspective.
- You are more people who can do important company presentations or key negotiations, etc.

And here are some motives against:

- The co-founders do not necessarily contribute equally, which can create frustration.
- You cannot decide on your own, which results in slower decision making and a risk of strategic disagreement.
- You must share the profits.

Generally, we believe that two or three founders is usually the best number, as long as they are a great match. A study in the US showed that there were two co-founders in 39% of all IT projects and that 35% of life science projects had two founders.[3] Second most common was three founders. In only 8–10% of cases were there more than four founders.

What works best? On average, it takes companies with only one founder 3.6 times as long to reach high growth than if they had had several founders.[4] This negates the fear of sharing the profit with others because if the company is growing 3.6 times as fast with several founders, it can easily be 5–10 times as valuable.

ON AVERAGE, IT TAKES COMPANIES WITH ONLY ONE FOUNDER 3.6 TIMES AS LONG TO REACH HIGH GROWTH THAN IF THEY HAD HAD SEVERAL FOUNDERS.

Most smart-money investors see a large warning sign in companies with only a single founder and, for example, it is difficult to find a leading accelerator fund that will accept single-founder companies. Why? One reason is the risk that the founder gets sick or does not want to continue. In the US Army, they use the expression 'two is one and one is none' to illustrate that everything which is critical must have a back-up – there must be no 'single points of failure'. To investors, a solo founder can be seen as a critical single point of failure and therefore a sign of danger.

'What if the founder becomes sick?' they might be thinking. Or 'What if he begins to threaten us with his resignation after we have invested our money?' Here are some other concerns they may have:

- 'Was he unable to convince other people in the industry that it was a good idea?'
- 'Is he perhaps a nasty person who does not want to share with others? A decidedly stingy stick, perhaps?'
- 'Is he a control freak?'
- 'Does he underestimate how much it takes to achieve success?'

The management at Y Combinator; one of the world's most successful accelerators, decided some years ago that they would no longer invest in companies with only one founder. Reason: after analyzing several thousand start-ups in the US as well as their own investments, they had seen that for technology companies there was a far greater likelihood of success if there was a minimum of two co-founders to start a business. Of course, this does not mean that all single-founder companies go down – Amazon was a single-founder company and thus one mammoth exception to the rule. Also, many, if not most, multi-founder companies end up having only one of those founders left in management – if any of them. Still, as a rule of thumb, multi-founder is by far the best option.

We should add something important to this. Many 'co-founders' did not join the business from the beginning. Indeed, founders in many start-ups reserve space for a new 'co-founder' in every 'C-suite' job, i.e. each job that starts with 'chief', such as 'chief technology officer'. Why? Because it motivates and creates a musketeer spirit in the management team. A co-founder is usually someone who thinks like an owner and will go through almost everything for the project and, if necessary, eventually go down with the ship. Real co-founders are fighting for their business even when everything seems hopeless.

Therefore, there are advantages in allocating co-founder titles even after the company has been running for a while. But there may well also be disadvantages. For instance, it is always problematic when a person with a co-founder title leaves a start-up. A co-founder can therefore never be a so-called fair-weather friend or an opportunistic personality. Team members who are in the business only to get a decent salary, easy opportunity for large profits, prominent title or to embellish their resume are not, as in not at all, co-founder material.

MANY 'CO-FOUNDERS' ACTUALLY DO NOT JOIN FROM THE BEGINNING.

Lars on taking in a co-founder after the company has already been founded

In 1997, I decided, together with a friend, to start a business, which we presented to a potential third co-founder, who had very complementary skills. This person, however, was fully occupied with something else and could not join at the time. We managed, however, surprisingly, to raise VC capital even before we had anything more than a name and an idea, and then we got started. Six months later, our friend joined our team and became a 'co-founder'. This was important both internally and externally to customers, the press, etc.

Important discussions between founders

In the case where there are several founders, it is crucial to compare your expectations. Let's say that you are single and able and willing to work 80–90 hours a week, while your partner is married, has two children and is in so-so health, which is why perhaps he will work only 50 hours a week, or even less. So, have you discussed these conditions? And what if he has far more money than you, or home equity potentially available as collateral for loans, and therefore acts as a backstop if the company unexpectedly needs more capital? What will this mean for the share allocation?

You should also discuss what motivates each of you in this project. Is it being together with the customers, to see the joy in their eyes when the product is delivered? Or is it to lead the company's staff? The joy of having to cope with all tasks in a company instead of only a narrow function? Or maybe to develop the product? Is one of you a control freak and therefore suited to checking all bills before they are paid? Is the other totally indifferent to such things? What do you each regard as fun and boring when running a business? Is there something both of you classify as boring? And if so, what are you going to do about it? If you envision the company in 3–5 years and imagine that it has been really successful by then, do you agree what that success will look like? How does each of you get the assignments that you enjoy? And what about all the other tasks?

It is also problematic if one of you wants to save the world but without much interest in profitability, while the other thought it first and foremost was supposed to become a great business.

The above conflicts are among the most frequent reasons a company has problems related to its development. If you cannot agree on these types of questions, you should perhaps not start a business together.

IN ADDITION, YOU MUST RECONCILE WHAT MOTIVATES EACH FOUNDER.

Entrepreneurs' deepest motives – from the investors' point of view

When business leaders and entrepreneurs are interviewed about their motivation, they often say that they wanted to create a better world. Steve Jobs and others have said again and again that you should follow your passion. However, if we look at what entrepreneurs express in deeper, scientific studies, their motivations are almost entirely divided into two main groups, which are slightly different from the motives above.[5] The predominant motives are usually:

- money
- control.

Money is apparently the most common motive, at least among technology entrepreneurs in the US. Indeed, a survey of 549 founders of US technology companies showed that the desire to create personal wealth was very important to 75% of them. After all, money gives you the opportunity to work with what you most want to do, to live well, to feel financially secure or to start many more companies later in life.

However, after money comes the control motive – 64% said it was important for them to control their own business.[6] The control motive may accommodate such desires as ensuring that their dream is implemented, leading other people, or not having a boss.

Of course, both of these motives can easily be aligned with the desire to improve the world. Creating a business contributes to the overall growth and development, and it also creates jobs and prosperity. And both motives may be aligned with personal passion – passion for the product and to see dreams come true, for instance.

However, here is a rather whimsical observation: yes, all else being equal, VCs prefer entrepreneurs with a desire to improve the world, and what might be even more important, entrepreneurs with a burning passion for their project. That sounds obvious. However, they tend to have another preference which is less obvious: they typically prefer the founders who have a strong financial motivation to those with a strong motivation for control. Here are the reasons:

- CEOs who focus primarily on money are more open to hiring people or having co-founders who can challenge them. They are also more willing to dilute their stakes to finance rapid growth. They are more likely to recognize when the company has possibly grown too big for them and therefore requires a new management team.

- Those CEOs who focus primarily on control tend to hire weaker employees in order not to be challenged in their position of power. Furthermore, they often grow their companies too slowly because they are worried about getting investors on board, which also means that they cannot afford the best employees. In addition, they often micro-manage too much and they maintain their position even after maybe they are no longer suitable for it. If there is a change of CEO, they will usually leave the company in anger due to the loss of control instead of staying and supporting the company's continued growth through a different role.

Of course, these are generalizations, but they are on most VCs' mind. Also, because it can become concrete very quickly. The money-motivated founder may seek an exit after 4–8 years, whereas the control-motivated one doesn't want an exit at all.

Another important consideration is how the structure can be changed from the early stages to the later stages. Some will agree on a high degree of control during the start-up phase in advance to ensure that the product is what they had in mind, after which they intend to switch to prioritize money. That approach may be rational. Others will never relinquish control or sell the company. Fine, but have you agreed on this strategy?

Who are the ideal co-founders?

The ideal co-founders must have a wonderful time together socially. It is about having compatible values, shared sense of humour and much more. But beware: most people have tried something like this. You have a great friend from school and the two of you go on vacation together for the first time. During the holiday, you suddenly begin to find your mate a bit annoying. A few days later, it gets worse. Finally, you are unable to speak to each other and when the holiday is over, the camaraderie is entirely dead. The point is that when people get closer to each other, tension can build up. Perhaps for this reason, when employees at McKinsey conduct interviews, they typically have what they call the airport test: 'If I was sitting in an airport and our flight was delayed by 10 hours, would I want to sit next to this person?'

A start-up is much more demanding regarding socializing than just 10 hours in an airport, and also way more demanding than a holiday with a school friend. The airport test is a fine rule when you are bringing people

Lars on the importance of humour and maintaining a positive attitude in start-ups

Once I and a few employees had to negotiate with the executive board of Deutsche Telekom regarding a potential investment in our company, as well as a possible joint venture. Their company was by some measures at least 1000 times as big as ours and when we walked towards their boardroom, I honestly felt nervous. However, just before we were to open the door, my colleague Peter began to dance bizarrely while in a whisper he sang, 'I'm so excited, I just can't hide it'. And then, just as we all laughed at him, he opened the door and together we walked into the meeting room – laughing. We got to an agreement and in retrospect I can see that a positive attitude and a sense of humour really mean a lot concerning whether things have succeeded or failed in my businesses.

into a larger team in a big company, but when it concerns the choice of a co-founder, you should raise the threshold. Think of a start-up as a small, decaying ship in which you and your partners are to sail around the world seven times – in a recurrent hurricane. The atmosphere should be good through all this.

Relevant work experience

How can you know whether your co-founder will maintain the spirit when things get really hard? How can you know whether that co-founder has an indomitable ability to shake off adversity and spread the joy and energy? You can't, but the best chance is if you have tried to work together. It is good to have been classmates, but much better if you have undertaken major work assignments together. Or at least you have been together in situations that were professionally and psychologically demanding. 'When the going gets tough, the tough get going', as the saying goes, so that's where you find out. It is therefore best if you have worked in another start-up – preferably in a start-up that is relevant for the new assignment – and even better if working there was difficult and often stressful.[7] Best of all, if we were to stack ambition upon ambition, if you have worked in a hyper-growth start-up, i.e. had come out of the first fumbling phase and had begun to hyper-scale. Below is a table showing how large a proportion of entrepreneurs had this background in different incubators.

Percentage of the founders of the world's top 20 business incubators, which had prior experience of hyper-growth start-ups.[8]

• Silicon Valley: 35%	• Austin: 18%	• Seattle: 26%
• Paris: 5%	• Tel Aviv: 17%	• Vancouver: 7%
• New York City: 18%	• Bangalore: 14%	• Berlin: 12%
• Sao Paulo: 13%	• London: 23%	• Amsterdam: 19%
• Los Angeles: 18%	• Sydney: 16%	• Singapore: 10%
• Moscow: 14%	• Chicago: 15%	• Montreal: 9%
• Boston: 13%	• Toronto: 5%	

Not surprisingly, the greatest number of hyper-growth veterans were in Silicon Valley and there was generally a bigger proportion of those in the US than elsewhere. Studies show that experienced serial entrepreneurs on average end up with around eight percentage points more equity in their companies than people who have not been serial entrepreneurs.[9]

ON AVERAGE, EXPERIENCED SERIAL ENTREPRENEURS END UP WITH AROUND EIGHT PERCENTAGE POINTS MORE EQUITY IN THEIR COMPANIES THAN PEOPLE WHO HAVE NOT BEEN SERIAL ENTREPRENEURS.

Moreover, another factor can be quite interesting: a co-founder who has 'star power' in the industry or generally as an entrepreneur will attract great employees who want to learn from this star. Similarly, if a start-up company generally has extraordinarily skilled and motivated employees, it will attract more like-minded employees. Success leads to success and talents attract talents. This effect is particularly important during the early phase, where the company lacks product as well as sales and profits.

The ability to understand each other

Experience shows that companies' founders often belong to the same culture – arguably because it gives them a sense of spiritual fraternity and makes it easier for them to understand each other. Although it does not sound politically correct, in the US there is an overwhelming tendency for founding teams to be very homogeneous – in fact, this is 46 times (!) as common as if they had been randomly composed.[10] There is also a tendency for founding teams to have almost equally as much or equally as little management experience. Either they are both (all) students or young people with equal lack of experience or they are both (all) seniors with equally great experience. That is what statistics tell us, but besides the obvious likelihood that you already associate with people much like yourself, there is a professional reason for it, i.e. the ability to read each other's minds.

The crucial difference

We have considered equality between founders. However, let us now look at the crucial differences. If the founders have similar professional competencies, networks and functional skills, there is less synergy between their social network and more potential for conflicts concerning their roles.

According to the Startup Genome project, if the business model does not have network effects, you have a great advantage if the founder team has great technical expertise. However, if the business model does build on strong network effects, it is statistically more advantageous to have relatively more commercial expertise among the founders. However, overall, studies showed that a founder team with one commercially focused co-founder and another technically focused on average raised 30% more capital, had 2.9 times greater user growth and was 19% less likely to scale too quickly than if the team was more one-sided concerning functional skills.[11]

Personally, we would say that if a start-up has three founders, it is often optimal if one is a technological expert, one is a product expert (good at creating the ideal user experience) and the third is a great sales person. However, what is rarely needed in a founder team is a human resources expert or a financier – those can be employed later when the company needs them more. And it is a great advantage if the team can appoint a single CEO early on – 2–3 or more co-leader CEOs may sound nice from a fraternity perspective, but that will probably not work in the long run.

TYPICALLY, IT IS A GREAT ADVANTAGE TO HAVE A COMMERCIAL + TECHNICAL FOUNDER TEAM.

Here is another angle on diversity: most people are either 'hunters' (people who sell) or 'farmers' (people who deliver), but few are both. Likewise, you should usually avoid finding a hunter if you are the hunter yourself; instead, you should find a farmer. It's better to start with, for instance, a programmer and a sales person rather than two programmers. You should be careful not to start a business without a sales person on board because it is not only the product that needs to be sold but, as mentioned, you must also sell the idea of working for less than the market salary to employees and probably also sell the idea of investing in the company to various critical investors.

The ideal founder team

Below is a list of some of the characteristics that increase the chance of an effective founder team.

Individual characteristics

- Show initiative (enterprising)
- Self-motivated
- Impatient
- Fast-working
- Mentally optimized for speed, chaos and uncertainty
- Resistant to adversity
- Look ahead, but learn from your mistakes
- Thinking of sustained improvements everywhere in the surroundings
- Have professional pride
- Can immerse in a task
- Curious
- Cooperative
- Persistent
- Can postpone gratification
- Optimistic
- Have had rather thankless routine jobs during youth
- Intuitive and interested in big pictures and broad patterns
- Creative
- Open to change and thus not inclined to seek a definitive answer to questions
- Talent for decision making based on objective principles and impersonal facts rather than on people involved and personal concerns
- Can be impulsive
- May have a moderate personality deviation
- Enormous propensity to get things done

Collective characteristics

- Have compatible social cultures and values.
- Have complementary professional backgrounds.
- Have worked together before, preferably in one or more start-ups which underwent hyper-growth.
- Agree on whether and how fast there should be an exit.
- Agree on the distribution of the workload.
- Agree on the allocation of the investment.
- Agree on the company's purpose.

The perfect teams often create companies with cultures that become so strong that they end up with a cult-like atmosphere. This can contribute to a special and sometimes even a little bizarre culture – which may actually be desirable because it stimulates bonding.

The shareholders' agreement

When you and your co-founders begin, there are frequently high expectations and no problems whatsoever. But problems will appear soon enough and therefore you must have a document that legally regulates the relationship between the shareholders, who at first usually are the co-founders only. This is the shareholders' agreement. If this is not a good enough reason for you, here is another: no professional investor would ever invest in a start-up without a shareholders' agreement.

NO PROFESSIONAL INVESTOR WOULD EVER INVEST IN A START-UP WITHOUT A SHARE-HOLDERS' AGREEMENT.

Therefore, we suggest that if you can possibly afford it, you always – fairly early – ask a lawyer to write this document, so that all co-founders are secured and can avoid spending time and money on a potentially expensive and damaging fight later. If you cannot afford a lawyer, find some templates online and use them. The agreement usually deals with at least the following questions:

- What if one founder leaves the company?
- What if one founder gets involved in a competing project?
- What if we need a new partner?
- What if we need to raise more capital?
- What if the founder is not able to deliver what they should?

- What if the founder does not dedicate enough time or finds another job?
- What if there is disagreement between the shareholders?
- What if there is an equal number voting for and against a solution?

Among these points, the most important ones relate to the exit. If the founder leaves the company and/or wants to sell their shares, who can or must buy those shares – and at what price? And what happens to their voting rights? The agreement must therefore have a take-back clause, which allows the company or other shareholders to buy back shares from a departing co-founder. The alternative to this is that the company ends up with 'dead capital', i.e. capital owned by inactive investors, which can make it harder to get future investments and which can be a waste of shares. Every shareholder in a start-up should be an active contributor to the business.

There are several models for this, including buy-back rights where the company or other founders have the right to buy a leaving founder's shares for 'fair value', which is defined by metrics such as last traded price or a multiple of revenues or profit, perhaps in combination. Alternatively, you might have a 'shotgun' clause, where, for example, one of two founders may offer to buy the other founder's shares at a given price. If the other refuses, they have the right to automatically buy the first founder's shares at the same price. This method takes into account situations where there is no profit yet.

Besides this important area, the shareholders' agreement may deal with strategy, goals and ambition, roles and other factors. The critical parts of a shareholders' agreement are typically wages and shares (co-founders rarely make bonus schemes during the first year). Regarding the salary, you should initially agree on:

- How long are we able and willing to go without a salary?
- What do we do when one or more of us needs a salary but we still do not earn the money to give it?
- What do we do if one of us works more than the other?

In most companies we have founded, the founders have not received a salary during the start-up phase, and sometimes even well after the start-up phase, when the company periodically needed money. It makes no sense – especially not tax-wise – to inject capital from one's own savings and then later withdraw this as a taxed salary. And investors will not be pleased if they notice that the founders receive a salary from a company that is faced with an acute liquidity shortage.

After the initial no-salary phase, the co-founders should, in our opinion, preferably receive identical salaries. An exception is where one founder has high fixed costs and the other has not or it is agreed that they don't take on the same workload. In these cases, they can obviously have different salaries, which then is balanced with different equity and option packages.

How much should the founders receive in salary? An American key rule indicates that a founder (and incidentally a CEO) in a start-up should not receive more than $150 000 annually in salary. This is obviously *only* when the company is up and running – if the company is short of money, the amount should be much less. If salaries are too high, it will burden a weak liquidity, but additionally it might encourage management to give a rosy impression of the business to investors and board members, simply to maintain their jobs for as long as possible. If, as we propose, salaries instead are far below what the person could receive in a big company, they keep their job in the start-up only because they believe in the project and thus in the value of their stock options.

This was salary, now let us look at equity. The distribution of equity may depend on who came up with the idea, the expected effort, as well as experience and competence. One approach is that one founder is the leader and receives 90% equity and the other (or the others) splits the remainder. If you do this, you may, however, run the risk that the other founder(s) begins to behave like an employee rather than an owner and thus you might just end up with overcompensated employees lacking owner instinct.

What is the value of previous experience?

Should you allocate more equity to a co-founder who has more start-up experience than the other? You may, but perhaps only if this individual has also succeeded before. One set of statistics showed that an entrepreneur who has previously received VC funding and taken a company public has 30% chance of success the next time. An entrepreneur who tried before but failed has 20% chance, and one who hasn't tried before has 18% chance.[12]

What is the idea worth?

Studies show that the founder who got the idea on average receives 10–15 percentage points more shares than other co-founders.[13] We think that makes sense. You might wonder how this actually ties in with the '2% inspiration and 98% perspiration' we mentioned earlier. Poorly? No, not really. The founders in most growth start-ups will get their equity diluted up to 10–20 times before a potential exit (a sale or IPO), which means that they *collectively* rarely end up with more than a total of 10–20% of the shares when an exit occurs.

THE FOUNDER WHO GOT THE IDEA ON AVERAGE RECEIVES 10–15 PERCENTAGE POINTS MORE SHARES THAN OTHER CO-FOUNDERS. WE THINK THAT MAKES SENSE.

What happens to the 10–15% of the shares allocated for the idea? They are now diluted to 2–3% of the exit value, which of course matches the 2% inspiration, 98% perspiration motto pretty well. If it still is a little more than 2% towards the exit, you should remember that by rewarding the idea, you can express an expectation that the person who got the idea will get more good ideas during the upcoming years.

Dynamic versus static equity allocation?

There are many arguments for allocating founders' shares partially dynamic. A dynamic allocation may be that you reward the idea with 10–15%, but then make a series of personal, forward-looking milestones for individual founders' effort, each rewarded with shares over a timeframe that can be 1–4 years.

You can, of course, combine a static and a dynamic approach. For example, half of the shares are allocated from the beginning and the other half are issued and allocated according to individually agreed KPIs (key performance indicators), related to product development, sales or fund-raising, for example. The norm is that the shares that you have obtained cannot be taken from you unless otherwise stated in the shareholders' agreement.

Statistics show that if there are multiple founders, in only 33% of cases will there be an equal distribution of the equity. This means that in 67% of the cases, the allocation is different, and in 40% of the cases there is at least 20% points difference in their mutual equity allocation.[14]

The best way to distribute shares by far is, in our opinion, a static allocation when the company is founded, followed by a dynamic allocation based on KPIs. For example, it may be a static allocation of 30–40% of the shares, where the founder with the idea gets a bit more than others, and the rest in future capital increases based on KPIs, which may simply include still being active in the company. For instance, we could suggest that full-time participation for four years would qualify for some additional equity.

However, it is a problem to use this time criterion solely, since you may end up in the situation called 'paying for a pulse', i.e. that a major shareholder is useless. However, this can be solved if the person concerned can be dismissed by the board and thereby loses prospective shareholder rights.

THE BEST WAY TO DISTRIBUTE SHARES IS BY FAR, IN OUR OPINION, A STATIC ALLOCATION WHEN THE COMPANY HAS BEEN FOUNDED AND THEN A DYNAMIC ALLOCATION, DEPENDING ON FUTURE PERFORMANCE BY THE FOUNDERS.

Which founder should be the CEO?

The best leader should be the CEO, but statistically there is an overwhelming tendency for the one who had the idea to end up being the CEO of a start-up. According to one study, this applied in 47% of the cases. Founders who were not the person with the original idea became CEO in only 12% of the cases.[15]

In companies with large system sales, the CEO is often the best sales person in the co-founder team, while the best strategist, technologist or organizer is one step below, the reason being that key customers like to speak with the CEO and therefore it is extremely helpful that the CEO is a great sales person.

Mads on who should have the most co-founder equity

Shares are usually distributed primarily to fill the difficult and critical positions. Some years ago, I, together with other people, founded what is today the largest online clothing company in Indonesia. When selling clothes online, there are typically three important functions: procurement, operations (inventory, shipping and so on) and marketing. After finding three co-founders, I asked them to find out what each should do together before I would come back two weeks later. When I came back, they had delegated the tasks, so one had to do accounting, one should take care of HR (human resources, i.e. hiring etc.) and the last had to do procurement, operations and marketing. However, the challenge of the project was not HR and financials. Apart from the fact that it can be easier to hire skills within these areas, there is far more critical value adding in procurement, operations and marketing. Thus, it was not fair to distribute an equal number of shares.

How do I work with boards?

Many types of companies require boards by law. A board hires the CEO and oversees that the management is professional and legal. In a way, one can also say that the board is the shareholders' representatives to the management. However, if the company has only a single owner, which can be a solo founder in a start-up, it will easily be a bit awkward as the chain of command and the right to fire each other runs in a perfect circle, as in action movies, where three people aim at each other with loaded guns. In these cases, the founder will typically consider the board as an advisory board instead.

This is one reason why the very young start-up rarely sees much value in a board and often has only the minimum legal setup. In these situations the board may consist of the founder together with a friend or family member and perhaps a lawyer. Later, and especially when the company gets external investors, it will need a professional board.

A great board

Small boards are generally the best. First, it implies that each board member has a real responsibility, and second, that you are far more flexible in terms of organizing board calls and meetings. Meanwhile, if you require additional oversight and advice, you can fix this by having an advisory board, a mentor or a coach, which we will address soon.

A good board preferably has an odd number of members so that it cannot become deadlocked in situations with 50:50 disagreement. Alternatively, the chairman must have the decisive vote in split-board situations.

Three or five are good numbers for start-up boards; you should begin with three rather than five. Often there are an equal number of founders and external investors on the board as well as one who is neutral. Typically, various external investors agree to be represented by a single board member, and the standard is that after a series A funding round, the board has five directors, who are normally the founder, the CEO (if not the same), two investor representatives and an independent.

When the company matures and the board grows, it often appoints board committees, where the most common are:

- compensation committee, which determines the stock options as well as salaries and bonuses (typically managed by the independent director)

- audit committee, which approves budgets and financial planning

- nomination committee, which designates new board members

- exit committee, which is accountable for the company's potential exit.

How should I cooperate with my board?

CEOs should know that it is time consuming to deal with boards, but it can be done foolishly or wisely. Here is what is the foolish do:

- Concentrate all dialogue with the board about formal board meetings.

- Disclose important board material only at the actual board meeting and not before.

- Make the board meeting into a sales presentation.

The wiser alternative is the following: first, book all board meetings one year in advance. Second, combine the formal board meetings with a continuous dialogue in the form of emails, board calls (conference calls) and short telephone conversations. Report regularly to the board, so that in principle, you can have a board meeting at any given time without necessarily having to prepare a 'presentation' for the occasion. Additionally, to enable board members to be well prepared, before every regular board meeting you should send everyone everything that should be spoken about in advance, as well as an agenda.

One format for regular updates to investors and board members is to mail them a link to a PowerPoint presentation with voice narration. Make a little slide show about the developments in the company, record your voice while talking over the slides (this is a standard PowerPoint feature) and send a Dropbox link to the presentation to your mailing list.

How should my board meetings play out?

The board meetings should always be led by the CEO. The nature of the physical board meeting should predominantly be a discussion, not a presentation, and if the meeting lasts two hours, for instance, you should as a rule spend only about 30 minutes on history – the rest of the time should cover discussion of solutions and ideas. If the management presents problems, it should simultaneously bring up potential solutions which the board then can discuss. These should ideally appear on the present agenda.[16]

Note that the dynamics between board members and management may become quite frustrating at times. A typical reason is that the board member acts more as a policeman than a coach. In good manager–board relationships, the dialogue is not a push from the board as much as a pull from the management: the management asks for advice. Also, whereas board members tend to be older and perhaps in some or all ways more senior than management, if their coaching becomes too insistent, it may break the entrepreneurial spirit.

How many formal board meetings must be held? Studies show that younger start-ups on average have roughly eight board meetings annually. This figure will decrease to around six when the company begins to report essential figures regularly, which provides a clear indication of how things are, and it will further decrease to around four board meetings annually when the company is more mature and is profitable.

A common approach is that if you have, for instance, eight board meetings annually, you make half official and the other half not, the difference being that official board meetings include approval of budgets and revisions to the overall stock option plans plus other major and formal decisions. At the unofficial board meetings, it is preferable that key management is present. In addition to this, it is a good idea for the board to meet at least once a year without the CEO so that board members can discuss the CEO – how to support him or her better or whether to replace him or her.

These are only the physical meetings. A well-functioning board in a dynamic start-up has countless emails and board calls where leaders are facing problems and opportunities with the board. 'Should we fire our sales manager?', 'Should we give this local distributor exclusive rights for 12 months?', 'Should we launch this product?' The relationship is therefore a continuous flow more than it is based on fixed intervals solely. If things work well in this way, you should expect that all board members have already agreed in principle to budgets and major items before the meetings where the formal approval of these should take place.

Also, remember that a great board should not only control and advise the company but its members should also be active ambassadors and an unofficial part of the company's sales staff. The management should therefore not treat board members as mentors or a jury but also very much as evangelists, ambassadors and sellers, and board members should always be equipped with the company's best demos, sales material, etc. They should feel comfortable with the level of information because they will not lend their reputation to something they feel uncomfortable about.

There are a number of great tools for board members on the site of the National Association of Corporate Directors (nacdonline.org). Check out the Knowledge Base section, which is full of templates, white papers and advisory documents. Another useful site is the Working Group on Director Accountability and Board Effectiveness, which was created by Pascal Levensohn from Levensohn Venture Partners. You can find this at pascalsview.com.

Do I need a mentor, coach or advisory board?

It can be helpful to have some solid advisors who are not a part of the board. These fall into three categories: mentors, coaches and advisory board.

Mentors and coaches do not appear in the official organizational chart. A mentor is a person who helps entrepreneurs with advice on company management. These can be found through social networks, but there are also quite a few mentor networks. A mentor is typically the person you can review things with, including crazy ideas that you might be a little embarrassed to bring up in front of your board. The perfect mentor has founded businesses and/or has worked in relevant management positions.

Mentors pay off

According to the Startup Genome project, American internet start-ups which had a mentor had 3.5 times as much growth and raised seven times as much capital as those that did not have a mentor.[17]

Furthermore, start-ups where the management followed thoughts from known start-up gurus – such as Steve Blank, Alex Osterwalder, Brad Feld, Fred Wilson, Guy Kawasaki, Seth Godin, Eric Ries, Dave McClure and Paul Graham – got external funding in 60% of the cases, whereas those who didn't got it in only 38% of the cases. Besides the practical knowledge you gain by following inspirational and experienced thinkers, it might be true that founders and leaders who can speak fluently on start-up phases and pitfalls inspire more confidence for a potential investor than ones who do not. Would you invest in an entrepreneur who seems quite unaware of the entrepreneurial process?

A different supporting role is that of coach, as often seen in elite sports. The difference between a mentor and a coach is, in our eyes, that mentors mainly help with the management-relevant problems, whereas a coach mainly helps with the more personal factors – a coach is a kind of personal motivator or industrial psychologist, if you will.

A third possible option is an advisory board, which is a group of people who advise professionally and normally appear in the organizational chart as well as in marketing material. Professionally, there are similarities between an advisory board and a mentor, the difference being that the former helps the entire management while the latter supports only the founders or the founder team.

11.
MY OUTSOURC-ING AND MY STAFF

During the last chapter, we looked at the core team, i.e. co-founders, C-suite managers, board members, etc. In this chapter, we will examine outsourcing partners and employees. We will consider why and when outsourcing is preferable or problematic, and also how you get the most out of it. In addition, we will study how to find the right candidates for your jobs, interview them, get them started, lead them, and finally motivate them with a sense of mission, communication, stock options, titles, bonuses, etc. We will also look at the tricky issues of management reshuffling as your company grows as well as at the unfortunate topic of layoffs.

Human resources is a big issue in any company, but it has unique opportunities and challenges in start-ups. Part of the reason for this is that these companies change significantly over time. How? Previously, we mentioned the Marmer stages regarding company development, but we also like another description dividing growth into (i) explorer, (ii) sprinter and (iii) marathon runner. A third one by venture capitalist Jeff Bussgang divides the start-up growth into three phases: (i) jungle, (ii) dirt road and (iii) highway.[1] In the jungle, he explains, you fight your way through the market while searching for the most appropriate path. At this stage, you are most of all a path-finder. When reaching the dirt road phase, you know where to go, even though the road is a bit twisted and there are plenty of bumps along the way – however, hopefully, at least there might be little traffic if your idea is unique. On the highway, everything happens rapidly and the traffic is denser with more structure.

Here comes the challenge: the first phase in Bussgang's analogy – explorers in the jungle – is great for people who thrive with uncertainty, creativity and an informal environment. What you need most of all for the next stage is sprinters who love to execute at a blistering pace. The people thriving in the last phase – marathon runners – may prefer a somewhat more formalized framework. So how do you hire for a company that will change culture so fast? Or should you instead focus more on outsourcing?

When should I outsource?

Many companies, without further consideration, choose to do by far the most in-house. This can potentially be a big mistake, partly because it can be hard to find, train and guide employees in all types of roles, and partly because it reduces flexibility and may be more expensive – often far more expensive. Thus, we are huge fans of outsourcing and try to delegate as much as possible. Perhaps you should not ask 'what can I outsource?', but instead 'what can I *not* outsource?' Then outsource everything else.

But, but, but. There are exceptions, including the company's first discovery phase, where you are still groping your way through. Here, you should do most of the work yourself to sense opportunities and threats more directly. In our opinion, you will rarely get away with outsourcing product development or business planning in a young start-up.

So, what *can* you outsource? Office cleaning, for starters. But also legal counselling, accounting and other similar assignments that are far away from the company's core competencies. What you *cannot* outsource are typically tasks that are crucial in maintaining an innovative position. If you position your production in China, it is doubtful that you will make major breakthroughs regarding the production technology.

About network orchestration

Li & Fung is a global billion-dollar company that produces clothes for a lot of major brands such as Walmart, but it does not own any factories. Instead it uses 'network orchestration', which simply means that rather than owning the production itself, the company lets others own and perfect it. Thus, the factory owners are also responsible for all the problems and they cover the capital needs, while Li & Fung instead gathers the threads and ensures that the finished product is made properly and gets to the stores.

Mads on companies with extreme outsourcing

Some years ago, I asked a person I met in Switzerland: 'How many employees do you have?' The answer was: 'We are three people in my business, but including all outsourced activities, we have over 1000 employees.'

However, outsourcing is not without challenges and you often see both companies and governments run into problems when outsourcing. These problems are rarely caused by the outsourcing concept as such, but rather by a lack of knowledge about how to find and continuously lead the right outsourcing partners, and also how to define a task and structure a contract. A few tips:

- Structure your outsourcing contract such that: (i) you can get out of it relatively quickly and easily, and (ii) you can get out of it immediately if the outsourcing partner does not meet your KPIs.

- Try to avoid paying for their working capital. This is done by paying after the end of the month or later.

- Realize that you might have to manage them as if they were your own employees, i.e. spend time with them, inspect their facilities regularly, ensure quality and train. In very large outsourcing projects, the customer often has a few employees permanently stationed at the company they have outsourced to.

Lars on his micro-multinational that became a money machine

I have founded companies that have had many employees, but the one which produced the most impressive financial results (it broke even the first year and produced a 25 000% return the first eight years) was actually a 'micro-multinational' which had only two employees – myself and my former wife, who worked part-time. The company made many international investments and had a turnover of up to several billion dollars a year, but we got analysis, administration and everything else done at least 99% outside the house. Thus, our time was very focused on the income drivers, not on administration.

Crowdsourcing – the coolest outsourcing

Note that you can use myriad crowdsourcing websites quickly and inexpensively and thereby find outsourcing solutions to numerous practical tasks. In fact, there is a huge range of online tools for all phases of product development, sales, marketing, etc. For example, you can find the following:

- All kinds of services such as design, animations and translations via Fiverr
- Software developers via Topcoder, Upwork and oDesk

- Freelance management consultants at Eden McCallum

- Freelance marketers, software engineers, designers, copywriters etc. on Elance and oDesk

- Translators on Gengo.com

- People to work on your concept, production, and distribution via Tongal

- Data aggregation and classifications via Mechanical Turk

- Test of user experience via Usertesting

- Standardized contracts which can be downloaded from Creative Commons

- User Feedback via apps such as UserVoice, Compare App, WebEngage, SurveySwipe, Apollo, Testimonial Monkey, Nicereply.

These are only a few examples among thousands, and in the case of smaller, individual tasks, which typically are what's required, this is called 'microwork'.

It is really worth the time to examine how much one's business can outsource. In your business, you can remove a lot of fat through outsourcing, including crowdsourcing.

How do I structure an employment process?

Let's now study development of your in-house team – hiring people and building your team. The process of finding an employee should, in our opinion, typically be standardized and be somewhat like this:

1. Define whether you even need to hire someone. Always ask whether the task could be outsourced and possibly crowdsourced instead.

2. Define the job as accurately as possible, including KPIs.

3. Create a job post.

4. Decide on how to find employees and who should run the hiring process.

5. Make sure that the candidates are interviewed by several people.

6. Give an offer, make the hire.

7. Get the employee started and integrated into the team and the organization.

Warning signs and detectives

It is vital that your partners and trusted employees are loyal and honest. Here are a few tips on minor warning signs. If an obvious candidate cannot be found on social media, it may be because the person wants to hide something – or perhaps hide from someone. This should set your alarm bells ringing.

Also, spend some of your time looking through the person's resume. Are there some strange gaps? There are companies and investors who use detective agencies to investigate candidates for major positions. We are not speaking about Sherlock Holmes kind of people with long coats and big hats, but companies that specialize in using primarily or only digital information to check candidates' professional and if necessary personal behaviour. Some will look at the digital traces only, others might investigate more intensively if there are any red flags. This is not necessarily expensive, and we have used such a service ourselves.

We have often seen that companies with too much money hire too ambitiously too early, while companies with too little money hire too late. A good idea can generally be not to hire from the first day you experience a need but rather to wait a bit to see what happens. Not infrequently we have seen immense pressure to hire for a special role, but then, astonishingly, the pressure decreased again. So think twice each time.

How do I find my candidates?

Essentially, you have two options to find an employee – either directly or through recruitment agencies. If you aim for directly, the following methods are popular:

- Post on social media such as LinkedIn and Facebook.

- Proactively, look for candidates on social media.

- Ask your employees as well as friends and acquaintances whether they can recommend someone.

- Mention the need in interviews.

- Advertise on recruitment websites and on bulletin boards at relevant educational or professional institutions.

- Be proactive at, for example, conferences. After a speech at a conference, let people know that you can talk/give out information about the role in an adjacent foyer or in the hall.

- Hire interns or graduates in an internship process and check out how they work.

- Hire freelancers/consultants and later offer them jobs if the cooperation has worked well.

- Post vacancies on your website.

- Create a link on your website for unsolicited applications.

- Let venture capitalists and other competent investors in your company assist in the search.

There are many other channels. We suggest that you always brainstorm about how you can get in touch with potential candidates.

The alternative to these methods is to use a recruitment agency – a headhunter. Here is how we look at this:

- Recruitment companies are often good at finding the candidates.

- They frequently use standard personality tests, mainly to check whether there are obvious reasons that candidates are *not* suitable for the job.

- But . . . only you or your management team can determine whether a candidate will fit into your culture.

About personality tests: professional recruitment companies often use standard intelligence and personality tests such as the Wechsler Adult Intelligence Scale, Keirsey Temperament Sorter, Calliper Test, and Myers-Briggs Type Indicator Test for their candidates. These can be extremely useful, but they do not necessarily show whether the candidate is the best for the job; they rather tell whether they are not. Neither do they tell whether the candidate fits the company culture; this can be determined only via personal interviews. Ultimately, you and your team must make that assessment. In this context, it should be emphasized that there basically are no right and wrong people per se. But there are right and wrong people for specific job positions.

Unfortunately, many companies make the mistake of hiring mostly people who are like themselves professionally. This is dangerous because it is often someone who is *not* like them professionally that they should hire – to complement them. Yes, the culture must be compatible, but the competencies should indeed be complementary.

No-go companies and preferred companies

Before you even begin to hire, consider whether there are companies you will not recruit from because, for instance, they are your business partners. This should be communicated internally, where appropriate. If you are still getting a job application from an employee of such a company, you can say that they can be offered a position only if this is agreed with their employer.

Moreover, there is the reverse situation where you would like to bring in a specific employee from another company, or perhaps a whole team.

In such cases, you can ask a recruitment agency to establish the initial contact against a (greatly) reduced fee, as their workload in these situations is minimal – you have already decided that you want the team, so the recruitment company is reduced to a go-between.

About the 'shouting' and the 'whispering' employee

Talents can be divided into two types: the shouting and the whispering. The shouting type is extrovert and possibly self-assured, flamboyant and well spoken. He or she is good at talking himself or herself into large compensation packages and pompous titles – the archetype is obviously the extrovert super-salesman. Sometimes, this master of the universe will later argue that he should have an executive position, which perhaps means that the company at the same time loses a great salesman and gets a poor director. Also, this type may be more inclined to look for new possibilities.

A so-called whispering talent, meanwhile, delivers a lot without making a fuss about it, and this person is not always conscious of his or her own value. Such a type will therefore typically be inclined to stay longer in your company. Therefore, in our experience, you should be careful not to underestimate whispering talents.

How do I cooperate with recruiters?

If you decide to use a recruitment agency, you must pay special attention to the following aspects in the contract with them:

- What is paid in fees and is this of the entire salary package, i.e. salary, bonus, pension, shares and benefits, or only the salary?
- Do you pay whether someone is hired or not?

- How long will the recruitment agency guarantee that the employee will stay, and will they give you your money back or try to find a replacement if the employee leaves early?

It is especially important to agree on what happens if they do not find the right candidate. At the same time, it makes sense to ensure that the recruitment company has no exclusivity if you find a candidate yourself.

THE CULTURE MUST BE COMPATIBLE, BUT THE COMPETENCIES SHOULD BE COMPLEMENTARY.

For a key position, it may be a good idea to spend some time with the person you might hire before deciding. Remember, no one is good at everything. Examine how the candidate has performed during their last five years at their previous job/jobs. Eat dinner with them, or learn how they act as a person through a more social interaction. You can also invite candidates to work with you for a few days and see what happens.

Who should be responsible for a hire? If you have given someone line responsibility for a division of the business, you should never hire someone within that division; instead let the division manager do it. Similarly, you should never fire someone within that division. If your company must fire someone, it is the direct manager who should do it, even if you have made the decision.

What about references?

You should always get references on candidates for key positions. There are two types: front door and backdoor. Front door are the references which the candidate provides themselves. The candidate will probably expect all these to be positive; some might even have asked people to provide references. Backdoor references are those that the candidate has not provided themselves. It is important to use both types if the position is of great importance.

IT IS IMPORTANT TO USE BOTH THE FRONT DOOR AND BACKDOOR REFERENCES IF THE POSITION IS OF GREAT IMPORTANCE.

When you speak with a reference, it is a good tip to ask them to rate the person's suitability for the job based on a scale from 1 to 10. If the reference says '8', for example, you can ask why two points were taken away. Another good tip, if practicable, is to ask for a 15-minute personal interview with the reference, maybe on Skype, or (much better) face to face. People become more open when speaking face to face.

How do I interview a candidate?

Depending on the role and the company, we have seen everything from two to seven interviews for a job. Some companies use up to 18 interviews, but start-ups do not have time for that many. We propose that other than for senior management positions, you have an employee who conducts the initial screening interview, so that the busy leader speaks only with candidates who seem appropriate. Thereafter use 3–4 interviews for a middle managing position, which includes 1–2 screening interviews.

Besides clarifying the suitability of a candidate, you must sell the job to the candidate. Most talented people will have many opportunities and you should therefore make sure that the candidate wants to get on board.

Wikijobs.com has a lot of proposals for tests and interview techniques. Here are some examples of questions, according to the website, you can get as a candidate at Goldman Sachs:

- How would you value a particular company?
- Try to sell me a share.
- How would China's growth threaten the German economy?
- What is the exchange rate of the euro relative to the US dollar?
- Mention some conflicts investors will face in the future.
- Where do you see yourself in five years?
- Give an example of a moral dilemma you have experienced.
- How do you handle stress?
- You are in a boat in the middle of a lake (alone) and throw the anchor into the water. Will the water level rise, fall or stay the same?
- Tell me about something interesting you have read recently.
- How would you convince a client that their request cannot be fulfilled?
- What do you do in your first year at Goldman Sachs?
- Give me a summary of your life in 30 seconds.
- How many manhole covers are there in London?

These are good questions for an early interview. If you have no interview experience, spend some time on Wikijobs.com or similar websites to find inspiration.

When you interview, it is generally good to get the candidate to speak a lot and spontaneously, as psychologists do. You must listen for signs that there is something that the candidate is enthusiastic about. However, our experience is that the most obvious is to ask the candidate to work on something directly related to the job, i.e. if you sell insurance, instead of asking the candidate to solve a Rubik's cube or sell a pen, ask them to sell insurance. If they do not know anything about insurance, give them some training material so that you can test their ability to sell insurance but also their ability to understand the product and learn quickly. If you want to know something about how they think in general, use a standard test such as the Wechsler, Keirsey and Myers-Briggs tests.

Mads on how to make companies attractive for job candidates

In our business, we say that we want a lot of people to want to work with us, so that we can choose the best among them. We ensure this by establishing a good process, explaining our business carefully, elaborating on what our goals are and building personal relationships with the candidates.

Mads on how to test candidates with realistic tasks

When we had to hire a new director for CompareAsiaGroup, we brought a lot of real data from the company to the interview and spent hours with the final candidates, where they examined this data and the real challenges that the company faced.

About highway builders in start-ups

A rather widespread mistake is to hire highway builders too early. This can obviously go well, but often it will not. Typically, such a candidate has a great CV from various executive positions in large, reputable companies.

However, these jobs are often completely different from working in early start-up stages. First, highway builders previously benefited from representing reputable major companies, which meant that they would speak from positions of power and authority. This is not the case in a start-up, where in the early stages one can feel invisible to the outside world. 'What is the name of your company, again?'

Second, highway builders are used to completely different working schedules than the ones you have in start-ups (unless during their career they did skunk works or were intrapreneurs). In large companies, leaders typically have calendars full of meetings from day one, as well as KPIs and milestones all well defined, and often they have someone who will prioritize for them. Thus, the days pass with meetings in which, among other things, they organize and optimize their teams and resources.

Great, but this is not the case at all in a start-up. In start-ups, you must define your tasks yourself. If you do not define anything, nothing happens. Additionally, there is not much time to ask others what you need to do, a question they hardly could answer anyway if they had time. Nor is there time to report much to others about what you have done. No, you must invent most stuff yourself, fill your own calendar, solve your own problems and in general create your own job, find your own resources, train your own people and to a large extent lead yourself. This goes for every day, all the time – including weekends, by the way.

There are other differences. In large companies, you are typically a specialist, whereas in almost all small businesses, people must largely be generalists. This can be a difficult transition for a highway builder. That is why it often goes wrong with highway builders in start-up companies. A typical symptom is that they make lots of plans and checklists at a stage where there is no one to perform them. They have experience as leaders but often have no one to lead. They are good at optimizing, but have nothing to do it with. They can report, but no one has time to listen. They issue commands without checking who will follow them. And at worst, they do not understand that they very often must do things themselves and so there is virtually no reason to make all those plans or issue all those orders.

For the record, we should mention that these problems do not occur every time a start-up hires a highway builder, but they do occur often. Thus, you should beware of employing people from big companies to run start-ups, and you should possibly check how well their qualifications really fit with the checklist of entrepreneurial qualities we mentioned in Chapter 1.

BEWARE OF HIRING PEOPLE FROM LARGE COMPANIES TO RUN START-UPS.

How do I remunerate employees in my start-up?

Remuneration can be predominantly (or exclusively) delivered through salaries, bonuses, competitions and options. On average, the bonus is about one-third of the remuneration for non-founders of start-ups,[2] which is quite a lot. This makes it possible to pay lower wages than the market standard for the same profiles.

ON AVERAGE, THE BONUS IS ABOUT ONE-THIRD OF THE REMUNERATION

FOR NON-FOUNDERS OF START-UPS.

A bonus scheme has several advantages. Employees are motivated to make an extra effort – and there will be far fewer wage disputes if there is a bonus programme. With bonus plans, employees are also motivated by the fact that if they do a good job, they will be rewarded. Additionally, it is a useful solution when you have hired the wrong people. In many countries, it is difficult and expensive to fire people, but if a large portion of their compensation is bonuses, it fixes the problem as they will leave voluntarily if they do not perform well enough to earn a satisfactory bonus.

Should bonus payments be daily, weekly, monthly, semi-annual or annual? That depends on the task. A telephone salesman with simple, quick and repetitive tasks could be rewarded daily, but the leader of a new subsidiary abroad might be rewarded annually.

For staff in routine positions, start-up bonuses are normally less than a third of earnings, but for the sales people it is typically about 50%. A good idea is to give the sales people a fixed salary for the first three months and then give them a much lower fixed salary as by then they should be able to earn a decent bonus. However, if these people are mainly paid by bonus, you should know that their loyalty to the company may be low or non-existent.

Another problem that we have experienced a few times with sales bonuses is an apparent sale where the client later backs out. Unless bonus agreements are structured well, this may mean that you end up paying a bonus for a sale that never occurred. To prevent this, the scheme may stipulate that bonuses are released when the client has paid. This also motivates the salesman to retain a client relationship after the first apparent deal closing.

Thus, bonuses have many advantages but also complications and some disadvantages. A bonus can create uncertainty and, in some cases, leave the impression among other employees that the individual employee cares only about their own little turf and nothing else. It can lead to employees not bothering to help each other because it might have an influence on their own performance and thus bonus. Therefore, a company often has an additional common bonus scheme for many or all employees based on the company's overall performance. Alternatively, you can award prizes and/or special bonuses to the employees who are best at helping others.

A variant of bonuses is competitions. This is typically in the form of sales contests, but there may be innovation contests, service contests, etc. This often leads to a fun atmosphere and we highly recommend this if your business has obvious targets that your employees can compete on.

You should note that it is important that the bonuses and prizes for winners of competitions are given out when you have said they would be – they should never arrive later. It can create turmoil among employees if, for instance, an agreed bonus is not ticking into their bank account immediately.

How do option schemes work?

Option schemes, or ESOPs (employee stock ownership plans), are rights but not obligations to purchase shares in the company at a pre-determined price. These are associated with shareholders' agreements so that the next shareholders cannot interfere with the company's future flexibility.

These options are typically issued at fair value price at the issue date and 'vest' over time. The vesting means that over a period you gradually earn your option rights. The typical vesting period is four years. If you leave the company after two years, for example, due to being fired or on your own initiative, you get only half of your options vested and thus the rest is worthless.

It is the norm for the earliest employees to end up with the most stock options in proportion to their job responsibilities, etc., since they took the biggest risk. For the same reason, it typically applies that employees who joined later, perhaps 'C-suite' executives who are not founders, will have far fewer shares than the founders themselves were given. This means that the overall option allocation can end up looking quite strange if you do not understand the history. This is why start-ups normally keep their ESOP programmes confidential.

An overall corporate ESOP is often 5–15% of the shares. According to the Startup Genome studies of young companies in the world's 20 leading entrepreneurial centres, businesses had on average the following ESOP allocations:[3]

Average ESOP allocations in the world's 20 largest entrepreneurial centres.

• Silicon Valley:	8%	• Austin:	8%	• Seattle:	15%
• Paris:	7%	• Tel Aviv:	10%	• Vancouver:	5%
• New York City:	10%	• Bangalore:	7%	• Berlin:	12%
• Sao Paulo:	5%	• London:	10%	• Amsterdam:	9%
• Los Angeles:	10%	• Sydney:	10%	• Singapore:	10%
• Moscow:	5%	• Chicago:	5%	• Montreal:	13%
• Boston:	14%	• Toronto:	9%		

As the table shows, on average, start-ups allocate about 10% to the stock option programmes. If the framework for your own business is 10%, for example, and you are fully allocated at some point, you run out of options unless some employees leave the company before they have fully vested, in which case it gives a little room to issue the non-vested options to other employees without exceeding the 10%.

However, if you need to issue more options while having none left to give, it can be resolved by a capital increase. For example, if you double the number of shares, the 10% that has already been allocated will be diluted to 5%, which then allows you to issue another 5% of options, etc. In addition, you should be aware that tax-wise, stock options are treated very differently in different countries.[4]

It is important to prevent an employee who will leave quickly from receiving options. The vesting period should ideally first be applicable after a trial period of, say, three months.

ON AVERAGE, START-UPS ALLOCATE ABOUT 10% TO THEIR STOCK OPTION PROGRAMMES.

What should happen when an employee starts?

A new employee's first day on the job can be quite daunting for them. 'Am I the right person for the job?' they might think. 'How are my colleagues?' 'Was it all a mistake?' As your company has invested a lot of time and resources in new hires, it is important that you build a good start-up programme for them. This can be done fairly quickly but can make a huge difference to how they feel, whether they will stay in the company and how quickly they will become fully productive. To give a new employee a great start, the following should be defined first:

- Make it clear who the employee reports to.
- Give the employee a mentor in a similar job during their first months.
- Arrange a series of meetings with relevant employees, customers or others.
- Give the employee written objectives, tasks and KPIs.
- Determine who the employee can go to when in doubt, and make sure that this is not their direct manager.

- Prepare a particularly detailed programme for the employee's first 3–5 days, which is structured down to the minute, so that they do not suddenly have nothing to do. The programme should include details right down to who to eat lunch with (the person must find and pick up the new employee, not the other way round) and meetings with the manager, colleagues, thorough review of their work, as well as someone who can advise them on salary, holidays, IT, etc.

If you hire many employees each month, you may want to make start-up teams. These can reduce the need for internal resources and create bonds with existing staff.

If new employees regret starting, they should preferably say this quickly

Online clothing company Zappos offers new employees $2000 to leave after the first week. This is a good method to get those who do not really feel at home out of the company immediately.

Tell your colleagues who you have hired

In our opinion, most people tend to forget one aspect of the recruitment process – to find out how candidates learn. Some people learn best by listening or by talking, others by reading or writing. If a company has had a CEO who learns best by reading, a culture where people write lots of reports to each other soon arises. If this CEO then is replaced with a dyslexic who learns best by speaking or listening, the writing culture will still be maintained for a while, after which it will die out. The point is that when you hire someone, you need to ask about things like this, and when you introduce this to their colleagues, you might as well make sure that their strengths and weaknesses, including how they learn, are communicated to everyone.

What about job titles?

During the recruitment process, there will often arise a sticking point:
which title can the candidate expect to receive? The candidate can sometimes have surprisingly high expectations, but here it is important to establish a clear strategy, so that no inflation in the company's hierarchy occurs.
It can be demotivating for a senior employee to arrive at a company and
have the same title as young employees with a lower status. Thus, you
should early on define the titles that should exist in your business. In general, hold back with titles that seem to be relevant to leadership and responsibility if the job does not really offer this responsibility; otherwise you will
quickly create unnecessary frustrations when the company moves from
the jungle towards the highway.

*HOLD BACK WITH
TITLES THAT SEEM
TO BE RELEVANT TO*

LEADERSHIP AND RESPONSIBILITY IF THE JOB DOES NOT REALLY OFFER THIS.

Young start-ups should rarely have a COO or CHRO

External investors will be suspicious if a young start-up company has a chief operating officer (COO). Instead, they will usually expect the CEO to take that role until the company has become a lot bigger. They may also be puzzled if early on you have a chief human resources officer (CHRO). Either a young company should have no personnel manager or it should have just a recruiter.

How should I fire people?

Having to fire an employee due to poor management is challenging for many people. However, if an employee does not perform satisfactorily, it soon becomes expensive and will quickly lead to frustration among colleagues, as they might think: 'Why do I work so hard and effectively, when the company tolerates that my colleague does not?'

In fact, the reality is that you create respect for the management and the company by firing when it is justified. Not doing so expresses the reverse – it shows that the ambitions and expectation levels are low. It is therefore no coincidence that experienced business people sometimes use the term 'hire slow, but fire quickly'.

Many will sometimes feel doubt about whether to keep an employee or not. But if you have reached that level, you should in fact no longer be in doubt – resignation is typically the only way out. However, you should often give the employee a brief chance to rectify. Here, it is good to have a conversation about the problems and then wait and see what happens. It is effective to give the employee a chance, but you should also do this so that a potential firing does not come as a complete surprise. The exception to this rule is when the employee is in a position to do great damage when they are feeling demotivated.

HIRE SLOW, BUT FIRE QUICKLY.

It is important that a dismissal takes place in the best possible way. Unless sabotage or dishonesty is involved, make it clear that it is not necessarily the employee's fault – there may simply be a poor match between the employee and the company. Ask how you can help the fired employee in the future. Remember that a dismissed person will never forget the day when it happened and therefore never forget whether it seemed fair and justified or not.

What if a CEO should be replaced?

Start-ups change their CEOs a lot. In fact, one study showed that 'at the Initial public offering (IPO), a founder is CEO of only 49% of the VC-backed firms and 61% of the non-VC-backed firms'.[5]

An obvious reason for changing a CEO may be that things have gone very bad. No performance? You are fired! But it could also be because things have gone quite well and thus the company has moved to a new stage, for which the CEO is not suited. Maybe the founder CEO is amazing in the jungle but hopeless on the highway – that is very common.

Another common reason is that the founder-CEO feels huge loyalty to the first employee and the original business and therefore prevents necessary change within the business and the team. A symptom of this could be that they invent job titles and organizational sidings where people from the original team will be parked.

Statistics show that 27% of CEO replacements in start-ups are based on the CEO's own initiative, while 73% are caused by the board.[6] In both cases, a CEO replacement works much better if the CEO leaving assists with the process, which, incidentally, may take up to a year or even more. In addition to having a general feeling of responsibility for the company, a CEO who helps to find his or her replacement has a great interest in protecting the value of his or her shares in the company.

And then what? Does the former CEO retain some position? Statistics tell us that if the CEO gets fired by the board, he or she leaves the company completely in 37% of the cases, but if it is the CEO's own proposal to resign, this happens in only 14% of the cases.[7] But note that this means that the departing CEO in 63% and 86% of the cases respectively maintains a position within the business, such as a chief strategist or director. This makes sense, because a retiring CEO can very well maintain an effective role as an evangelist, an ambassador or a networker, or to develop spinoffs or take care of important ad hoc projects. However, it is rarely good for the new CEO if the old is chairman of the board – this invites conflicts. Sometimes a potential CEO will reject the job if the old CEO will be chairman of the board and thus a constant smart aleck interfering too much in the tactical decisions.

In our opinion, there are often clear benefits when a founder-CEO maintains a connection to the company even after his or her resignation – this person is indeed a key part of the history and culture and can act as an excellent advocate with the customers, in the media, at exhibitions, etc., a role that otherwise may strain and distract a busy CEO. It is handy, for example, if the current CEO is primarily focused on leading the team as well as key negotiations, etc., whereas the co-founder and former CEO takes care of making speeches, giving interviews, etc.

Is the 'founder' role more fun than the 'CEO' role?

In relation to the founder's potential resignation as CEO, you should be aware that typical founder roles, such as evangelist, may be more fun than typical CEO roles.

Should no. 2 in the hierarchy be promoted to no. 1?

It is fairly common that there is a no. 2 below the CEO who automatically takes his or her place when he or she resigns. This may seem a natural choice, but you should consider that skilled CEOs usually have a decision-maker mentality, while the person below the CEO often has an advisor mentality. And the advisor may not be comfortable shifting to the position as decision maker.

Purpose, virtuosity, culture and autonomy

We have looked at salary, bonuses and stock options, which obviously are tools to attract and retain employees. However, employees will generally be motivated by four factors beyond remuneration:

- the feeling of having a general purpose
- personal development
- the degree of freedom
- the culture in general.

Some call this purpose, virtuosity, culture and autonomy.

Let's start with the feeling of purpose. The company must of course exist for some reason, i.e. it is contributing to the world with something useful. Typically, it will fulfil some specific users' or customers' needs, but often it also serves a much broader purpose. For example, by selling LED lamps, you make some customers happy, but you also contribute to fewer coal-fired power plants, innovation and job creation, etc. You can communicate this effectively using anecdotes and statistics.

One tool to promote the sense of purpose is corporate incentive events on or off campus. These can be for a division or for the entire company, possibly including partners. The second non-financial incentive is the employee's personal development. Almost everyone needs to feel that they are learning all the time. One obvious tool is training programmes. It is motivating and stimulating for managers to train others and it stimulates an optimization process because it entices them to think about their working structures. Learning by teaching is very effective. That said, you should be aware that small businesses are rarely as good at creating training programmes as larger ones are. Therefore, they often prefer more experienced employees and may find it difficult to take in students because no one has the time or tools to engage them.

LEARNING BY TEACHING IS VERY EFFECTIVE.

Train them and keep them

Serial entrepreneur Richard Branson once tweeted: 'Train people well enough so they can leave. Treat them well enough so they don't want to.'[8]

Who are the best coaches?

As people develop their abilities in some field, they typically start out being (i) unconsciously incompetent: they do not know how much they need to learn. Then they become (ii) consciously incompetent and realize how difficult the job is. Next step is to become (iii) consciously competent, which is where they are aware of how much they have just learned. And finally, they become (iv) unconsciously competent because they have forgotten how long the journey to their current knowledge was.

Here is the point: they are best at explaining their position to others when they have reached stage three, i.e. when they are consciously competent. At stage four, it becomes harder when they have forgotten what beginners do not know and understand. And at stages one and two, it is impossible.

Freedom was our third non-financial employee motivator. Often start-ups provide far more personal freedom in the workflow than do older companies. This can be very motivating and in start-ups people often can come and go as they please, as long as they are effective, and they can speak in a way that more or less suits them, bring their dog to work, listen to rock music while they work, etc., which makes it easier and more fun to make a great effort. Don't ignore this advantage, which brings us to the general issue of culture.

Thoughts on culture

A good culture can be extremely motivating and can minimize the need for formal rules, which is exactly what start-ups need to do. Is there a special culture you should cultivate in a start-up? The answer is in a way 'no' because it is attractive that each company has its own, unique culture, which will mean that the staff feel they are part of something special. This culture may very well be a little bizarre in some ways so that employees get a feeling of fraternity. At the same time, an interesting corporate culture may actually give a lot of free PR.

In practice, a company's culture can be communicated through everything from employees' expected attire to various rituals, offices' and factories' interior communication, and moral principles. At Saxo Bank's headquarters in Denmark, you will find Ayn Rand's moral principles etched into a glass wall which separates the reception and canteen. Other companies celebrate completely different values, from eastern spiritualism to ecology, physical discipline or bravery, and so on. Elite sport teams are usually good examples of rather bizarre cultures. The ice hockey team the Detroit Red Wings throws a dead octopus onto the rink before each match; other teams have their own uniforms and rituals, which they often cherish.

However, even if it is generally good for a start-up company to have a unique culture, there are two cultural traits that you should want in almost *any* start-up business:

- Keep the lines of communication short and use delegation.
- Avoid politics, communicate freely and sell the truth in a positive and constructive way.

The monkey's world

Short lines of communication require a flat organization with few management levels, so employees can get decisions and information through without having to struggle with bureaucracy. However, this can cause managers to become overloaded with tasks and problems.

A good way to minimize this problem in flat organizations is described in the classical theory of monkeys on the shoulder from 1974.[9] This highlights the situation where you as a manager encounter an employee who says, 'Boss, we have a problem'. In this situation we say the employee has a 'monkey on their shoulder'. Anyway, as the boss, after you have listened to the problem, you say you will think about it and get back to the person. Problem: this problem is no longer the employees', it has become yours. Now *you* have the monkey on *your* shoulder.

This keeps happening everyday until you are burdened by 60 screaming monkeys on your shoulder and can barely make it into your office for people queuing up outside waiting on your decisions. In fact, the whole company has slowed down because everyone is waiting for you. And you begin to feel stressed.

The solution is, roughly speaking, the following: Do not say that you will consider the problem and come back with your answer later. Instead, you must either provide the employee with a mandate to solve this alone, or you need to make an appointment where you will discuss it again more deeply, in person or over the phone. If such a conversation is agreed on, the monkey – and this is important – must end up still sitting on the employee's shoulder, not yours. For example, the employee can come up with a solution, which is then discussed straight away or at a later meeting. Also: do not ask the employee to send you an email describing the problem unless this is exclusively a presentation on the previous conversation – otherwise, the monkey will end up on your shoulder again.

The whole point of this is that the decision should not wait for you but for your employee – the 60 screaming monkeys should always be delegated. This gets the organization up in speed and at the same time ensures that you can spend time on the major challenges – so-called gorillas – while employees maintain the responsibility for the many monkeys.

How to avoid politics

The second big potential problem to avoid in your start-up is politics, where people in secret agitate their ideas and slander each other in their attempt to gain power. One of the methods to prevent this is to maintain openness. For example, a company can have frequent short meetings with the following fixed agenda:

- Positive stories: what has gone well since the last meeting and what can we learn from that?
- Positive criticism: what has gone badly and what can we learn from that?
- What is it that we do not do that we should consider doing?

All three aspects are important. The positive stories provide knowledge about core competences and create a winning atmosphere. But you cannot have an artificially positive leadership because there are always problems which must be resolved and the staff will typically find out about these problems sooner or later. It is therefore better to share problems and give people a sense of responsibility for solving them. As mentioned earlier, it sometimes helps when you include a little humour, but mixed with action points and delegation of responsibilities.

The third point is important, partly because it inspires change and improvement, and partly because if everyone leaves the meeting having had the opportunity to state their thoughts about the issue, they have less reason to agitate behind the scenes.

A general purpose of such meetings is that everyone senses that the company is going through a constant learning process – and that it is willing and able to constantly adapt and innovate.

We are still discussing how to avoid politics and another important aspect is to communicate that the remuneration is never negotiated during the year. However, this rule may create a problem if a key employee has been offered a higher-paying job in another company and thereby 'blackmails' you. What should you do then? If you give in, you have created a bad precedent; if you do not give in, you lose the employee immediately. So again: what to do? One possible solution is to negotiate in cooperation with the company seeking to hire your employee that he will stay with you long enough to complete his projects and enable you to find a replacement. You can then possibly provide a temporary income-contingent bonus to achieve this, but no change in salary. These measures in combination will serve to prevent a culture in which people can beg or threaten you to receive higher wages.

Start-ups are unpolished

One last comment about culture. Start-ups often display rough and direct communication and language, which comes naturally to the daredevil types who are comfortable with the often-brutal challenges the team must tackle. In his book *The Hard Thing About Hard Things*, former entrepreneur and now venture capitalist Ben Horowitz writes about an episode at his start-up Netscape when the company seemed to be destroyed by Microsoft and therefore had decided to launch a new product in response.[10] Two weeks before the scheduled launch date, Ben's partner Marc Andreessen told a journalist about the product, which should have been a surprise. Ben then wrote a short email in which he politely made Marc aware of the problem. And then, around 15 minutes later, Marc, replied:

To: Ben Horowitz

Cc: Mike Homer, Jim Barksdale (CEO), Jim Clark (Chairman)

From: Marc Andreessen

Subject: Re: Launch

Apparently you do not understand how serious the situation is. We are getting killed killed killed out there. Our current product is radically worse than the competition. We've had nothing to say for months. As a result, we've lost over $3B in market capitalization. We are now in danger of losing the entire company and it's all server product management's fault.

Next time do the fucking interview yourself.

Fuck you,
Marc

So . . . is it OK to sign an email to the management and the board with 'fuck you'? We will pass on that, but we do not believe that a rough start-up can necessarily have a polished form of communication, although some employees might ask for this. When some Netscape employees complained about the company's outspoken language, management discussed it but concluded that if they forbade that kind of language, they could not hire from Intel and Microsoft, where people were used to the same tone. This they communicated to the staff, after which the complaints stopped.

Culture is people

One cannot build a strong culture without being careful to only hire people who fit into this. Therefore, job candidates must be clearly confronted with the culture prior to their employment, just as the recruiters must consider very carefully which candidates really fit into this culture.

PART 4.

ABOUT MY COMPANY'S GROWTH, STRATEGIES AND CHALLENGES

Let us assume that you have your idea, your first funding, your business and your team in place, and now you need to do business!

But, how? How, for example, is operating a small start-up different from working in a well-established, large company? Which stages will your start-up go through? And how can you as manager in a start-up plan while going through the huge uncertainty you will experience? Which strategies can you choose from? When does each of these make most sense?

This chapter is about where the greatest strategic start-up opportunities lie and how you can create home runs. It touches on the typical traps that make start-ups fail. To address this, we present a selection of models, working methods, checklists and tools that we have found useful in our own entrepreneurial work.

12.
MY GROWTH PHASES

The Marmer phases include (i) discovery, (ii) validation, (iii) efficiency, (iv) scaling, (v) maintenance and (vi) sale or renewal. It is important to realize that start-ups going through phases 1–4 should not try to be small versions of large companies. Instead they must be completely different from large companies and they should master rapid organizational changes as they move from phase to phase. In this chapter, we will discuss the transitions that a growth company goes through and how you deal with them.

Babies and teenagers are not just small or young versions of adults, they are completely different. The same applies to young and small versus old and big companies. We will now study this. Let's start with the discovery phase. In this phase you should, as mentioned, primarily identify your product/market fit. An interesting definition of this is given by serial entrepreneur Sean Ellis. It goes as follows:[1]

'In my experience, you should, to achieve a product/market fit, have at least 40 percent of your customers saying that they would be very disappointed without your product. Certainly, this threshold is a bit arbitrary, but I defined this by looking at the following comparison of results across nearly 100 start-ups. Those who had problems with demand were always below 40 percent, while most who received strong traction exceeded 40 percent.'

So a product/market fit means that many customers are very pleased with the product and would be disappointed if it disappeared. But how do you find or develop such a product/market fit? This can be done in three different ways: (i) product-centred development, (ii) traditional marketing cascade and (iii) agile business development.

Product-centred development

Product-centred development assumes that a single person or a small team has a strong, innovative idea which is forced through. That is how artists work – they cannot and obviously should not conduct market analysis; their product is expressive and arises out of their soul and passion. Fortunately, Picasso did not ask art collectors what percentage of red they preferred in a painting before he swung the brush.

The product-centred development form is used, among others in the luxury industry, where the product is an artistic or emotional expression more than the solution to a practical problem. This also applies to fashion and supercars. To a great degree, you can argue that Steve Jobs turned Apple into a luxury company both in the way it developed new products and how it sold them through its 500 or so sleek designer stores. However, you should know that even if a product is developed without market research, it may be necessary to test it through such research once it is developed.

Product-centred development may make sense for a start-up, and it certainly worked for Apple. However, it can also become a dead end.

Traditional marketing cascade

The classic marketing cascade is different. With this method you begin with formal analysis, then you make documents such as market requirement, functionality specification and detail specification, after which you proceed with launch plans and budgets to ultimately reach the first customer milestone.

This method may prove useful to start-ups with complex capital expenditures, seen within the biotech and hardware industries, but in more flexible and less capital-intensive projects such as most software development, new media or services, the third of our methods – agile business development – is usually the proper method.

Agile business development

Agile business development assumes that you create a customer discovery loop where you (i) produce a minimum viable product or a mock-up/demo/simulation, (ii) test it with customers, (iii) modify it, etc. You will repeat this method with short intervals until you believe you have got it right. So: build, test and learn. Rebuild, test again and learn again. Once more. And so on until everything is perfect. If the company is in a particularly dynamic market, the process never stops, it just keeps forever spitting out new products.

BUILD, TEST AND LEARN. REBUILD, TEST AGAIN AND LEARN AGAIN. ONCE MORE. AND SO ON UNTIL EVERYTHING IS PERFECT.

One of the reasons agile business development is popular among start-ups is that they often need to make major strategic changes repeatedly during their early stages. Groupon, for example, began as a website where people could get together and find solutions to some sort of greater cause or goal. However, the management soon discovered that the most popular group of solutions was very simple: joint procurement of . . . half-price offers for pizzas. This was not a greater cause, but it was popular. This feature, initially marginal, then became the company's only purpose. In other cases, the opposite has happened: the original purpose is reduced to one feature among many in the final product. Or everything might have changed.

Such radical course changes, or pivots, might seem to be signs of failure. However, according to the Startup Genome project's studies, they are actually clear signs of health. In fact, the companies that had made at least one abrupt pivot managed to raise 2.5 times more capital than and had 3.6 times as much growth as those which did not make pivots.[2] Besides, it was 2.3 times more likely that a company doing those pivots had more than one founder, indicating that creativity increases when you have more founders. Additionally, Startup Genome's studies showed that companies that had made several pivots early on (when it was cheap) made fewer later when it would have been more expensive.

THE COMPANIES THAT HAD MADE AT LEAST ONE ABRUPT PIVOT

MANAGED TO RAISE 2.5 TIMES MORE CAPITAL AND HAD 3.6 TIMES AS MUCH GROWTH AS THOSE THAT HAD NOT MADE A PIVOT.

About the risk of skipping the discovery phase

There are countless examples of magnificent but failed product launches, such as Webvan, Sirius, WebTV, Vista, MSNTV, Apple's Newton, etc. Many of these could probably have been avoided by testing the product/market fit more thoroughly first. Webvan, which launched internet shopping for groceries in 1998, invested more than $1 billion and employed more than 2000 people – all of this within 19 months and without having tested the concept first. Then, in 2001, the company went bankrupt after losing more than $800 million. Webvan used a traditional marketing cascade and that was an expensive mistake.

The founder of online shoe retailer Zappos, which also offered internet shopping, instead used agile business development. He made agreements with local shoe retailers enabling him to photograph their shoe selection and try to sell them online. This gave him a sense of how it should be done and whether the shoes could be sold that way. It turned out that they could, and only when he understood *how* did he start to invest and build infrastructure.

Webvan could have followed a similar strategy. It could have purchased the products in a supermarket, for example, and done test marketing in a local community before developing and building its enormous infrastructure.

Start-up companies' many pivots should have an impact on the use of outsourcing. As mentioned, you should outsource a lot, but not what is most important for the company's learning process. Startup Genome found out that software firms which failed had 15–19% of their product development outsourced during their discovery and validation phases, whereas the more successful companies outsourced only 3–4%.[3] Finding the product/market fit obviously requires full personal commitment.

Something else to be aware of during the discovery phase is that it is dangerous to agree on a launch date too early. If you do that, you could easily end up launching the wrong product to the wrong market.

Agile business development has become particularly popular within software and electronic media businesses, where it is easy to practise. If you work with an online product, you can often obtain real-time feedback and make new releases almost daily to see the reaction (which, to put it mildly, is not the case if you produce aeroplanes). In many cases, you do it by making 'fake doors' where perhaps 1% of users are taken to an alternative version of your website, or by doing 'split releases' or 'A/B testing' where typically half the customers receive one version of a website, for example, and the others get another. You can then continuously compare the results with Google Analytics.

With physical products, it tends to become more complicated, but you may still test product variations using 'one-night stands', where you briefly and locally offer a changed version of your product, or where you change the price or packaging to see what happens.

Inquisitive Tom

An essential element of the discovery phase can simply be to chat with knowledgeable and inspiring people about your thoughts. Elaborate, and listen to what comes back. Alternatively, if you are the type of person who learns best by reading and writing, write memos about your ideas and ask for people's reactions. However, you must remember that most knowledgeable and inspiring people are extremely busy. Therefore, if you ask for a coffee meeting with such a person just to get some feedback, they are likely to avoid the meeting. A coffee meeting sounds like 30 minutes, and most successful people cannot or will not set aside time for such a meeting with a stranger without a clear agenda. David Cohen from the accelerator Techstars has described how these people perceive inquiries about business ideas:[5]

- Tiny = email response, one or two simple questions in a short email
- Small = email response, 3–5 questions in a longer email
- Medium = 15-minute phone call
- Big = 30-minute phone call
- Huge = in person meeting

Very sensibly, Cohen recommends making first contact with a simple email question and then asking for more if the initial contact goes well. We would like to add: if you contact busy people and then waste their time, you have hardly begun a relationship which you can later develop; rather you have made all further contact impossible. Moreover, another effective way to irritate busy people is to share their email address with people they do not know.

IF YOU CONTACT A BUSY PERSON BUT ARE WASTING THEIR TIME, YOU HAVE HARDLY BEGUN A RELATIONSHIP WHICH YOU CAN LATER DEVELOP. RATHER YOU HAVE MADE ALL FURTHER CONTACT IMPOSSIBLE.

Testing with one-night stands

Does greater product variation help the business? There is a phenomenon called 'the decoy effect' where you can get people to buy more by adding a 'decoy' item to the assortment.[6] This was illustrated in an experiment where a cinema sold two portion sizes of popcorn: a small for $3 and a large for $7. Almost everyone bought the small one because the large one seemed expensive in comparison. Then the assortment was changed to a small for $3, a medium for $6.50 and a large for $7. From then on, the vast majority bought the large because it seemed cheap compared with the medium. In other cases, however, increasing the assortment may pull in the opposite direction. A company established a jam jar booth outside a supermarket. It sold more when the customers had four jam jars to choose from, compared with having 20. Sometimes people should not have too many products to choose from.[7]

These are observations that are useful to do on your own, especially during the company's discovery phase. If in doubt, test with the one-night stands.

Customer development during the discovery phase

A special variant of agile business development is called customer development. This is about being very close to potential customers and about developing while you watch their response. In fact, your entire young start-up company can initially be a customer development team and nothing else.

It does not need to be complicated. For example, if you dream of opening a restaurant with Korean food, then invite your friends and family home for Korean dinners and ask for their opinion. Tell them to be honest and critical. It may also be that you dream of designing suitcases. In this scenario, you can have some cheap prototypes made in the Far East and have them tested among a variety of friends and acquaintances before initiating actual production. In these two examples, your meals and your suitcase prototype are your MVP.

In some cases, a start-up arises through the customer development situation where you as a consultant have developed a solution for a concrete paying customer. Since the customer was happy, you consider this your MVP and create a business where you replicate and develop this for many clients. In such cases there might be a copyright problem, but then you might make the client an offer, such as a 20% discount against releasing copyright, or whatever. If the client is reluctant, you might even offer a stake in the new project as compensation.

User stories

Regarding all three development methods – product-centred, marketing cascade and agile – it can prove helpful to write 'user stories' that describe a customer's activities with the product. User stories are, like customer development, split tests and the other methods described above, attempts to find the right product/market fit.

The 'Pinocchio' approach is a 'fake it until you make it' way of using a non-living product to test an idea. A great example of using the Pinocchio method came from Jeff Hawkins, who founded Palm Pilot. Reportedly, he always walked around with a block of wood in his pocket, which would appear as a prototype computer that he was in the process of developing. In any situation where the future Palm Pilot could be used, Jeff would pull out his wooden block and imagine how it would work in that given situation and then adjust the design, buttons, etc. accordingly.

Use apps to test your website

If a website is an important part of your business, you can use apps such as Optimal Workshop's Chalkmark to test how people use your site. For example, it may be important to know what is the first thing they click on.

The earliest market analysis – desk research

During the earliest stages of your company's development, you will probably use cheap or free methods to gather information. Most of these methods are called desk research because you can do them from your desktop. For example, you can estimate your market via Google Trends, where you look up likely keywords that customers will use and then see how many Google keyword searches there are (such as 'pizza', 'delivery' and 'Birmingham'). An additional tool is Facebook Ads to identify potential customers' demographic distribution.

There are many apps to make online surveys on your website or social media (SurveyMonkey is among the most well known). And there are plenty of marketing research web services such as Illuminate Content, MetricWire, QuickTapSurvey and Survtapp.

Start-ups often overlook asking banks whether they have free analysis of the relevant markets. You can also ask a direct-mail agency how many addresses they have within a given market space – this can give you a feel for the market size and structure. Do they have 500 restaurants in Birmingham? Or 5000? And you can study annual reports, websites, etc. within the relevant industry.

Additionally, there are a lot of good journals on most markets (you can google this, or alternatively most are available on Ulrich's International Periodicals Directory). Regarding more comprehensive analysis, you can look for multi-client studies, which are very structured market and technology analysis. These are rarely cheap, but even a (free) glance at the table of contents can give valuable information. Also, try Google Scholar, which has a wide selection of free scientific articles, dissertations, etc.

If you plan to establish traditional exports, you can contact the embassies abroad for advice. You should be aware, however, that they will find it difficult to answer questions about aspects such as 'an evaluation of the local market for product X'. It is better to elaborate on your organization and present potential distribution. You should describe your relevant export experience, your product, its audiences, its use and important competitive strengths and weaknesses. Provide them with detailed product documentation and possibly price lists and delivery conditions – preferably in the local language for the export market (if you cannot speak the language, find a cheap translator at, for example, gengo.com). And do not forget to inform them about any other contacts and activities that you already have on the market.

The earliest market analysis – field research

Should you move on to do field research where in contrast to the desk research, you actually have to leave your office to do interviews etc., the most common methods to use during the discovery phase are (i) informal interviews, (ii) key interviews, (iii) focus groups and (iv) supply mapping – for more on these, see the box at the end of this chapter. You can arrange some of this by yourself, but if you must use an agency, you should expect them to use about 20% of their time (and costs) on planning, 65% on interviews and 15% on data analysis and presentation.

Moreover, an effective field research method is to visit relevant trade shows. If you do not know which shows are most relevant, try googling some of the names of suppliers to your sector or your product descriptions and combine these words with 'visit us at', 'fair', 'exhibition' and 'show'. That will show you where the action in your sector really is.

Business plans versus business canvases

Of course, whatever you learn from your customer development, fake doors, split releases, A/B testing, one-night stands, Pinocchios, online surveys, desk and field research, etc. needs to feed into your planning. But how should the plan look? Well, it's a business plan, right? Like MBA students have been taught for decades? Well, actually not necessarily. In early 1982, when Microsoft was seven years old, the management decided to create an international division. Bill Gates gave the job to Scott Oki, who after some time told Gates that he had made a business plan, to which Gates famously replied: 'What's a business plan?'

So, do you need a business plan during the early development stages? A study of 100 ventures started by Babson College alums who graduated between 1985 and 2003 concluded as follows:

> 'There was no difference between the performance of new businesses launched with or without written business plans. The findings suggest that unless a would-be entrepreneur needs to raise substantial start-up capital from institutional investors or business angels, there is no compelling reason to write a detailed business plan before opening a new business.'[8]

The alternative to the traditional business plan, which is typically 15–50 pages of elaborate detail, is our business canvas, which is an informal tool for making your continuous business model design. Its visual form can be something as simple as a large sheet – consider A3 – with space for each of many strategic areas. This canvas is now filled with bullet points and possibly also small diagrams, but no long text. Below are two examples of items that may be included:

Example A

• Value proposition	• Resource requirements
• Market segments	• Necessary activities
• Customer relations	• Partners (ecosystem)
• Distribution channels	• Price structure
• Profit models	• Cost structure

Example B

• The problem we solve	• Distribution channels
• The solution	• Funding
• Value proposition	• The first customers
• Critical success factors	• Cost structure
• Unique competitive advantage	• Income sources
• Customer segments	• What we don't know

This canvas is adjusted continuously, for example several times the first day and then ad hoc or once a day, then maybe once a week, and so on. In practice, this may be done on an A4 sheet, which is probably easier to complete by hand. However, it can also be done with a permanent marker on a whiteboard, with sticky notes on a paper sheet on a wall, or in many other ways. Even using lipstick on a mirror could be useful. Old versions can be saved (or photographed) so that you and your team can rethink ideas and remind yourselves how unstable the process is.

Can it be done more formally? Yes, there are excellent creativity tools, such as the website LaunchPadCentral.com or the app Trello, which are great at making virtual bulletin boards and putting structures to ideas or tasks.

What if you are the type who learns best by writing and therefore still have an urge to make a full, long-form business plan? Then by all means, do it, but just remember that the malleability of the business canvas is extremely useful and should not be replaced by the less adaptable long Word document. And remember this: if an entrepreneur at an early stage of the development presents a comprehensive 'business plan' to experienced VCs, they might see this as a danger sign.

The validation phase

We have discussed the discovery phase of the start-up development, so let us now move to the validation phase. Let's say that via the discovery phase you have found a proven product/market fit. This means that your business probably must focus a lot on:

- developing and improving its product features
- increasing its sales
- examining its user needs more in depth
- developing its metrics for monitoring product/market fit
- expanding capacity.

Furthermore, you may need to raise some additional capital – perhaps in the order of $4–500 000.

It is during this phase that your team probably evolves from being just a few founders plus probably some freelancers to actually having staff on the payroll. This can be a frustrating step where you and your co-founders must implement staff administration, and you suddenly also get the responsibility of motivating and setting goals for your first employee(s). This can feel like a big step. Keep in mind that it is much easier to hire employee number 11 than employee number 1, and it can also be easier to manage 3500 employees than 10. In large companies, there is a process for everything – as there is for McDonald's. There is not a process for everything in a small company where you will have to define and undertake so much yourself.

On average, the validation takes around 3–5 months, unless the product is either very complex or extremely simple. If we include the extremes, it may very well take from just a few months and up to many years.

A key task in this phase is to begin following key metrics for the company's success. These should be directly relevant for your bottom line instead of just having metrics on how many people have visited your website, for instance. How important is this? Very. The Startup Genome studies revealed that only 31% of the start-ups which did *not* use metrics to measure their progress were given external funding. Among those that did use metrics, 50% received external funding.[9]

According to the Startup Genome studies, the most used tools to monitor metrics are Google Analytics (which is for websites), self-developed tools and spreadsheets. However, please be aware that there are plenty of off-the-shelf dashboards for this purpose, such as MyDials, Workday and PivotLink. Some of these are very good, and if at all possible, we strongly recommend you to use dashboard tools for monitoring your business.

IF AT ALL POSSIBLE, WE STRONGLY RECOMMEND

YOU TO USE DASHBOARD TOOLS FOR MONITORING YOUR BUSINESS.

The efficiency phase

After the validation phase comes the efficiency phase. Working on efficiency is essential for a young company once it has found its product/market fit, as in the early days, lots of things have typically been done quick and dirty, if not worse. The efficiency phase can involve improved standards for accounting, finance, contracts, trademarks, production, quality control, staff, production and everything else. In software, it can include writing proper source code, setting up better test environments, etc. It is also during this phase that you need to understand your costs down to the smallest detail, so that you can cut these where possible.

When working on efficiency, it is important to gain an understanding of the customer life value, i.e. how much you earn on a repeat customer from the first time that person purchases or pays for your product, to the last time. You must also analyze whether the company's processes are sufficiently scalable and include insights about whether the variable costs have a form of economies of scale – will they be higher or lower, the more products you sell? And if not lower, how can you change that? Note here that production costs per unit have a greater tendency to decrease with increasing revenue than sales costs – in other words, production usually scales better than sales, unless it is web sales, where the opposite is the case.

One way to view the efficiency phase is that it is part of the 'nail it before you scale it' process. Perhaps some entrepreneurs feel that they have nailed it once they have proven a product/market fit, but in our opinion you also need to build a streamlined execution machine before you have nailed it and are ready to scale – we will address this in more detail in Chapter 14.

Perhaps the company may raise, say, another $700 000 or so during this phase, which might fund the next year and a half year, and it is normal that here you bring your staff up to about 20 employees. But again, staffing and financing depend on the nature of the project, and this can vary enormously.

PERHAPS SOME ENTRE-
PRENEURS FEEL THAT
THEY HAVE NAILED
IT ONCE THEY HAVE
PROVEN A PRODUCT/
MARKET FIT, BUT IN
OUR OPINION YOU
ALSO NEED TO BUILD
A STREAMLINED EXE-
CUTION MACHINE
BEFORE YOU HAVE
NAILED IT AND ARE
READY TO SCALE.

From nailing to scaling

Hereafter comes the scaling phase. In confidence that the company has control of everything, you raise perhaps $3 million (as with the other funding examples, this is used as an average sum of raised capital among many companies. Each situation can be immeasurably different). With funding in place, you can increase the staff further and really put the pedal to the metal with sales, marketing, production, product launches, recruitment of skilled managers, the establishment of well-defined departments and development of workflows.

During this phase, you will also typically begin to expand the product range and/or market penetration. This can happen in 10 basic ways:

Ten strategies for strategic expansion.

	Existing products	New products
Existing markets	• Increase the usage from existing users • Increase the market share • Identify new applications or usability	• Increase the assortment • New product versions released • Launch new products targeted towards the same market segments • Add new functions to the existing products
New markets	• Target new geographical areas • Target new market segments	• Diversification

The safest method to expand is typically to stick to where you are directly improving what is already working. Either way, you should be most careful with a new market and new products.

Tactically, expansions can be carried out mainly in the following ways:

- *Internal development.* The company's own staff is responsible for product and market development.

- *Internal venture.* You create a new unit within your company where your staff can work as intrapreneurs.

- *Obtain licence.* You buy the licence to distribute other companies' products.

- *Sell licence.* You sell distribution rights for your products to other companies.

- *Market-oriented acquisitions.* You buy a company that has good market access.

- *Knowledge-oriented acquisitions.* You buy a company because of its products or development expertise.

- *Marketing alliance.* You agree on cross-selling, cross promotion, joint promotion, system integration, etc.

- *Joint venture.* You make a new company with a partner company.

- *VC investments.* You invest in small companies with which you have synergy.

An important element in the scaling phase is expansion of distribution, unless you have an electronic product which is already global.

Early on, companies often expand according to the opportunities they randomly encounter. An example: at an exhibition, you meet an interested distributor in Portugal and therefore you go into the Portuguese market. This is an unplanned, bottom-up approach. Later, as you become more sophisticated and have more resources, you will be more strategic and will systematically start to attack the most accessible markets, which may be those closest to you physically, unless you do pure ecommerce. And finally, as a truly global player with strategic planning, you will study the international markets systematically before actively selecting the next target based on their overall attractiveness.

Parallel to this, you will initially rely mainly on indirect distributors and then later will try to get greater control by establishing your own sales companies in local markets, plus possibly buying out previous distributors and franchisees. The table below provides an overview of the alternative ways to develop your distribution.

Twelve strategies for product range expansion.

	Via domestic organization	Via foreign organization
Direct	• Directly from your own country • Subsidiary • Affiliate • Production in a foreign country	• Import company • Sales agent • Sales representative
Indirect	• Export company • Export agent • Export administration company	• Import company • Franchise

How the market for a product evolves

In this chapter we have so far studied in some detail how your company evolves through its growth phases. But how does a market grow overall, and what does it mean for suppliers such as you? Let us start by defining the five traditional phases of a market development:

1. Emerging market

2. Growth market

3. Shake-out market

4. Mature market

5. Dying market

Each of these five phases has its own characteristics:

- First, early products in the emerging market will typically be launched as stand-alone solutions with basic functionality.

- In the later growth market, many variants and applications follow. As this happens, you frequently see products converge or become embedded in other products. The product quality will also improve constantly and common technological standards will often evolve (especially in the electronic markets).

- In the shakeout and maturing markets, many companies die while others merge as part of consolidation plays and product integration.

- The final stage, the dying market, can evolve in many ways. The product may disappear entirely here or (more likely) become a niche or a feature in something bigger.

As this happens, one or several companies will aim for the role as category king, but only one of these will end in this role. This process tends to happen faster in business-to-business (B2B) markets than in business-to-consumer (B2C) markets. In any case, the winner of the category king battle will subsequently command a large percentage of overall profits in the category.

How distribution structures change as markets evolve

Distribution will typically initially be based largely on 'push' strategies, which focus on getting distributors to carry the product. Later on, there will be an increased focus on 'pull', i.e. to stimulate the demand from end users. As the markets evolve, there will be many informal business alliances – informal because the market is still too fluid for companies to be willing to bind too strongly. These early alliances can relate to joint marketing, for example. Later, more formal and long-term agreements will be made, and during the maturing and dying markets there will be many mergers and acquisitions.

How promotion strategies evolve as markets mature

How do typical promotion strategies evolve as markets develop? The early-stage activities will typically be centred around creating awareness – and often in the distribution chains. Later, it will be necessary to provide more factual information as well as to create a positive attitude about companies and products. During the shakeout phase and beyond, there is frequently a great need to build confidence as people can see that there is a shakeout. In this late phase, promotion is increasingly purely simple reminders, such as showing the product only, without any additional information.

The most important formal field research tools for start-ups

Analysis method	Scenario	Typical duration
Focus groups	You do not yet have a structured view of the respondent's attitudes to your (still) loosely formulated ideas about potential products, advertising or packaging concepts. You may be looking to create the basis for later quantitative tests. Respondents are specialists, or the topics to be discussed are sensitive/personal.	Roughly four weeks
Informal interviews	Purely exploratory conversations to find out where the big opportunities and problems might lie.	1–4 weeks
Key interviews	You need information on market structures and competitors, etc. and you are looking for qualified opinions and advice beyond facts.	Varies

(Continued)

Analysis method	Scenario	Typical duration
Distribution studies	You must assess relevant opinions and attitudes among leaders in the distribution chain. Additionally, you want to understand your competitors and your company's image, competitiveness and product development through distribution channels.	Varies
Retail panels	You want to identify how specific retail chains buy, store and sell your brands and competing brands.	Subscription based
Radar	Mapping of your product's audiences and their attitudes to your product.	1–4 weeks
Supply mapping	You must register which products are available in any sector of the market. It may include brands, prices, packaging and shelf space and identify distribution patterns, competition, pricing structures and sales parameters.	A few days
Consumer panel	You are interested in tracking how clients in different end-user segments are buying your competitors' products and how this changes over time.	Varies
Concept tests	You need an evaluation of product concepts to find out if they will work, what their strongest and weakest elements are and, if there are several alternatives, which one is best. The test can be performed separately for products and packaging. Similar tests can be conducted for products, product features, packaging and advertisements.	Roughly four weeks

Assessment of the competitor situation

The Startup Owner's Manual by Steve Blank and Bob Dorf contains some key rules on competitors' market shares, which, curiously, are derived from military research:[10]

- If a business has at least a three-quarters share of the market, this is in practice a monopolistic condition. To attack in such a market, you need to spend at least three times as much on marketing as the monopolist, and you should know that this competitor may very well respond by lowering its prices and increasing its marketing budget.
- If the two largest suppliers together have at least three-quarters of the market, and the largest of these two companies is 1.7 times as big as the other, there is a duopoly, which also makes the market very difficult to attack. An attack will thus require that you use at least three times as much on marketing as the two duopolies use amalgamated. And here it also applies that they can respond by lowering their prices, for example, or increasing their marketing budget.
- If the largest provider has about 40% of the market, the market is unstable and subject to rapid change. If you use more than 1.5 times as much on marketing as the largest provider, you have a chance.

What you should be aware of is that if your product is fundamentally different from those of existing suppliers, you may in fact be competing in a different market. Also, many start-ups circumvent these draconian demands on marketing spend through effective use of virtually free PR, where they build on having a good story to tell that the press finds interesting.

About market analysis and statistics

Following are two rules on statistics which will surprise many market analysts. First rule: the cost when increasing statistical reliability increases exponentially. Suppose, for instance, that you select a representative sample of 100 people to check whether they know product X, and let's say that the result is that 50% know the product. Your research agency tells you that the statistical confidence interval is ±10% (i.e. 90% confidence interval). How many people would they need to interview in order to bring this uncertainty down to within ±5%?

Answer: They must interview 400 instead of 100. It would probably make the study about three times as expensive (but not four, as the data collection as mentioned above is only part of the total analysis cost).

Second rule: the number of interviews for a given measurement uncertainty is surprisingly small related to the size of the total 'universe' (market) you are investigating. A simple example: you prepare a quantitative study in two countries, one with 100 million inhabitants and a second with 5 million inhabitants. You want to know the percentage that knows your product and you assume that it's about 50% in each country. You require 90% probability that the analysis result is less than 1% different from the true value. So how many interviews do you need to conduct in each of the two countries?

In the small country, you must conduct 5755 interviews; in the big country, the figure is 5764. The difference is just nine interviews, despite a difference of 95 million people in the population! Actually, the size of the universe begins to be statistically significant only if the number of interviews comes close to or above 10% of the universe. Which means almost never.

What should I include in a brief to a market research agency for a field research task?

Here is what they normally need to know:

- *Universe.* What is the total 'universe' (people, companies, etc.) that is relevant to the marketing problem?
- *Problem.* Which decisions should the study support? Are we looking for the unexpected or should we answer something specific? Should the information be quantitative or qualitative?
- *Hypothesis.* Can you formulate a relevant hypothesis based on previous studies or your general commercial experience?
- *Statistical reliability.* Is it sufficient to get a rough estimate of the market or do you need a high degree of statistical confidence? Again, will the study support a quantitative decision?
- *Time pressure.* When do you need the preliminary results and when do you need the final report?
- *Budget.* What can you spend on it?
- *Method suggestions.* Do you have suggestions or requirements for the selection of sources and research approach?
- *Logistics.* Who is responsible for design of the questionnaire, translation, demo material, tabulation plans and personal participation?
- *Presentation.* What do you expect to find in the report – text, tables, size of the report, possible tabulation and presentation of the report?
- *Secondary information.* Are you interested in incorporating data from previous studies or any other related information into the final report?

13.
MY MARKETING MIX

Many people believe that marketing is all about PR, advertising and sales. In fact, this discipline is much broader and is ultimately about optimizing the use of the company's total resources to achieve well-defined goals. Because it is focused on resource allocation, it is also very much about what not to do. For instance, usually, you should not stray from your core competency. And usually, you should neither start projects without synergy to the rest nor scale parts of the company if the others cannot follow. In this chapter, we will walk through most of the important marketing tools that are available for you through your company's expansion.

A good starting point for the company's marketing strategy is its elevator pitch, which we described in Chapter 9. In more classical marketing terms this is an expression of the company vision and mission.

This leads directly to segmentation whereby you normally divide the target market into groups (segments). Yes, 'normally', because with the emergence of big data in more and more businesses, you can largely skip segmentation and go straight to individualization – more about that in a minute.

Segmentation approaches

Let's start with classical segmentation. Here, you ask questions such as 'Which groups of customers do we sell to?' and 'How are they different?' If it is manufacturers, distributors or other companies, one speaks about business-to-business markets. If you sell to the public sector (government), it is sometimes called B2G. Otherwise it's called business-to-consumer.

However, your target market may be segmented much further, where each individual group typically must be treated differently regarding product, price, promotion, distribution and processes. Therefore, you should consider *why* customers buy your stuff, i.e. what basic needs does or will the product fulfil? You should also consider how customers prioritize, how they decide on their purchases, where they live, etc. At the end of this chapter, you will find a box with examples of such considerations.

Once you have been through this analysis, you can choose between five segmentation strategies:

- *Niche strategy*. Choose one or a few segments and target them with a dedicated approach. You should often use this strategy during the first growth phases, so that you can get local dominance, even if you are a small player in an otherwise big market. For instance, Facebook started at Harvard only, while Amazon focused initially on books only.

- *Long tails strategy*. Long tails refer to the outer segments in a normal distribution curve, i.e. small niches. Some companies specialize in selling many customized products to many small niches. This may be a portfolio of specialized magazines, for instance.

- *Differentiation strategy*. Choose many or all segments within a broader market, but customize the marketing mix to each of them.

- *Aggregation strategy*. Ignore segments and instead target the market as a whole. This is rarely a good approach, but if a company has a short window of opportunity (time-limited great advantage), it can be meaningful to operate aggressively and simply.

- *Mass customization/segment-of-one.* Because of big data and the ability to carry out mass customization through e-commerce and smart production, you ignore segments and deliver instead whatever is requested by any individual client. This is also called segment-of-one marketing.

What are mass customization and big data?

Let's just elaborate a bit on segment-of-one marketing. In recent years, big data has become ever more important in marketing. Simply said, this involves massive data streams, often combining text, numbers, video and audio, which are analyzed non-stop, in real time, for patterns. The analysis is frequently made with machine learning software, and apart from finding proven patterns, the software will often extrapolate to make assumptions, where data is not present. Examples of companies that excel in big data and mass customization are Amazon and Facebook, which soon will know enough about any single user/client to enable them to make highly customized offers to a particular person. To explain, IBM's CEO Ginni Rometty made a speech in 2013, in which she said:[1]

> 'The shift is to go from the segment to the individual. It spells the death of the average customer. Take the data and do things like real-time pricing, you're going to do omnichannel . . . you're going to bring out the latency in the data.'

She was right – the use of real-time data about the behaviour of every single client provides a significant change to marketing in more and more sectors. However, we still believe that classical segmentation is and will remain an important exercise, if not for anything else then for figuring out which overall strategies you want to pursue. This includes decisions relating to our next point in the marketing mix, namely product policy.

Becoming 'category king'

Studies of many business areas show that a large part of overall profits accrue to a single company. For instance, in their important book *Play Bigger*, three Silicon Valley veterans describe their investigations of a number of market categories, where they found that up to 80% of all profits and on average 76% of market value in each category went to a single company.[2] This was typically the acknowledged category leader, or, as they called it, 'category king'.

So how may a start-up end up in that lucrative position? First of all, it has to be an ambition. As a company, you will work not only on your product–market fit, team, business model, etc., but also on defining and promoting a new category which you can subsequently dominate. For instance, Apple invented and dominated the tablet computer category, and when it was launched, Steve Jobs said the magic words:[3]

> 'iPad creates and defines an entirely new category of devices that will connect users with their apps and content in a much more intimate, intuitive and fun way than ever . . .'

Yes, 'an entirely new category'. In similar fashion, Xerox, Google, IKEA, Netflix, Salesforce.com and Airbnb became clear category kings – companies that all invented or at least in the public mind became associated as the leaders of entirely new categories. They did this not only by delivering great products, but also by being great at defining the new category and evangelizing its advantages. In fact, in order to become category leader, you don't need to invent the product, you just need to make it clearly different and then communicate very strongly about why you do what you do. For instance, Miles Jones created several new categories in music, Muhammad Ali in combining showmanship with sports, McDonald's by delivering fast food, etc. In other words, to become category king, you don't need to set the scene – if you can steal the show instead.

Here is what category kings don't do: they don't try to implement every feature that their clients ask for. Instead, they define the category they are in, including (this is important) the problems they solve. And then they drive the product development to solve that problem or create that benefit.

Also, when describing their category, they never mention product features. Just bear in mind here the rule we described from the sales compass: 'The most important rule in the sales compass is that you must not describe the product before you have sold it'. The same goes when you describe your category: talk about problems, desires and solutions, but do not go into your product. Just don't. And then remember that once you reach category leader status, a lot of things will become a lot easier. Category leaders tend to attract the best people, get the most press coverage, have the most client data, etc.

How do you define your category? First, it must be something simple that every client, partner and employee can immediately grasp and feel empathy for. This is typically something that can be explained as an elevator pitch and reduced to a slogan or 2–3 words. Second, it must be something ambitious, but not insanely so. For instance, Amazon didn't start out as a leader of the web shopping space in general; instead it started out by defining itself as leader in the book shopping space. Only later did it move on to lead the online shopping category in general, then cloud computing, e-readers and possibly more in the future.

Last piece of advice: if you want to launch yourself as a category king, don't make the launch event into a sales or marketing event. No, this is a *company* event, because from that moment on, your new ambition should penetrate *all* your strategies.

Product policy

How do you make a product sellable, perhaps apart from being associated with category leadership? By making it particularly attractive on at least one and perhaps many parameters, such as these 20:

1. Location in relation to the customer	11. Delivery
2. Usability	12. Lifetime
3. Design	13. Fashion
4. Exclusivity	14. Meeting of standards
5. Packaging	15. Personal customization
6. Flexibility	16. Reliability
7. Impermanence	17. Service competence
8. Features	18. Stability
9. Speed	19. Variation
10. Compatibility	20. Performance

One thing is a particular product, but another is the company's entire product portfolio. One of the most well-known management models for portfolios is the Boston Consulting Group Matrix.

Boston consulting group matrix.

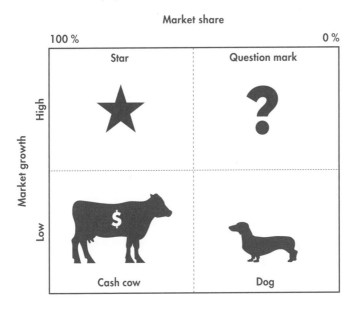

Market share

Products usually begin their life in the upper right corner, i.e. as a question mark. Here you need to gain market share, and if that fails, the product ends up being a dog. Being a dog is usually an unsustainable position, where the best decision may be to sell or terminate the product. A well-functioning company will always try to find new question marks as its other products become cash cows or dogs. For sure, the question mark-to-dog route alone will not make you rich.

Conversely, if you are successful, your question mark instead becomes a star – see the upper left quadrant. In this position, you typically earn good money and should invest in further growth. Due to the high market share, you will probably have economies of scale and/or network effects, which means that you are able to finance significant development costs and that you can tolerate a possible price war.

However, you should watch out for the following trap: if the market grows rapidly, the company may thus experience rapidly increasing revenue and therefore this may divert attention from whether you may, in fact, have declining market share. Decreasing market share is *always* a danger signal, even if your revenues and profits are rising, and in case you have a decreasing market share in a rapidly growing market, while you might perceive your product as a star, it might in fact already have become a question mark!

Cash cow is a position where you typically make money but it does not make sense to invest a lot of resources in the product. Often, cash cows are used to fund the development of entirely new products. You milk them to feed the stars and create new question marks so that the show can go on.

Which pricing strategies can I choose from?

Products have prices, so let us now look at this. For some companies, the pricing policy is rather passive – you just follow the market standards. But there is a lot you can play with, and for many companies the pricing strategy is a key differentiation parameter – in some cases *the* key parameter. Below are 38 pricing strategies, which are all explained in Appendix A.

· Aperiodic discounting	· Member offers
· As-a-service models	· Minimum prices
· Auction pricing	· Pay per use
· Complementary pricing	· Pay what you want
· Customer differentiation	· Penetration pricing
· Discount coupons	· Performance-based contracting
· Dynamic pricing	· Periodic discounting
· Fractional ownership	· Premium pricing
· Free	· Price bundling
· Freemium	· Price signalling
· Frequent-user benefits	· Real-time pricing
· Frequent-user discounts	· Second market discounting
· Frequent-user exclusives	· Skimming pricing
· Geographical price differentiation	· Solo supplier discount
· Hidden revenues	· Subscription
· Last-minute discounts	· Token pricing
· Leasing	· Up-front pricing
· Licence	· Volume discounts
· List prices	· White label

Companies are typically using a combination of these pricing models, and there are other strategies – only creativity (and in some cases the law) limits the alternatives.

What is crucial to my promotion?

When speaking about communication or promotion, you must first identify whom to communicate with, then how. Let us start with *whom*:

- *Direct stakeholders.* Shareholders, employees, potential employees, suppliers, authorities, directors, mentors and advisory board, etc.
- *Opinion leaders.* Beta testers and test users, power users, bloggers, media contacts, opinion leaders on mass media and market analysts, etc.
- *Distributors.* All selected segments in the wholesale, retail and e-commerce markets.
- *End users.* All the selected end-user segments.
- *The general public.* For instance, people who may follow you on social media.

Thereafter, the question is *how* to communicate – which instruments do we have in our marketing tool box?

We can begin with public relations, where among other things you can make press kits, including for example background information and pictures, which typically can be downloaded from the company website. Additionally, your PR efforts can include press releases, press conferences, press interviews, newsletters, participation as advisor to industry committees, speeches, launch events, participation in exhibitions and fairs and assistance with information to analysts.

If the company is relatively technically oriented, or if it sells B2B or B2G, it is quite common that the company prepares white papers, which are objective (!) analysis of market needs and how your product fits into that solution. A part of a white paper or a separate document can be a return on investment (RoI) calculation for the clients. For instance, 'if you spend x buying these LED lamps, your investment will have paid itself back within z and your annual return of investment is Z'. This may also be expressed in an Excel calculation model.

Advertising is another aspect which may include the company's website as well as paid advertisements in print and electronic media and brochures. There are also demo products and product illustrations, such as online tutorials and user guides, free demonstration versions, etc.

And finally, there are digital and social media. These may include tweets, Facebook posts, LinkedIn posts, Instagram, Pinterest pins, livestreaming events, webinars (web training and briefing events), Wikipedia references and blogs. Such media can be used to send out information and advertisements (preferably viral), but also to establish and support user groups and for tutorials and discussion forums, etc.

It is extremely important to consider how anything you do anywhere can be amplified to the max with social media. For instance, if you give a speech somewhere, why not live-stream it on Facebook? Why not post photos of it on Facebook, LinkedIn and Instagram? Think of yourself as running two companies: i) your start-up (95% of your job) and ii) a media company that covers your start-up 24:7 on social media (5% of your job). Use of social media is free, convenient and the easiest way to reach a lot of people in a lot of ways and learn from their feedback. So when something interesting happens in your business, by all means do a video shot, hit the Hootsuite app on your smartphone, add a little text, tick the platforms you want it shared on and . . . share!

WHEN SOMETHING INTERESTING HAPPENS IN YOUR BUSINESS, BY ALL

MEANS DO A VIDEO SHOT, HIT THE HOOTSUITE APP ON YOUR SMARTPHONE, ADD A LITTLE TEXT, TICK THE PLATFORMS YOU WANT IT SHARED ON AND ... SHARE!

And then test what happens when you use social media. What generates the greatest response?

In addition to posting, you can use the web and social media to create listening posts on your company, your products, your competitors and yourself, e.g. by using Google Alerts or more integrated tools such as Falcon Social Media. This allows you to get alerts whenever anything important to you is mentioned, so that you can respond and have a dialogue with customers and other stakeholders, opinion leaders, distributors or end users.

Thirty-six instruments in your PR and marketing toolbox.

• Analyst briefings	• Launch events	• Selfie-video statements
• Blogs	• LinkedIn posts	• SlideShare posts
• Company website	• Live-streaming events	• Speeches
• Demo products	• Newsletters	• Tweets
• Demo reels	• Online tutorials	• Twitter posts
• Elevator pitches	• Paid advertisements	• User guides
• Exhibitions and fairs	• Pinterest pins	• Vimeo posts
• Facebook posts	• Press conferences	• Webinars
• Free demo versions	• Press interviews	• White papers
• Go-home briefings	• Press kits	• Wikipedia references
• Industry committees	• Press releases	• Workshops
• Instagram posts	• RoI calculations	• YouTube posts

Start-ups should always concentrate mostly on 'earned media', which is publicity they do not pay for – for example, product reviews, blog posts, press releases, interviews, publicity in the media industry descriptions, white papers, social media including viral marketing and dialogue through social media, and encouraging Facebook likes. The alternative to earned media is 'paid media', such as Facebook and Google advertising and paid bloggers and exhibition participation.

Promotion on earned and paid media can have different primary purposes during your corporate development phases. In the beginning, you are primarily focused on raising awareness so you are discovered. 'Hello! Look here! We are interesting', you should say. As a next step, it becomes important to create a positive attitude and to provide information for retailers and end users. 'Well, now you have discovered us. Thanks. Here is more about what we stand for. We think it is good. Hope you like it'.

Later, when the company or product is fairly well established, a shake-out phase will often occur in the market where the wheat is separated from the chaff. During this phase, you need to focus on creating trust and reminding people of who you are and what you stand for. 'Remember us. We are still here. You can trust us'. And when the business or the product is very well known, you focus a lot on making people remember you by, for example, showing the product without any explanations.

Guerrilla marketing

A special approach that some entrepreneurs are particularly good at is called 'guerrilla marketing'. This is to generate attention without spending the money it would normally cost. As a rule, it is about creating a moment of surprise, which in turn creates publicity, and it includes a variety of creative techniques with names such as ambient, ambush, grassroots, stealth and street marketing, not to mention astroturfing, wild posting and viral buzz.

It sounds funny, and if you do well, it is. Furthermore, it can provide great PR, perhaps even viral – often virtually without paying a dime. A classic example of successful guerrilla marketing was performed by Finn Paavo Beckman, who with a friend launched a record label called Merceedees Production – a name which by playing on both the Mercedes and the phonetics of CD smelled of guerrilla marketing already. But their creativity did not stop there. As they needed to act as managers for a new band without spending money at all – because they had none – they started with the grand total of 19 existing fans (that's right, all of 19!). Fortunately, they had email addresses for these fans, so they began emailing them 'confidential' inside information stating that the band was close to getting a publishing contract, which undoubtedly was true, as Beckman and his partner, who were both managers and publishers, negotiated this contract with themselves. So instead of launching official news, they launched an insider tip, which is clearly a guerrilla tactic. This access to inside information got fans to spread rumours, which increased the fan base considerably – almost without cost.

Later, Merceedees Production would hand out 40 000 brochures in Germany, but again without spending money. How? They found fans to distribute them voluntarily and a company that would publish them for free against getting its own advertising in the brochure in return – thus, the whole campaign became free.

Unfortunately, the band members started fighting on stage during their first concert, and they actually ended up throwing instruments at each other. After that the band was dissolved, to the dismay of Merceedees. But the marketing was brilliant.

Optimization of the marketing mix in head-to-head competition

Let us look at how companies optimize their efforts in tough competition. Any of the marketing tools we have mentioned could be used here, but there are four competitive features which can be particularly effective:

- Very fast product launches
- Creating network/viral effects
- Capturing critical deals by being first
- Creating switching costs

The first one is simply to be blisteringly fast. Often, start-ups excel by being able to get new products launched much faster than larger and more mature companies. In certain industries, the main head-to-head strategy is to have the fastest launch cycle, i.e. to constantly be one step ahead with the latest products. The second is to create network effects, possibly including viral effects. If this works, you may create a competitive position that becomes extremely hard to attack.

Third, if you are first out with something, use this advantage to go for the best deals in the eco-system. For instance, you can try to win big parts of the distribution channels or even block some of these for your competitors through exclusive distribution agreements, package deals (possibly all-or-nothing), volume discounts and combined sales of branded and white label. The latter means that if the distributor is a retailer of your product, they can make a version of the same product but within their own product assortment, which they earn more on. But they cannot take a competitor's product.

The last strategy is to increase distributors' switching costs, i.e. the cost and inconvenience of switching a distributor. This can be done by establishing joint production or joint shipping facilities with the distributors, for example, or by offering system integration or a very high level of service. Large distributors typically have enterprise resource management software (ERM), which takes care of order execution, inventory management, etc.

If you as a supplier can interface your own ERM with the distributor's, it facilitates the logistics of both parties and increases the distributor's switching costs.

Similarly, you can create switching costs for end users in a number of ways, such as having several of your products interface with each other, etc.

Self-ordering can promote rapid scaling

It is useful to create solutions where customers can buy themselves, i.e. so called self-ordering. This may happen via an automated online ordering system, where customers can pay by either credit card or PayPal, for example, or where they can purchase via existing ecommerce websites such as Amazon. Companies with well-functioning self-ordering can scale rapidly – sometimes explosively.

How the company can be strengthened through alliances

Instead of thinking solely of competition, it can be interesting to look at alliance opportunities. Here are the obvious alternatives.

Twenty strategies for strategic alliances.

Financial and strategic:	Promotion and distribution:
1. Joint venture companies	11. Affiliate marketing
2. Know-how exchange	12. App stores
3. Acquire licence	13. Co-branding
4. Sell licence	14. Co-packaging/co-pricing
5. Market-oriented acquisition	15. Co-promotion
6. Knowledge-oriented acquisition	16. Common marketing organization
7. Venture capital investments	17. Common sales logistics
Development and production:	18. Cross-sales
8. Joint product development	19. Original equipment manufacturer (OEM) agreements
9. Joint production	20. Value-added reseller
10. Open platform	

When and how do I make a marketing plan?

As we mentioned, an entrepreneur rarely needs a business plan from the beginning. Instead, they typically make a business canvas, a back-of-the-envelope-like spreadsheet with simple business models, and a PowerPoint. However, as the business matures, this might change, and eventually it may very well become meaningful to have a normal business plan. So how should this be structured? The example below could be an inspiration.

1. *Executive summary.* This is typically 1–2 pages summarizing the main findings, threats, opportunities and conclusions. The summary should quote the elevator pitch and elaborate the company's goals, vision, value-creation models, business segments, core competencies, marketing strategies and organization.

2. *Analysis of the outside world.* The purpose of this analysis is not (!) to prove how much you know about the market but solely to describe the key underlying trends in the environment and their strategic implications.

   2.1. *Market.* Elaborate on your ecosystem. Which part of it is most important to the company? Which problems does this part of the eco-system solve? You should indicate the main influencing market factors, ranging from general conditions (political, legal, economical, etc.) down to micro factors. The next step is a study of your industry. What Marmer stage of development is the company in and what are the implications of that? Should the company pursue general consolidation, penetration, market development, product development or diversification?

   2.2. *Competition.* List the main key competitors and their activities and strategies. You can include a prediction of what the strongest of them are expected to do in the future and how your company should respond. It may be helpful to try to imagine for a moment that you were head of each of the competitors' businesses. What would *you* do if you were them? Maybe they will do exactly what you imagine. So how should your company respond to that? (Granted, this is a bit like playing chess against oneself, but it can be enlightening.)

3. *Core competencies.* List your key skills and what you primarily want to do to ensure lasting growth in the selected markets. Here you may find it helpful to imagine how an outside investor would justify an investment in your business. What makes you special? Why not invest in the competitor instead?

4. *The main strategies.* Taking the previous points into consideration, you should sum up your core idea, your basic business model and your essential marketing strategy. Describe product, price, distribution, promotion, sales, service and processes.

5. *Marketing.* Since you have listed the main strategies already, it is now time to move on to the specific methods where each must be described with a short justification. Which marketing tools are key to your business? Sub-points in this chapter may include elaboration of each of the key strategies in the previous chapter.

6. *Alliances.* This is potentially very important – describe how you will work with others in your ecosystem.

7. *Organization.* The company's organization is often complex, so there is one structure based on line features, another for activities and a third describing the so-called meta-organization, i.e. activities in your entire ecosystem. Describe how it looks and how it should be developed.

8. *Quantitative level.* This is a quantitative summary of sales, income, investment, profit and liquidity. It should also include the most important KPIs and all the other indicators to measure the success of the company. This can include financial data, but also measurement of web activity, customer complaints, delivery times, service ratings, brand ratings, percentage returns, etc.

9. *Follow-up.* This will typically include a combination of routines for quantitative follow-up: how will you check and respond to developments in markets, sales, quality, profitability, etc.?

14.
MY FIVE BIG-GEST COMMER-CIAL THREATS

As we saw in Chapter 1, a large proportion of the world's entrepreneurial projects – and especially of potential high-growth start-ups – go out of business quickly. This problem has obviously been analyzed a lot and these studies show that there are five dominating reasons for the failures. In this chapter, we will walk through these and address how you deal with them.

In the first chapter of this book, we referred to some horrible statistics concerning how often start-ups (especially growth start-ups) fail. However, mitigating circumstances were applicable. First, we showed that there are a lot of entrepreneurial roles such as skunk works, intrapreneur, franchisee and so on which are less risky than the traditional way, where you create a new company based on an innovative idea. Second, we mentioned that a lot of entrepreneurs go through many mistakes and at times spectacular failures before they hopefully succeed. If a statistic shows that 75% of companies fail, it does not necessarily mean that 75% of entrepreneurs never achieve great success. However, the bottom line remains that a lot of entrepreneurs do fail. Research shows that the five main reasons are:

- poor product/market fit
- internal disputes
- premature scaling
- unbalanced scaling
- misguided transition from early adopters to mainstream.

So let's now see why that happens and how it can be prevented.

IF A STATISTIC SHOWS THAT 75% OF COMPANIES FAIL, IT DOES NOT NECESSARILY MEAN THAT 75% OF ENTREPRENEURS NEVER ACHIEVE GREAT SUCCESS.

Mistake #1: poor product/ market fit

If the business idea is simply poor, the project will be like whipping a dead horse. The reason that some investors (not all!) nevertheless say that they often prefer the best possible team to the best plan is that great teams have the skills to make necessary pivots until they reach the proper product/ market fit, where they are also capable of implementing the business.

We believe that three of the typical mistakes concerning a poor product/market fit are (i) the project is simply too small to be worth the work and risk, (ii) missing dominance strategy and (iii) confusing lifestyle and growth projects.

Regarding the first: today, marketing people speak of the total addressable market (TAM), which is a theoretical customer base, and of the served available market (SAM), which are the potential customers, who might in principle purchase the product from a supplier. The third level is the target market, which is the number of clients that the company believes it could sell to. Finally, there is the sales budget, which is what the company expects to sell during a given period.

Entrepreneurs often misjudge this by a lot. And we mean by a lot. How much? Studies from Startup Genome show the following: start-ups that have not made their product yet overestimate their future sales by 100 times on average.[1] We will just let this simmer. Yes, roughly 100 times! Typical reasons are that they overestimate the market potential and they underestimate the competition. Oops.

START-UPS THAT HAVE NOT MADE THEIR PRODUCT YET OVERRATE THEIR POTENTIAL BY AN AVERAGE OF 100 TIMES.

Overestimation of their sales potential can also be because they do not combine sales potential with the demand for local dominance – they miss a dominance strategy. Many entrepreneurs make the mistake of saying something like, 'If we can just obtain 3% of the global market, we will have a revenue of a billion and a profit of 100 million'. What they forget may be that companies with a low market share of 3%, for example, typically *lose* money. A better approach is to find a much smaller share of the market, where you might be able to obtain 50% market share. You should therefore not point out a large market where you can get a small market share, but instead a sufficiently small segment of the market where you can get a large market share.

COMPANIES WITH LOW MARKET SHARE TYPI- CALLY LOSE MONEY.

Our third widespread problem with the product/market fit can be that you confuse a lifestyle project and a growth project. Either your project can scale or it cannot, but if it realistically does not have potential to scale, and if you nevertheless still treat it as a potential growth project, then you may run head first into a wall, since you will assume that you can get external investors on board, which you most likely can't. Therefore, remember that to scale, your business must be replicable, have decreasing marginal costs and maybe even have viral potential. Does it have all of that? Or any of it?

Mistake #2: internal disputes

As we have seen already, statistics show that internal disputes very often are the main reason why start-ups fail. So how does this happen?

Missing or poor shareholders' agreement is a typical part of the reason. Therefore, make an agreement early on which takes into account surprises by allocating at least some of the shares dynamically. Also, agree on the expectations of the company's goal, both businesswise and financially.

Another way to counteract internal disputes is to inform employees that they will not always be able to report to the founders if the company grows. For the same reason, as mentioned, you need to hold back with the pompous titles and be careful with hiring executives from big companies (highway builders) for leadership positions in your start-up.

At the same time, it is important that the leaders, including you, can grow with the task. When the company is tiny, the founders are involved in every single little detail – they use micro-management. Later, they should become more tactically and strategically orientated, and when a company reaches several hundred employees, they should focus more on developing their leaders rather than the operations of their business, since their great leaders will manage operations for them. However, remember that it is not necessarily the one who was extremely good at developing the initial products who is great at strategic leadership, let alone developing leaders.

Finally, they should also learn that while they had 60 screaming monkeys on their shoulders when there was just a bunch of founders, now there should be zero monkeys so that they can focus on the gorillas instead.

IT IS NOT NECESSARILY THE ONE WHO WAS EXTREMELY GOOD AT DEVELOPING THE INITIAL PRODUCTS WHO IS GREAT AT STRATEGIC LEADERSHIP, LET ALONE DEVELOPING LEADERS.

Mistake #3: premature scaling

The Startup Genome team has found a strong tendency for start-ups to fail because they scale too fast. Let us say you have a small software company that sells customized solutions to fairly few customers. Suddenly, you decide that you want to be an international supplier of software products. Let's do it!

Great, but what does this require? It will most likely need a comprehensive test environment, a professional test team, a documentation team, several development teams, international sales staff, a marketing team and of course human resources (HR) to control the now way bigger organization. And suddenly it is no longer a company with 25 employees but instead an organization with 250 or more employees. Can you cope with this transition economically, physically and mentally? Management wise? And financially?

Also remember the 'nail it before you scale it' advice. As we mentioned before, to us, nailing it is not only to find the product/market fit but also to make the company into an efficient, streamlined execution machine. Do this first. Then scale aggressively. But not before.

Mistake #4: unbalanced scaling

A variant of the scaling problem, which almost all start-up companies struggle with, is to accelerate parts of the company before other parts are ready. This creates unbalanced growth, as in the following examples:

- Employ more people than they can afford
- Try too hard to earn money on the first users/customers without, for example, a good user experience
- Aggressive marketing on a product that is not market-ready
- Create too many features for a product before consumers have understood the core function
- Spend too much on new customers
- Appoint senior leaders too early
- Create more than one management layer too early
- Compensate for product-related problems with PR rather than with fixing the product
- Invest in scalability before the product/market fit is in place

- Hire people when freelancers easily could have been used

- Create too many detailed plans too early.

That may sound stupid, but it is quite unavoidable in the typical start-up situation where everything is fluid and much is unknowable.

Mistake #5: unsuccessful transition from early adopters to mainstream

Now we have looked at four typical causes of failure in start-ups, namely poor product/market fit, internal disputes, premature scaling and unbalanced scaling. The fifth and final cause includes problems with the transition from the first customers to the mainstream market.

An example: You start a business and quite quickly manage to sell to some enthusiastic customers. In other words, the discovery phase, validation phase and efficiency phase are now behind you. 'Wow, that's great', you think. 'Now we can go full speed and conquer the entire market!'

Well, it surely feels pretty cool and macho giving it full speed, but what you might not have thought enough about is that not all customers are alike. The most enthusiastic have already signed up – the less responsive are an entirely different matter.

For the less responsive are much harder to deal with. For perspective: tech markets often use the following description of the sequence of customer groups: (i) technology enthusiasts, (ii) visionaries, (iii) pragmatists, (iv) conservatives and (v) sceptics. The first buy it when it is new *because* it is new. The last buy it *despite* it being new. The first are perhaps those who might stand in line all night to get the latest Apple product. The last group, perhaps, may include your grandparents. In between these two you have the group who are reluctant to change their 15-year-old television because they only recently discovered how its remote control works.

WHAT YOU MAY NOT HAVE THOUGHT ENOUGH ABOUT IS THAT NOT ALL CUSTOMERS ARE ALIKE.

This vast difference between the openness to new things becomes a problem for you because there can be a huge difference between selling to the first groups, which are small and eager, and to the latter, which are big but reluctant.

Here is what can make the problem even worse: marketers sometimes say there are approximately 200 000 people in the world who enthusiastically want to try anything new but do not want to pay much, if anything, for it. If it is those who praise your product early in the process, it can give a false signal. One of the best descriptions of this problem is found in Geoffrey E. Moore's classic book *Crossing the Chasm.*[2] To quote:

> *'The transition from selling to enthusiasts and visionaries to sell to the early majority is not continuous.'*

Instead, it is a chasm you can fall into. The main market – the early and late majority – places high demands on the company. They can require a lot of features and support that early adopters don't demand, for example.

This is not only an end-user problem; distributors that may be required for reaching the masses can also place high demands on the company. Often the company will therefore find that it needs to go from 20 to several hundred employees to make the leap from early adopter niches to the mainstream, for which it may not be able to organize the funding, management and procedures. The obvious risk is that the transition brings it straight towards the premature or unbalanced scaling problems – as well as financial problems.

One solution can be to choose a few applications and market niches and then create the full solution for these areas first. Moore calls this approach a 'bowling alley' where the company crosses the chasm with one niche product at a time, until it finally as a whole has made it to the mainstream. Such a successful crossing of the chasm brings the company to the 'tornado' phase, where growth seems almost automatic.

Problems concerning the transition from early adopters to mainstream.

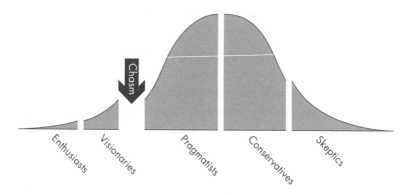

PART 5.

ABOUT MY EXIT AND WHAT COMES AFTER

Everything has an end, and if your entrepreneurial project survives the first, challenging years, maybe a time will come when you will make an exit. This can be done in one big strike, gradually or partially – the possibilities are many and include divestment, strategic sales, merger, management buy-out and stock exchange listing.

In this chapter, we study these and other forms of exit, and we discuss the considerations and exercises that must happen before a successful exit such as a trade sale or an IPO can take place.

In the last chapter of the book, we look at what you as a (so far) successful entrepreneur can do with your life and work after a successful exit. Most often, the priorities seem to be combinations of starting new companies, spending money on fun lifestyle projects, investing financially and doing good. That sounds like great fun and gratification, and generally it is. But there are snakes in this paradise and we also spend some words on them.

15.
MY ALTERNA-TIVE EXIT ROUTES

For some entrepreneurs, an exit is the primary goal, while for others it may be a necessary evil. Whether it is one or the other, the time of an exit can be filled with joy, relief and sadness – maybe all at once. From our own experience we know that it is hard to understand how much you may have become attached to the people in your start-up, to their mission and to the whole company, when you suddenly leave it.

But sometimes an exit is really the right thing to do, and in this chapter we will tell you more about how it can be done.

What is an exit? Some may think of an exit as an initial public offering, but IPOs are normally only potential pathways to exits and there are plenty of variants, which we will get to shortly.

Why should I sell out?

There can be many reasons for selling your business or parts of its activities and assets, including:

- You have no choice, for example for health reasons, because other shareholders or managers push it through, or because you simply do not have the economy to be able to continue.

- You are bored, tired or do not care any more – you may have been doing the same thing for 20 years and want something new.

- You want money to do something else or retire.

- You think others will pay more for the company than what it is worth to you or under your leadership.

- You fear a serious economic or trade crisis.

- You see a possible synergy with a different ownership.

- You are subject to tax laws that make you taxable before you sell your shares and therefore you must sell some of them to pay the tax.

- Your spouse or family may suffer from your huge work effort and all the castles in the sky you are constantly building. If you take out some money to buy a better home, for instance, they see that it is real and also for them.

- There are bidders for your company, which makes you think: 'Wow, it's a high price. At that price I would like to sell my shares.'

In which ways can I make an exit?

There are many exit strategies and these can be divided into four main categories, as shown below.

Fifteen exit strategies.

Selling assets	Selling shares to strategic partners
• Carve-out	• Corporate earn-out
• IP rights sales	• Joint venture with divestment right
• Hard asset sales	• Merger with divestment right
• Mushrooming and strategic spin-offs	• Take in partners
	• Management buy-out
	• Trade sales to a capital fund
	• Strategic trade sales to a commercial company
Secondary sales of shares	Selling shares to the public
• Selling into a fundraising round	• IPO
• Selling through public secondary market	• ICO

The two strategies that typically give the highest price for your company are either a trade sale to a strategic partner who can get a lot more out of your company than you can, or an IPO in a good stock market. Also, in some cases, an ICO has been tremendous, but often for the wrong reasons (naive investors). However, there can be lots of reasons for preferring other exit strategies, as we will discuss below.

THE TWO STRATEGIES THAT TYPICALLY GIVE THE HIGHEST PRICE FOR YOUR COMPANY ARE EITHER A TRADE SALE TO A STRATEGIC PART- NER WHO CAN GET A

LOT MORE OUT OF YOUR COMPANY THAN YOU CAN, OR AN IPO IN A GOOD STOCK MARKET.

Selling assets   The basic idea here is to keep the company but sell some of its assets. This might enable you to pay out dividends and thus gain cash, for instance. One way of doing this is to establish a subsidiary with existing or new activities and then sell a minority of the shares either through an IPO or directly to selected investors. This is sometimes called a 'carve-out'.

An alternative approach is 'rights sales', whereby you sell a patent or exclusive sales rights to marketing of your products in a region against an up-front payment plus an annual minimum income plus sales-dependent commission. Such rights are often called IP for 'intellectual property' and are thus IP rights. This may mean more revenue in the short term, but of course it reduces your control and longer-term upside.

You can also sell assets that are not IP-related. These are often referred to as 'hard assets'. A classic example is the company that owns its office or production properties but now sells them to a pension fund and makes a long-term lease for them instead. This is called 'sale-and-lease-back'.

Another variation of asset sales is to make spinoff companies and then sell these, one at a time. This will enable you to achieve a 'mushrooming' effect, whereby innovations are placed in new subsidiary companies which are then sold off for a profit. Every successful spinoff company is then a small exit. This makes sense if you think the company is relatively better at innovation than at the scaling process. In some way, this strategy makes your company an incubator or accelerator for its own ideas.

A variation is simple spinoffs. This is about selling the company in several stages for overall strategic reasons. Especially if the company consists of a slightly messy mix of activities, you often get a better price by dividing it into separate units that are more focused and then selling these one at a time.

How do I sell shares on secondary markets?

Approximately 5% of total venture activity is in secondary markets.[1] Even as your company is going through successive fundraising rounds, there may be possibilities to sell some of your shares. Until quite recently, investors would be alarmed if founders or key management sold out while investors were still piling in. Generally that makes a lot of sense, but there is now greater understanding that sometimes a founder needs to take a bit off the table to stabilize the home front. But not too much – 5% of your shares is fine; 10% perhaps also; but if you seek to sell more than 20%, expect more than raised eyebrows. In fact, you might expect an investor revolt.

How do you do it? There are secondary VC funds that specialize in purchasing secondary shares, and many normal venture capitalists will also do it on an opportunistic basis, whether from the founders or (preferred) from some earlier investors such as angels. There are also secondary markets on SharesPost and SecondMarket.

How do I sell to strategic partners?

Then there are sales to strategic partners, which can take many forms. An interesting possibility is this: a corporate earn-out model, where you undertake to develop a product or market for another – and typically much larger – company. However, instead of doing this for a fixed fee, you get an agreement stating that your own business is acquired by the other if or when the KPIs are reached. Here, the buying price will often be adjusted after your fulfilment of specific KPIs.

A somewhat related approach is a joint venture with divestment right. Some companies make joint ventures with others in structures where one part has an option to buy out the other at predefined terms. Let's say that your start-up makes a joint venture company with a bigger and older company. Your team runs the joint venture, but they have an option to buy it after three years at, say, 10 times revenues.

A parallel situation is the merger with divestment right. This is a merger with another company – perhaps a 'merger of equals'. This, in itself, is not an exit, but it can become one if is agreed that your shares can be automatically sold to your merger partners after a while. Incidentally, a merger can also offer you the opportunity to initially retire from daily management and later sell your shareholdings. A similar option is to take in new business partners. These will then buy parts of your company and take a role in management.

The more definitive exit strategies to strategic partners come in three major forms: (i) management buy-out, (ii) trade sales to a private equity fund and (iii) strategic trade sales to a commercial company. As for the former, the management (apart from you, if you are the selling founder) buys the company's shares, or in case they are already shareholders, the remaining shares. The typical management buy-out situation concerns older entrepreneurs who orchestrate a generation change by allowing the younger management to buy the company. However, the managers can rarely afford this, but they can then join forces with external investors and seek loan capital, as well as arrange for a gradual payment over several years, thus in a way buying the company with its own future earnings. This element is call an earn-out.

Our next option is the sale to a private equity fund, which, as mentioned earlier, invests in – and works with – companies that are not listed. In some cases, they actually buy first-hand controlling items in listed companies and then de-list them, which is called a buy-out, but the most common approach is that they invest in companies that are already non-listed (private), which in this context means the ownership is a smaller circle instead of public stock investors.

Like venture capital funds, private equity fund companies typically let each of their funds run for 10–12 years, where they primarily make their investments for the first 3–5 years and then seek exits through, for example, a trade sale or an IPO. In many cases, former management remains in the company, but now with the capital fund as a dominant investor or sole proprietor. In such cases, the management usually receives significant stock options. If management and owners are the same, they can first get a nice, safe amount for their shares and later an upside of the company's added value.

The third approach to a definitive sale of the company is the strategic trade sale to a commercial player in the relevant business sector. Often, a start-up company has a greater value – sometimes even much greater – for a commercial buyer than it has for its current owners. Such a buyer may be a customer, supplier or competitor which wishes to strengthen its business by acquiring your products, distribution agreements, employees or patents, and development capacity. Alternatively, it may see significant cost synergies where administration, production or sales become significantly more effective in aggregation. In general, this is called a trade sale and the point is not only to figure out what your business is worth for you but also what it is worth for them. The selling price may be a compromise in between.

For a strategic sale, you can either be paid with (i) shares in the buying company, (ii) cash or (iii) an amount that depends on how well your company is doing under the new ownership. The latter is an earn-out. Earn-out is a relatively widespread structure for company sales involving small and medium-sized companies, which are particularly dependent on individuals. Such earn-out means that you typically receive a portion of the sales price in the form of cash and/or shares in the purchasing company when you sign and the rest over the following months or years after the company has been sold, depending on how the figures are for some previously agreed KPIs. However, our advice is to show caution with such agreements. There are countless examples of such earn-outs that end in frustration and legal disputes.

You should note that potential buyers may want you to sign a 'no shop/ no talk agreement' whereby you will not play off prospective buyers against each other and you will keep the discussions confidential. This can be acceptable if you have a strong indication that they are indeed serious and there is a letter of intent on the table. However, if you do sign such an agreement, make sure that none of your friends and business associates is peddling the deal and that none of your employees or anyone else talks about it.

Even if you have signed such an agreement, it's great to have alternative potential buyers lined up to step in. It is fairly common for prospective buyers to bail out at the last minute, perhaps to shake up the seller and enter later with a lower offer. Having alternatives here is great.

Dual track negotiation

The best BATNA, if someone is looking to buy your company, is to be in the process of raising money through a venture round. The prospective buyers will then know that if you succeed with a funding round, the participating VCs will probably not sell at less than 3–4 times what they paid. So if the potential buyers pass on a $100 million valuation, their next chance might be a $300–400 million valuation a few years down the line.

M&A chain reactions

Any experienced investment banker and venture capitalist will know the following phenomenon: a sector has very few or no mergers and acquisitions. Then one big player makes a high-profile merger or acquisition, after which you see a stampede among other players who suddenly see this as a game of musical chairs, where the last player will be left without the right partner or technology. For this reason, a start-up company may experience significant difficulties in finding a buyer for ages and then suddenly everyone is knocking on its doors.

Selling shares to the public

Instead of selling assets or shares to strategic buyers, you can list the company so that anyone can invest in it. This is the ICO or IPO, but before we dive into this, we should mention a strategy that may in some situations prepare well for it. It's called inversion. This is where you find a company that is smaller than your own but has a better location. You then arrange for this smaller company to buy your company, perhaps for money that you lend to it. The purpose is often to move your headquarters to the smaller company's location, perhaps because that location has lower taxes or for other reasons is more attractive. For instance, a Swedish start-up with 300 employees may do an inversion with a company in Silicon Valley with five employees to swiftly move its headquarters to Silicon Valley. American companies have taken advantage of inversions to move to Canada for lower taxes. It should be mentioned here that technically this is not an exit strategy, but it can lead to one.

Which brings us to listing. Normally people think of that as an IPO, and typically it is. However, as we have described, an ICO is also a tool that makes shares publicly traded – but it does it even before any commercial activities have begun.

Now, back to IPOs, where we should mention that there exists a short-cut called a reverse IPO. You do this by finding an 'empty shell', a listed company which has no or very little activity. Since it is empty you can buy a controlling part of its shares cheaply. Your start-up subsequently lends money to the listed company, which then uses your funds to acquire your company. However, stock exchanges require a meaningful valuation, free flow of publicly owned shares and trading volume for a company to stay listed. If they de-list the company, you are back to square one.

The far more common form of IPO is a simple first listing on a stock exchange. It is not cheap to be listed as a public company, neither in the listing process nor regarding the formalities required forever after. But it gives the company visibility in the market and can thus be a kind of marketing tool for your products and for attracting staff. Also, since the shares become liquid, they become more suitable for stock options and as a currency with which to buy other companies.

What about my own role after a sale?

When you sell your company, it is not necessarily a given that you can or should stop working there. For example, if you are a CEO, you typically do not stop immediately as you may be needed there for several more years to ensure continuity. Whether it is expected that you continue may depend on how important you are for the company and its results and opportunities.

If you do not want to continue after a sale, we suggest that in good time, and certainly long before initiating a sales process, you hire another CEO who can continue after the business has been sold, thus ensuring continuity.

Sometimes you may not want to stop because you like the job and feel you are needed, even though you are selling your shares. In the technology world, we often see CEOs of acquired companies get an even greater role with the buyer than they had previously. Perhaps they go from managing their business with 50 people to leading a division of 500 people in the acquiring company. What we also often see, however, is a certain frustration because of the shift from an entrepreneurial culture into a much heavier and more formal corporate culture.

16.
MY EXIT PROCESSES

An exit is normally time consuming and can last for longer than many entrepreneurs would have expected. And it can be complex as it involves strategic decisions, preparing the company for the exit situation and perhaps beauty contests, difficult negotiations, tons of paperwork and more.

Let's go back to the time when it first occurred to you that you should consider an exit.

Your first choice here is obviously to decide which of the options described in the previous chapter is best for you: asset sale, trade sale, or IPO? Here, you should ask yourself: 'Who are my most obvious potential buyers?' 'Who will pay the most?' 'Why do they want to buy us or part of our activities and assets?' 'Why would someone invest in my IPO?'

How do I increase the exit value?

Once you have found out who you are looking for as potential buyers, you should look at your company and ask: 'How can I make the company worth more for this buyer – or those buyers?' Here you must think about what your business's valuation will be based upon. It could be users, customers, revenue, gross profit, patent, or surpluses, for instance. Find out what drives the valuation and then look at how to increase those numbers. Capital funds, which typically buy more established companies, are extremely good at exactly this, i.e. to see the opportunity to create or sell value that the owners cannot see for themselves. When they buy a company, they typically invest heavily in growth at the start, but towards their exit, where companies are typically valued on profit margins, they begin to reduce costs. In addition, they often make sales, acquisitions and possibly mergers to create the good story and a better economy.

So, you should think like skilled capital fund owners by identifying potential buyers and what they will want. It also makes sense to decide very early on the minimum terms you are willing to accept for the exit.

The good story   This goes hand in hand with thinking about the company's story. Let us explain: in the finance industry, you often hear portfolio managers and analysts saying that a given company has a 'good story'. This does not mean an imaginary fairytale. No, what they mean is that the company's goals, vision, value-adding models, business segments, core competencies, marketing strategies and organization seem to add up to a coherent, logical and strong story that an investor should like. The convincing story of such a company should feel focused and compact, i.e. leaving the feeling that there is everything that is required for success, but nothing else. In other words, the good story should not point in many different directions or be flapping loosely in the wind.

THE CONVINCING STORY FEELS COMPACT, I.E. IT LEAVES THE FEELING THAT THERE IS EVERYTHING THAT IS

REQUIRED FOR SUCCESS, BUT NOT ANYTHING ELSE.

The outcome, once you have thought what makes the good story for your company, is almost certainly that you need to change something. Perhaps you need to make changes to management or staffing in general, get some shareholders out or in, develop or terminate some projects, buy or sell something. Some examples:

- If, for instance, you have a company that covers four out of five countries in a promising bigger region, you can consider starting up in number five.

- If there are parts of the company that the expected buyer is not interested in, you can sell or make spinoffs to make your story more compact.

- If your company has too much debt, you can also sell parts to reduce the liabilities.

- If certain parts of your activities are risky and others are not, you can split them up into two companies.

- If the company doesn't own technology, and if you think owning them would significantly raise its valuation (which typically means a higher multiple), you could develop or buy some technologies.

- If the management team seems incomplete, you can hire some stars to complete it.

- If your business is too dependent on a few large customers, you can merge with or acquire another company to improve diversification.

Next comes the spring cleaning, which is similar to what you did prior to getting external funding – conduct a legal audit, check that all processes are optimal, etc. A clean and transparent company will get a higher valuation.

Third, and probably in parallel: try to refocus some of your marketing and PR away from how great your products are and instead towards how fantastic the company is.

How do I make a trade sale?

Now let us look at the sales process in a trade sale. This typically consists of seven stages:

1. Determine goal and strategy

2. Find financial partners for the process, if needed

3. List potential buyers

4. If expressions of interest come in, shortlist qualified buyers

5. Support them in their due diligence

6. Collect offers

7. Close deal with preferred bidder.

Note that while this entire process can be done in less than a week – when, for example, a bank becomes insolvent and quickly needs a buyer – most companies take many months to ensure they get the greatest number of potential buyers and hence the best price. In fact, it is not atypical that the process takes 12 months or longer – even up to several years.

In the first phase, when you are still pondering your strategy, you can make a list of potential buyers. If possible, ask a corporate finance house or investment bank for their opinion – they will basically come up with advice that you can use for free.

At this point you probably need to find a financial advisor. Some choose to use a corporate finance house, such as PwC or Deloitte, others an investment bank, such as Goldman Sachs, to sell their businesses, while still others sell the company themselves. In many cases you may find a boutique finance house specialized in the sector.

When you sell through a financial advisor, they typically take a percentage of what the company is sold for, if the sale goes through. Some sellers choose to offer a bonus to the advisor if the sales price exceeds a given amount. Corporate finance houses or investment banks can sometimes ask for a payment, a 'retainer', regardless of whether the sale goes through or not, but we suggest you do not accept this.

There is no clear answer to whether you should sell on your own or use an advisor, but as a starting point we can say that if your company is very small, you should probably sell on your own, as the amount a corporate finance house can make is so small that they would not spend time on it anyway. If it is a medium-sized company, consider a corporate finance house, and if it is a large company, consider an investment bank. But as we said – there is no fixed rule.

If you want financial advisors involved in the process, hold a 'beauty contest', where candidates present what they think they can do and on what terms. These presentations will probably not only guide you to the best partner choice but also give you insights into your task. For instance, they might help you understand which kind of buyer you should look for and what you should consider changing in your company to get a better exit.

When your financial advisor has been chosen, you should update the list of potential buyers with them. The advisors or you (or both) will now start the search. Set a deadline for indicative offers, even if you really do not have a special reason to choose that particular date. Once you have received a quote, select a few potential buyers ('qualified buyers') and support a due diligence process with those, where they can go into deeper detail with the company. But remember to set a deadline for final bids; otherwise they will not rush and may not dedicate enough resources to the due diligence process.

It is not uncommon for sellers of companies to negotiate to keep a corner of the store that they want to further develop themselves. This is sometimes called a carve-out, although the term is used more to establish subsidiaries selling a minority of the shares.

Finally, we must offer a warning. There are countless cases of bigger companies interested in buying smaller ones which end up attacking them aggressively instead if the deal falls through. A typical approach can be to hire their key staff. Therefore, before entering negotiations, ask them to sign a 'non-solicit agreement' or NSA, which prohibits them from hiring any of your employees for a period of, say, two years.

Now you are ready to choose a buyer. Close the agreement and get the money. In the first place, it may be a good idea to insist on proof of funds. Later, this money is paid into an escrow account by a lawyer or secured by a bank guarantee.

What is my role after the trade sale?

Trade sales will often include clauses about your continued participation – for example, you and your potential co-founder might be obliged to remain 100% in the management for 1–2 years and then be available 'on call' for another period. Furthermore, parts of your payments will often be paid on earn-out terms. To ensure that they get as much of their payment from the earn-out as possible, most founders wish to stay in the company until the earn-out is over, and they try to hold on to their best employees to increase the likelihood of a good result. You should take that into consideration.

A variant of a trade sale is that the buyer acquires all your company's assets, after which it is liquidated. The typical motive can be to safeguard against unknown 'skeletons in the closet', so that buyers know exactly what they are getting. If so, you should subsequently be able to conclude a solvent liquidation of the company so that it closes after all creditors have been paid. After the transaction, the previous owners will be left with the empty shell, including its net cash and perhaps other assets such as real estate that the buyer didn't want. After costs relating to liquidation, they share the remaining net cash.

A successful trade sale often requires competitive bidding for your company. You can create this competition through corporate finance houses or investment banks that can run the process for you, by contacting more buyers yourself or by being more in the press. While we do not necessarily recommend the latter approach, stories appear in the press about companies being sold and which buyers are involved, and these have probably been leaked to create competition. However, competitive bidding has its complications as it may also scare away prospective buyers who don't want to potentially waste time on due diligence if the company may well end up being acquired by some of the other bidders.

How does an IPO play out?

The IPO process can be divided into the following phases:

1. Selection of advisers/banks

2. Due diligence and preparation

3. Preparation of documentation

4. Pricing

5. Roadshow

6. Allocation.

An IPO is managed by a financial house, which is almost always a bank or a group of banks with a lead bank directing the show. In many cases, banks begin to circle early around companies that are ready for an IPO – they have a nose for these things! You will find yourself invited for lunches, presentations, and so on. But when your board decides on a possible IPO, regardless of previous contacts you need to hold a beauty contest.

Ideally, one would like to use one of the world's leading investment banks such as Goldman Sachs, Morgan Stanley, JPMorgan, BofA Merrill Lynch, Credit Suisse or Deutsche Bank, but you should be realistic about how big and attractive the trade really is going to be for the banks. None of those mentioned would probably take the task of listing a fairly small company.

Anyway, in their presentation, each bank will tell you which stock exchange they think your company should preferably be listed on, how they would value it, which investors they have access to, which similar IPOs they have made previously and whether your company is better off with a trade sale (which they can arrange!). Also, they will explain what they will charge for their work and how the process will evolve. One of the obvious points is that they will typically seek other banks as partners, so that they themselves will act as the lead bank and the others as support, in order to find more investors. All serious banks will at least do minor due diligence before they even show up for a beauty contest for a given company.

What is the due diligence process and what is the red herring?

Once the agreement with the bank is in place, it conducts more extensive due diligence, for which you must put material in an electronic data room. At the same time, you must designate employees whom the bank can contact at any time to answer any questions, whether they are technical, financial, legal, commercial or other. They will also typically conduct a comprehensive legal audit, i.e. review of the entire contractual basis of the company, and, in general, point out which conditions, in their opinion, should be properly coordinated before the company can be listed.

When the bank and its possible consultants feel that everything has been put in place, the preparation of presentation material will begin, which will include a teaser, i.e. a brief presentation, and partly a disclosure document, popularly called a 'red herring', which is comprehensive documentation with descriptions of the company as well as many warnings against anything that can go wrong. A red herring is made by several lawyers appointed by the banks and with the support of your own lawyers, and can take an astonishingly long time for the lawyers and management to work out. Assume that you must submit your own comprehensive descriptions of the company, after which there will be at least 5–10 half- or full-day meetings, where your C-suite staff will discuss this with the lawyers and representatives from the bank. One of the reasons for this carefulness is that there must be nothing left in the red herring document that could ever be used against the bank or the company in a later lawsuit, and therefore every sentence is considered carefully.

In addition, the bank, in cooperation with lawyers, will prepare a cap table before and after the transaction, as well as subscription documents and more.

At some point, it will also be discussed whether some of the existing shareholders wish to sell shares in connection with the listing. This is a secondary sale, whereas the rest of the share sale is primary and gives money to the company instead of to existing shareholders. However, major secondary sales can scare many investors – why should they buy if the management who know most about the company will sell?

How do the lock-up period and green-shoe work?

In relation to the subscription documents, a 'lock-up' is also agreed, which is a period after the IPO during which the existing shareholders cannot sell and there are agreed rules for periods after financial statements when they may sell. A typical lock-up is six months, but sometimes it is up to 12 months. In addition, when a lock-up is over, you may still be unable to sell all your shares in the short term as a major shareholder, as an excessive offer may adversely affect the price.

The exception from the lock-up is that at the stock exchange, there may be a 'green-shoe option' whereby the banks have the right to sell up to 15% more shares than the original amount determined by the issuer, if demand allows. If the IPO goes well and the stock rises immediately, they will buy these shares from the company, and if it goes poorly but the bank thinks they will rise later, they can instead buy them in the market. This allows the bank to generate greater profits and helps stabilize the market immediately after the IPO.

Once the formal documents have been completed, the focus changes to the preparation of the company's roadshow.

Roadshow, quiet period, pricing, book building and allocation

The roadshow is a sales trip. The company initiates a quiet period beforehand, during which no one can comment to the press or the public on anything which may affect demand for the shares. The period is prescribed by local law and is typically 40 or 90 days. If you violate this rule, you risk the entire process being cancelled and the company will find it difficult to return to the financial market.

Before the roadshow starts, your lead bank will work with you to make a Q&A list and hopefully subsequently will hold one or more sessions during which it will play critical investors and try to shoot down everything you say. Only when the bank feels very sure that the team can handle the process professionally will it dare set the start day for the roadshow.

When the IPO itself is quite close – often just a few days before – the bank makes a so-called pricing meeting, where a price range for which the shares will be offered is agreed. This range is not binding and can be changed during the process, but if you come out with a price range that is too high and therefore is lowered during the subscription period, it scares investors, unless the entire stock market has fallen accordingly – so you should rather do the opposite.

In the roadshow itself, you travel for a period of typically two weeks and visit important potential investors. This usually includes breakfast presentations, lunch presentations and dinner presentations (plus lots of meetings in between), where you and 2–4 other members of the company's management present and take questions while investors are eating and listening (and you are starving – remember to bring snacks!).

Along the way, there may be parallel meetings, where one of you is asked to leave the group and hold one-on-one meetings with key investors who cannot or will not go to your other presentations.

The dynamics around pricing range

Pricing of shares in an IPO has a special dynamic. For example, if investors believe that the stock exchange will be 20–30 times oversubscribed, they will typically make much larger buying orders than they actually wanted to see executed, as they know the distribution will be rationed. For example, an investor may ask to buy 1 million shares, although the person actually wants only 50 000. If the opposite is true – it is rumoured that the subscription take-up is slow – people will bid only what they actually want. Small psychological differences can therefore lead to huge differences in subscription interest. And if the price range is lowered in the process, many investors disappear completely.

Following the roadshow, the bank and any consortium banks will produce a combined 'book' with purchase interests, after which you and your management will typically be called for an allocation meeting, assuming there is a significant oversubscription. Here you go through the interested investors, some of which are pools of anonymous small customers and others are big well-known investors. The bank will advise on a mix, with typically most long-term investors who are expected to hold the shares for many months or years but also a minority of small investors, so that there is a high trading volume every day.

And then the shares start trading, which makes a member of the perhaps 0.01% of hopeful entrepreneurs who actually made it that far. So if you do experience this, please have a glass of champagne.

17.
MY NEXT PROJECT

Now we have come to the last chapter of the book, which should not really have been included and therefore became wonderfully short. It is about what entrepreneurs do after an exit. Why is this interesting enough to be included in this book? Because entrepreneurs, as far as we can see, often make big and catastrophic mistakes after an exit.

Try to imagine the following situation. You are one of the very few entrepreneurs who actually made a home run, including a successful exit. And therefore, after many years of intense work, your work pressure has suddenly abated – and you have a lot of money in the bank account. What do you do now?

We and our hubris

Perhaps you do something brilliant – but perhaps not at all. Here is why it might not be so brilliant: entrepreneurs like us might not be the most humble people on the planet. In fact, let's face it, most entrepreneurs are very self-confident and entrepreneurs who have just made a home run might tend to play a bit of fancy-pantsy. Therefore, after a good exit, we propose you ask yourself: 'How much did I actually work to get to where I got?

Was it a consequence of many years of back-breaking work to get to learn some business and professional discipline inside out? Were there massive preparations involved? Training, training, training? Countless fights and endless work?'

Our guess is that there probably was. Yes, you did all that.

We mention this because if part of the explanation of your success was an exceptional willingness to work, train, study, prepare and fight, then there is no clear reason to believe that you could make another home run without the same effort and dedication. So . . . are you willing to do this now that you have become wealthy?

Our point is this: talent cannot compensate for knowledge or work. The fact that you are smart probably doesn't mean that you could make another great home run without working really hard again.

TALENT CANNOT COMPENSATE FOR KNOWLEDGE OR WORK.

Another question: were you perhaps lucky in the sense that you happened to be in the right place at the right time? If so, do you think you could succeed another time being exactly in the right place and at the right time?

As far as we can see, there are lots of successful entrepreneurs who fall into the trap of starting other projects where their dedication and luck aren't the same. And then they fail, fail, fail.

These thoughts bring us to what your personal core competence really is. Are you an eminent seller? Is that the only thing that makes you special? Or are you a genius leader? An outstanding technologist? Analyst? Or something else? Whatever it is, it is worth considering letting your future activities build on the same talent that led you to success, rather than thinking that you are now something you have never been before. In this connection, it may be a good idea to take the same personality tests that you might have used for personnel recruitment, such as the Wechsler Adult Intelligence Scale, the Keirsey Temperament Sorter and the Myers-Briggs Type Indicator Test. They can tell you more about where your talents lie.

With these thoughts in mind, we will now briefly comment on what typically are entrepreneurs' next projects after an exit. We will begin with what, in our experience, former entrepreneurs almost never do. As we wrote in Chapter 1, we have never personally seen them park themselves on a beach after they have sold their first business. Instead, here is what we see them do:

- Start new companies
- Spend money on fun lifestyle projects
- Create a financial investment portfolio
- Make angel investments
- Do charity.

Should I become a serial entrepreneur?

Many successful first-time entrepreneurs end up as serial entrepreneurs. They start another company. And then more. One could say that in principle the easiest way would be to remain in the same industry for every start-up on which they embark. However, that is often not the case, and the reason is probably that they sold their previous start-up because the sector was not that hot any more. So, for the next one they need to find a new sector which is now hot. Each new company a serial entrepreneur starts is often in a new sector – at least if the person is specialized in tech.

However, one thing frequently stays the same – they often bring some of the same people with them from start-up to start-up. Once you have found a winning team you want them with you each and every time – and they will follow you because you are good at what you do.

So that can work very well, but perhaps you should consider putting some of your wealth aside and not invest everything you own and have in every start-up you can think up. Even if your talent and dedication are enormous, your luck might not always be.

Lifestyle projects

Some entrepreneurs don't like to spend money privately; it doesn't give them pleasure, but rather brings them pain. This is perhaps a personality disorder, or perhaps some moral or social consideration, who knows, but it can certainly make them extremely wealthy for purely mechanical reasons. Wealth equals income minus expenditure.

However, as far as we can see, most do like the good life in some measure – typical post-exit entrepreneurs' lifestyle projects can range from hunting to playing golf, skiing, collecting wine and driving luxury cars. Some also focus on 'investments of passion', which may include collector cars, luxury homes, boats, private aircraft, sports clubs, art, boutique hotels or restaurants, bars and nightclubs. To this, we will simply say that there are certain economic rules of thumb for investments in these areas.

And not all of them are good. We can start out with luxury homes, where the value of the building itself as a rule must be gradually depreciated due to technological obsolescence as well as wear and tear. If a building is 40–50 years old, it is often cheaper to tear it down and build a new one than to renovate it, which tells us that many buildings lose their entire value plus demolition costs over 4–5 decades – at least if you correct for inflation. Yet the land on which the building is located may well increase significantly in value if it is an attractive place. That is why real estate experts say 'location, location, location', to which we would like to add that it is a great advantage to buy properties in a recession rather than in a boom. And never buy during a real estate price bubble unless your passion for the property clearly exceeds your interest in the investment value.

About other investments of passion, the following rules of thumb apply: the annual operating cost of having a boat typically corresponds to 10% of its new-build price and as a rule it should be used more than eight weeks annually before it becomes cheaper than renting one instead. Nevertheless, many people enjoy spending time on their yacht and plan its tours throughout the season, a privilege they wouldn't enjoy if they were renting a boat. It should be noted that with modern satellite connections and mobile telephones, it is possible to be online from a boat and thus it can be used as a floating office and, for that matter, as a mobile meeting room.

With private aircraft, a key rule states that one must fly for 500–600 hours a year before it becomes cheaper than renting. However, the equation is improved if you are a pilot or a co-pilot and use, for instance, the low-maintenance Pilatus. In practice, however, there are also arguments for renting instead of owning – that one can, if appropriate, for each flight choose an aircraft that fits the specific needs in terms of number of passengers, required runway length and cruising speed.

As for investing in sports clubs, hunting areas, art, boutique hotels, restaurants, bars or nightclubs, we will just remind you of this: maybe you think these are fun areas to go into, but do you also have the necessary knowledge and the right talent? Are you also ready to put in the necessary work? And remember the key rule that applies to the hotel industry: 'The third owner earns money'. This says something about what happens to the first and second owners.

Financial investments

After an exit, it may be a good idea to put a portion of one's post-exit funds into financial investments, which means investments into stocks, bonds, funds, etc. However, for many entrepreneurs this is a new and unknown world, in which they often end up suffering major losses. Alternatively, they are so suspicious of banks and financiers that they never get started and thus never create a core portfolio with stable returns to stabilize or build up their finances and purchasing power in the long run.

The problem for many is that financial investment is a completely different discipline than building a company, and there are completely different rules – rules that are often counter-intuitive and potentially devastating to the charismatic entrepreneurial type. No, you cannot force your will in the financial markets in the same way that you did in commercial business as an entrepreneur. It works conversely: the financial markets always enforce their will on you. So, it is with shrewdness and analytical talent that you can win in the financial markets, not with charisma and willpower. That change of role doesn't work well for everyone.

What should you, as an entrepreneur, do with the financial markets? Our recommendation is to forget trying to trade – you will be up against some of the smartest people in the world who do nothing else. Instead, think of your task as asset allocation, i.e. strategic allocation of the funds in different active classes. The intellectual Mount Everest in this discipline is probably the way in which the university fund Yale Endowment has allocated assets for decades and a good start is thus to read a book by its long-standing boss, David F. Swensen.[1]

After reading this, you can contact some banks that are large enough and ask them to propose a strategic asset-allocation model with a global exposure to non-correlated assets, such as primarily shares and perhaps private equity and venture funds as well as bonds, real estate companies or hedge funds.

Angel investments

A great hybrid between launching start-ups and not is to become an angel investor, which is something lots of entrepreneurs turn to after their first major exit. This can give them a combination of fun, the pleasure of building stuff up, plus on average very nice returns. Also, it is a route that can bring more diversification than simply starting your own new company.

Do charity

Many former entrepreneurs like to get involved in charity work. What you perceive as the right charity varies from person to person, but we want to draw attention to the fact that an entrepreneur can not only do good for example by helping distressed people in poor areas or protecting the environment (East Coast charity), but also by working as a mentor or investor in and for start-up companies (West Coast charity). While there are probably many who can figure out the first, there is clearly a lack of people who have the time, experience and talent to help young people start new companies. This isn't charity, perhaps, but it can certainly do some good.

Final words . . .

Here is the end of our story – we are sorry that it became this long! Our last words: we all have only one life. We are each born with human potential and we each try to realize some of our dreams. Perhaps your dream is to become a professional football player, an auditor or a cook. Maybe it is to have five kids and a little house in the country, or to become a rocker with Harley and all. But if it is to be an entrepreneur, we just want to say this: try. You should probably try carefully first, but please do try. And train yourself, because entrepreneurship is something you must learn over time, just like any other skill set. Think about it: people who complete an Ironman are not necessarily created differently than people who are in front of the TV every evening – but the former have trained themselves hard and consistently.

Entrepreneurship is surely demanding and always risky, but just as you can train yourself to become a musician, athlete or anything else, you can also train yourself in entrepreneurship. And if that is really what you dream of – to become an entrepreneur – once you sing the last verse in life and think back, would it not be great to know that at least you tried the best you could – and maybe even succeeded with it.

And then you can have the evening's third glass of wine and think: 'I lived out my dreams'.

Good luck!

APPENDIX A: 116 BUSINESS STRATEGIES FOR ENTREPRENEURS

Product and product portfolio strategies

1. **Fusion product** – you merge product concepts that were previously sold separately. An example is Cirque du Soleil, which merges concepts from restaurants, sports, circus, dance and rock concerts.

2. **Central aggregator** – you collect other people's products in an integrated solution such as a media platform or an IT solution. This is very often used in IT.

3. **Blockbuster** – you make a big hit such as a movie, a music album or a video game, which is an enormous success and maybe goes viral.

4. **Target the poor** – products are designed specifically to accommodate poor people. The profits from each unit may not be great, but the supplier can use this to lift its overall production volume, which can give other commercial advantages such as economies of scale or building brand awareness among poor who will later reach middle class. This is often used by consumer goods providers such as Unilever.

5. **Trash-to-cash** – you collect used products or mere trash and upgrade or transform them so that they can be sold well. The key business edge is the low purchase price (in some cases, companies are actually paid money to take it) plus in some senses the great marketing story about re-usage (environmental awareness).

6. **Ultimate luxury** – your product is not only good but among the very best within its category. Instead of promoting good value for money, you make the high price a part of the product feature: you may literally promote how expensive it is. And instead of promoting it directly, you may make it clear that not everyone can buy it. Examples are supercars, the most expensive watches or ultra-premium credit cards and travel clubs.

7. **Counter-trend** – when there is a major trend in the market it attracts virtually all major suppliers but leaves a space for deliberately counter-trend products. The name aikido refers to a Japanese martial arts technique whereby you use your opponent's strength against them.

8. **Low-cost business design** – you focus intently on bringing your costs below those of your competitors, for example through automation, scaling or outsourcing. Think Ryanair.

9. **Customer is king** – no one is better at helping customers than you. A typical strategy for high-end hotels, but can be used in many businesses.

10. **Mass customization** – you have automated how each customer can get their product personalized. Maybe you use computers equipped with algorithms that learn from the customer's choice and use this knowledge to advise new customers. Many car vendors do it to the extent that hardly any of the millions they produce are identical, Levi Strauss pioneered it in 1994 with its Spin jeans, Dell does it for PCs, My Unique Bag did for, well, bags. Online shopping or design is often involved. Interestingly, the company not only gets far more happy clients but also learns from their choices.

11. **One and You're Done** – make an existing product extremely simple for the user to purchase and use. Amazon's 1-Click Ordering or Microsoft's plug and play in Windows 95 were great examples.

12. Profit multiplier – you reuse the same product in many ways. Example: movies in the cinema are later relaunched via TV broadcasting and Netflix, while the soundtracks are released on CD and on digital download platforms, while toys, T-shirts, games, books, computer games are also developed.

13. Revolutionary invention – your product is innovative and simply much better in some respects. GoPro is an example.

14. Secondary sale – your basic product is cheap or free, but you earn a lot from services or accessories. For instance, printers are often sold very cheaply but then there are high margins on ink cartridges. Or a telco network gives away phones against getting subscriptions. Or you buy a cheap Nespresso coffee machine, after which the company makes lots of money on the capsules. This is also sometimes called an 'add-on' business model.

15. Solutions provider – the customer does not want a standardized product but a customized solution. As a full-service provider for this market area, you offer total coverage of products and services and make sure it all works together. Typical examples include many IT service providers, plus building contractors.

16. Guaranteed availability – you ensure that the availability or function of the product or service is guaranteed. This means no waiting time or downtime. Examples include NetJets (waiting time) and many server farms (downtime).

17. Ingredient branding – focus your marketing on an ingredient in your product, such as the cocoa beans that were used to make your chocolate or the quality of a specific part of a car.

18. Long-tail product assortment – instead of focusing on one or a few great sellers, your strategy is to provide a wide range of niche products within your market area. Even though each of these offers limited profit, the overall business model may be sound because you have many of them and possibly little competition.

19. No frills – focus only on the essential product features to bring down cost and price. Examples are discount supermarkets, budget hotels and the cheapest airlines.

Pricing policies

20. Aperiodic discounting – discounts at unpredictable times, so potential buyers cannot plan to buy in the next discount period.

21. As-a-service models – sell access to the use of a product, for example monthly subscription conditions.

22. Auction pricing – sell via an auction system, where the price is determined by competitive bidding.

23. Complementary pricing (loss leader pricing) – subsidizes the core product and instead earns on spare parts, accessories, refills, etc. The product you possibly lose money on is called a loss leader.

24. Customer differentiation – different types of customers pay different prices for the same product.

25. Discount coupons – can be used as partial payment for the products.

26. Dynamic pricing – let prices fluctuate constantly depending on statistical real-time measurements of supply and demand.

27. Fractional ownership – several clients have usage rights to a given asset but at different times.

28. Free – you give away everything for free for a period.

29. Freemium – a basic version of a product or service is given away in the hope that some users will upgrade to an improved paid version.

30. Frequent-user benefits – if you buy more, you receive upgrades.

31. Frequent-user discounts – the more you buy, the cheaper it gets.

32. Frequent-user exclusives – valuable customers can buy limited-edition products that others may not purchase.

33. **Geographical price differentiation** – sell at different prices in different geographic areas.

34. **Hidden revenues** – all or a part of revenues are generated though product placements, sponsors, advertisers, kick-back from suppliers, etc. This enables you to offer the product for free or at a discounted price.

35. **Last-minute discounts** – if you buy a service at the last minute before it is executed, you get a discount.

36. **Leasing** – offer to lease rather than buy; optionally with redeeming rights.

37. **Licence** – the company develops intellectual property rights, the usage rights of which are licensed to other companies.

38. **List prices** – insist that all distributors have an identical price which you control.

39. **Membership offers** – offer discounts for frequent users or members of a club.

40. **Minimum prices** – the customer can buy as much as they want, but there is a minimum price that must always be paid.

41. **Pay per use** – instead of paying a fixed price for usage rights, you pay for only the actual usage, which is metered.

42. **Pay what you want** – the price is up to the user. This appeals to the feeling of gratitude and obligation.

43. **Penetration pricing** – start marketing with a very low price to get through the market.

44. **Performance-based contracting** – you get paid according to how well you solve a specified task.

45. **Periodic discounting** – compile discount offers or sales at regular times.

46. Premium pricing – make a low-cost product to attract customers; earn money on other products which are more expensive.

47. Price bundling – offer discounts when customers are buying several products.

48. Price signalling – maintain a high price with the expectation that customers thereby will conclude that the product has a high value.

49. Real-time pricing – prices vary in real time to reflect fluctuations in demand and supply (such as in Uber pricing).

50. Second market discounting – sell the same product but under two different brands and at two different prices.

51. Skimming pricing – begin with a high price to obtain an exclusive image or reach the most enthusiastic buyers; thereafter, reduce the price.

52. Solo supplier discounting – give a better price to a supplier if they guarantee not to use competing products.

53. Token pricing – products/services are paid with blockchain tokens.

54. Subscription – the customer subscribes to regular delivery.

55. Up-front pricing – a service paid in advance.

56. Volume discounts – offer lower prices by higher sales volumes.

57. White label – the same product is sold at a higher price when branded by the company and at a lower price when branded by its distributor or not at all.

Speed and timing strategies

58. First-mover advantage – you are the first to go aggressively into a new market and therefore you can get the best partner deals – and maybe get the entire market associated with your name. If there are economies of scale, network effects and viral effects, you can also ensure a lasting competitive advantage. YouTube did it.

59. Second-mover advantage – you are rapidly copying what the first mover does except that you avoid their mistakes. This may mean that your clients become happier than theirs. Only when you have become market leader through this strategy do you switch focus to original innovation.

60. Trendspotting – you predict a big trend and ensure a spot in the upcoming boom. Can be a domain, a patent, a plot of land, etc.

61. Turbo-business – you can spit out products faster than anyone else, for example due to shorter lines of communication, delegation, floating procedures or automation in another way.

Marketing ideas, including distribution and promotion ideas

62. Brand building – everyone knows your brand and branding is your core competency (Red Bull is an example).

63. Revenue sharing – build an ecosystem of contributors to your business and share some of your profits with them. For instance, pay clients to refer new clients or bloggers promoting you for referring leads, etc.

64. Shop-in-shop – you create a hosting service where other vendors can set up shop. This could be web hosting, retail warehouses and shopping malls or online shopping sites.

65. Self-service and self-ordering – a part of the value creation is transferred to the customer as they begin to service themselves, such as booking flights online (self-ordering) and checking in with their mobile (self-service). IKEA, Mobility Carsharing and buffet restaurants are other examples.

66. Supermarket model – you provide a large variety of products within some market categories so that the shopper gets all the choice within a simple space. Examples are classic supermarkets (Walmart), financial supermarkets (Citibank) and e-stores (Amazon).

67. Direct selling – you disintermediate the distributors and start selling directly to your clients. This saves you money, enables you to cut prices and may even provide a better and more convenient solution for clients.

68. Experience selling – the process of buying your product becomes a great experience in itself. When you are in the shop or showroom, you have an awesome time. Or perhaps the car manufacturer that sold you the car lets you pick it up at the factory after a tour of the facilities.

69. Franchising – you own the intellectual property rights such as trademarks, patents and brand names, and you develop products, services and corporate identity, etc. But instead of making a lot of subsidiaries or retail outlets, you license the usage rights to it all to independent franchisees who use their local expertise and carry the risk of local operations. Great examples include McDonald's, Marriott and Starbucks.

Networking-related strategies

70. Network effect – your product is designed so that it becomes more attractive for each user, the more people who use it. LinkedIn is an example.

71. Viral effects – many of your users recommend or share your product.

72. Digital marketplace – electronic commerce can be made through your platform. Amazon is the king of them all, but this is also what electronic stock exchanges do.

73. Dominating network – your network is the largest and thus everyone wants to be there. Facebook is a great example.

74. Platform/standard – everyone loves to shop on your platform and eventually it becomes a de facto standard. Then you will automatically take advantage of the market's overall growth. For instance, eBay or NASDAQ.

75. Two-sided network – you create a double network effect which enable interactions between interdependent groups of customers. A network effect builds up, but only if both sides expand in parallel. This is complex to build up but can become robust once it works. Credit cards, online market places and stock exchanges are examples.

76. Peer-to-peer (P2P) network – you set up a platform such as an online database or other communication service that connects players with each other. eBay, Craigslist, Airbnb and TaskRabbit are examples.

77. Open business model and open-source software – you deliberately give external access to your business or software platform so that others can add to it or build on it. In software, this is ensured by releasing the software source code so that anyone can understand what it does.

Commercial-alliance strategies

78. Affiliate marketing – you create a network of marketing affiliates which boost your product and/or distribution. These affiliates – bloggers, brokers or online shopping network affiliates, for instance – typically make money per sale. They may also use the association with you to boost their own core business, which is something else. An example is Amazon Associates.

79. Co-branding – joint branding for advertising and products.

80. Co-packaging/co-pricing – offers where customers (end users) buy two (or more) companies' products as a single package and for one price.

81. Co-promotion – joint marketing campaigns, for example on exhibitions, fairs, press conferences, launch parties, etc.

82. Cross-selling – companies agree to sell each other's products. This provides an increased assortment and more income.

83. Joint marketing organization – several companies (sometimes a lot) create a joint sales organization for cost savings and greater impact. This organization can handle market research, sales and marketing.

84. Joint product development – shared research facilities, for example.

85. Joint production – several companies produce from a jointly owned facility.

86. Joint selling logistics – several companies share logistics such as storage and shipping facilities.

87. Joint venture companies – two or more companies co-found a new, jointly owned company.

88. Know-how exchange – establish forums such as professional groups and trade organizations that exchange experience and data.

89. OEM agreements – OEM stands for original equipment manufacturer and means that manufacturers sell another company's product under its own name and branding, i.e. private label.

90. Open platform – a company makes it easy for others to develop applications and variants via, for example, SDKs (software development kits).

91. Value-added reseller – sale of a core product from one company added additional benefit from another. In the case of complex solutions, for example within IT, they use the term 'system integrator'.

Value capture/business structure strategies

92. Build to be bought – you create a company with the ulterior motive of making it an obvious acquisition target eventually. This is particularly common in life sciences.

93. Consolidation play – you merge companies in a given industry, for example through acquisitions, merging or the creation of cooperative structures. Sometimes this is called a 'roll-up'. You can make roll-ups of anything from dental clinics to law firms or the watch industry (Swatch).

94. Critical scaling – you manage to grow your business to a critical size, so through economies of scale or network effects you may dominate. ArcelorMittal did this in the steel industry.

95. Arbitrage – you can buy something cheap from one channel and sell it for a higher price in another. For instance, buy wholesale and sell retail. Or buy in a low-cost nation and sell in a high-cost area. Or borrow cheaply and invest with a higher yield.

96. Business model cloning – if something works extremely well in one country or one industry, then copy it elsewhere. The copying is sometimes referred to as reverse engineering if it involves a complex analysis of how the copied product was made. Rocket Internet is a prime example.

97. Niche dominance – your market is limited, but you almost own it.

98. Purchasing cooperative – you create a network that allows purchasers or consumers transparency and collective power compared with providers (like Groupon).

99. Recycle capacity – one of the big business models is to look at the society and identify unused resources. For instance, cars that are not used most of the day, empty summer houses, factories running partly idle, unused computer capacity, etc. Figure out how these things can be used better through crowdsourcing, for instance (Airbnb and Uber are examples). A variant is to find resources that can be used for multiple things at once. For instance, a high-street upscale car dealer showroom becomes a restaurant at night.

100. Cross selling – I sell yours if you sell mine is a great model for mutual help. This can partly be to utilize logistic synergies, but companies may also cross-sell to combine complementary images. Bentley has the sporty Breitling watches and Breitling are the watches used by Bentley.

101. Crowdsourcing – let the solution to a task be provided by an anonymous crowd on the web. This is typically done for small rewards to each (microworks) or for larger prizes such as in innovation awards. Sometimes it's solved simply because people like to help each other, such as with Wikipedia. Examples: InnoCentive, XPRIZE and DesignCrowd.

102. Layer player – specialized in solving the same small part of the value chain for a lot of companies. By doing this it develops an expertise and economy of scale within its narrow field that none of its clients has. Furthermore, it removes a management complication from them. Examples include airline catering companies, web service companies and cleaning companies.

103. Mass customer data mining – a rapidly growing business model is to use online services to collect vast amounts of data about clients and then use this knowledge to offer highly targeted advertising platforms as well as any service where detailed client information is important.

104. Lock-in model – customers are brought into a situation where the costs of switching to another supplier are substantial relative to the situation if they stay with their current supplier. This is often seen in complex software systems, but also on a smaller scale when you buy a device and many expensive add-ons. For instance, if you buy a Canon camera and many expensive Canon lenses, you are unlikely to shift to Nikon where your Canon lenses won't work.

105. Make more of it – you use your existing platform to make more of the same products for other brands and clients, thereby creating additional revenues, stimulating economies of scale and inhibiting growth of competitors.

106. Orchestrator – the company defines which eco-system or value chain it wants to create but systematically tries to outsource almost every part of the related work. This enables it to run a lean organization and benefit from the combined expertise and economies of scale of its suppliers. It also ensures a focus on the efficiency of the overall system rather than on countless operational issues.

107. Category king – the company defines a new product category and takes a lead in it. This means that while management builds the company, they also invest strongly in building awareness about the entire category.

Expansion strategies

108. Internal development – the company's own staff is responsible for product and market development.

109. Internal venture – you create a company within the company, where your staff can work as intrapreneurs.

110. Obtain licence – you buy the licence to distribute other companies' products.

111. Sell licence – you sell distribution rights for your products to other companies.

112. Market-oriented acquisitions – you buy a company that has good market access.

113. Knowledge-oriented acquisitions – you buy a company because of its products or development expertise.

114. Marketing alliance – for example, cross-selling, cross promotion, joint promotion, system integration.

115. Joint venture – you make a new company with a partner company.

116. VC investments – you invest in small companies with which you have synergy.

APPENDIX B: 46 TYPICAL CRITERIA FOR SUCCESS IN START-UP COMPANIES

Below is a list of 46 signs that show whether a start-up company has a good chance of future success (or continued success).

Founders and their cooperation

1. The company has at least two founders.

2. If its business idea includes both technical and commercial challenges, it is a great advantage if there is at least one founder with each of these backgrounds. Only if there are very large network effects may it be advantageous to have a 100% commercially oriented founder team.

3. At least one of the founders has a 'star power' that will make it easier to attract talent to the company.

4. It is a plus if some or all of the founders have attended top universities (irrespective of whether they graduated or dropped out).

5. Although the founders have different professional backgrounds, they have compatible social and cultural values.

6. The founders show many of the following characteristics: (i) enterprising, (ii) self-motivated, (iii) impatient, (iv) fast-working,

(v) thrive in the face of speed, chaos and uncertainty, (vi) resistant to adversity, (vii) forward-looking but nevertheless learn by mistakes, (viii) constantly think about improvements in their surroundings, (ix) have professional pride, (x) ability to immerse themselves, (xi) curious by nature, (xii) cooperative, (xiii) persistent, (xiv) good at postponing reward, (xv) have had unpleasant, unrewarding jobs during their youth, and (xvi) are happy and optimistic by nature.

7. The founders should preferably know each other well in advance. It is best if at least some of them have worked together before and even better if this happened within a young start-up company with high growth.

8. The founders agree on the distribution of the workload.

9. The founders agree on the conditions for an exit – what it might require and when it might happen.

10. The founders have a shareholders' agreement and agree on the fundamental purpose of the company and their individual roles and effort.

11. The share allocation among the founders is partly dynamic, i.e. based on some performance criteria.

12. The founders reserve the 'founder' title to most of the C-suite team, although some of these positions are filled later.

13. The founders are well versed in sharing economy, crowdsourcing, productivity-enhancing apps and other ways to minimize costs and increase efficiency in a fast-moving, cost-constrained company.

14. Ideally, the founders have an experienced mentor and follow blogs from leading entrepreneurs.

The planning processes

15. Initially, the management team does not make a comprehensive written business plan, but rather a simple business canvas, which they change often during the first many months.

16. They probably make several pivots, i.e. high-speed strategic re-adjustments, in the early phases.

17. They develop and test a minimum variable product before starting on a finished product.

18. They outsource activities such as bookkeeping, etc., which are not relevant to their core competencies. However, during the early phases they engage personally and intensely in the product and marketing development, and they spend a lot of time with customers to learn about how to evolve the product.

19. The product that the company seeks to develop as a rule should be so good that about half of its users would be 'very disappointed' if it disappeared again.

20. They develop well-thought-through metrics that make it easy for them to keep track of the extent to which they meet their strategic goals.

21. The company does not begin aggressive scaling until there is clear evidence that it has a strong product/market fit.

22. If management expect many funding rounds, they consider a physical presence near a leading venture capital centre.

23. When the company scales, there is a strong focus on lifting all elements synchronously, so that they do not, for example, sell an unfinished product or over-develop a product without focusing enough on its marketing.

24. The management shows great attention to any possible challenges concerning the transitioning from an early adopter to the mainstream market.

The business models

25. The business models contain elements that are original.

26. The business models enable extreme scaling with decreasing or unchanged marginal costs. Likewise, they can lead to very high earnings, clearly worth the investment and the risk.

27. The company's strategy points to a niche that it can dominate. Only when such niche dominance has been achieved does it plan to expand further.

28. If the company introduces a new product to an already mature market, the product with respect to at least one important product features at least 10 times better than what it will compete against.

29. Ultimately, it is an advantage if the product is relatively simple and easy to promote – or sells itself through word of mouth.

30. The company offers not only features but a complete product.

31. The company does not have a product or technology that is looking for a need. Instead it shows a clearly identified need that can be met with the company's product.

32. The business model contains elements that can clearly counteract competition, such as network effects, patents or exclusivity agreements.

33. The company operates within an area dominated by core technologies that develop hyper-exponentially and therefore offer opportunities for start-up companies.

34. The company focuses on locating itself in commercial ecosystems where payments are made.

35. Its project has low capital requirements.

36. The company's product invites repurchases and habit formation.

The funding patterns

37. They have participated in prominent incubator/accelerator programmes.

38. They have received funding from some of the most successful VCs – preferably at an early stage in their development.

39. The early investors have participated proportionally in the subsequent rounds (especially important if these are high-performing, prominent VCs).

40. Their funding has taken place at short intervals, preferably with a maximum of nine months between each round (this also means that they raised many rounds if they are no longer at the seed stage).

The business momentum

41. The company is seen as a category king, thus leading its space.

42. There is clear positive momentum in how often it is mentioned in the press and on social media. The best is if the company had a low profile from the outset and then built it up rapidly as the business evolved.

43. There is clear positive momentum in its following on social media.

44. It has been able to attract more competent staff as it has progressed.

45. Its business reach, sales and gross profits follow an exponential path.

46. There are repeat or referral users.

APPENDIX C: LIST OF USEFUL WEBSITES, APPS AND WEB-EXTENSIONS FOR ENTREPRE- NEURS

Find sales leads, journalists, etc.; including email addresses

- https://hunter.io/ – helps you find email addresses.

- https://salestools.io/ – input company domain and find contact persons in the company.

- www.findthatlead.com – find emails. Can be used in collaboration with Rapportive.

- www.hey.press – find journalists.

Develop business ideas

- https://evernote.com – an online bulletin board that you can use to organize ideas and aphorisms.

- https://flippa.com – Flippa is a marketplace for web domains as well as web shops. It can help to provide business development ideas and provide access to the quick launch of an online business.

- www.google.com/keep – an online bulletin board that you can use to organize ideas and aphorisms.

- www.trello.com – an app that lets you to create multiple virtual bulletin boards. Trello lets you structure your ideas and tasks, and you can share your bulletin boards with others, even integrate and combine bulletin boards.
- www.solvrgroup.com – looks like a common search engine, but when you "search", the answer comes up as a problem that you can add an idea to. A new problem arises, as an idea must be attributed to. These issues can be shared with others via a link and in this way you can make the process collective.
- https://www.uservoice.com – an app where you can set up user-generated poles. Great for evaluating solutions to a problem.
- www.surveyswipe.com – an app where you can do mobile surveys.
- www.surveymonkey.com – an app (mobile and web-based) that can be used to generate surveys. The results of the surveys can be stored on your website and social media accounts.

Develop company name, product name, logos, slogans, styleguides, business cards, etc.

- www.vistaprint.com – design and produce business cards.
- www.tongal.com – a platform where you can receive feedback and ideas for your concept, your production and your distribution.
- https://www.fiverr.com – early-adopter crowdsourcing site.
- www.99designs.com – a crowdsourcing website where you can help on logo design, website layout, product design and other graphical solutions for an affordable price.
- www.squadhelp.com – crowdsourcing of brand names.
- www.sloganslingers.com – crowdsourcing of slogans.
- www.designcrowd.com – a crowdsourcing website where you can help on logo design, website layout, product design and other graphical solutions for an affordable price.

- www.templatestash.com – templates for websites.
- http://thenameapp.com – an app you can use to search for available domains.

Manage patents and trademarks

- https://www.42patents.com – renew patents at a low price.
- www.brandit.com – helps you pick, register and protect trademarks.

Organize work groups and internal communication, etc.

- www.atlassian.com/Confluence – website and app with tools to organize complex work tasks.
- https://trello.com – easy-to-use tool to organize groups and work in a company.
- www.skype.com – video chat platform.
- www.tango.me – online platform for video conferences.
- www.linkedIn.com – an absolute must-have tool for staying connected with important contacts.
- www.stride.com – social Media service to organize projects.
- www.hivedesk.com – an app to manage our freelance workforce.
- www.whatsapp.com – simple communication tool to manage smaller groups.
- www.slack.com – simple communication to manage smaller groups. Create many channels and groups, share documents, ideas, etc.

Crowdsourcing of work tasks

- https://www.fiverr.com – one of the leading crowdsourcing sites.
- www.99designs.com – a crowdsourcing website where you can help on logo design, website layout, product design and other graphical solutions for an affordable price.

- www.crowdio.com – 24/7 customer service chat for your business.

- www.designcrowd.com – a crowdsourcing website where you can help on logo design, website layout, product design and other graphical solutions for an affordable price.

- www.edenmccallum.com – a website for freelance management consultants.

- www.gengo.com – a website for freelance translators.

- www.mturk.com – a website where you can obtain data aggregations and classifications.

- www.sloganslingers.com – crowdsourcing of slogans.

- www.squadhelp.com – crowdsourcing of brand names.

- www.survtapp.com – good for market research.

- www.topcoder.com – find freelance software developers.

- www.upcall.com – outsource your calls.

- www.upwork.com – find software developers- and engineers, freelance marketers, designers, etc.

Legal tips and templates

- www.liveplan.com – a website with word templates to various tasks, e.g. marketing plans, legal documents, etc.

- www.creativecommons.org – a website where you can download standardized contracts.

- www.fortune.com/tag/term-sheet – Fortune Magazine term sheet templates and news on startups and the venture capital industry.

- www.entrepreneur.com – a website with word templates to various tasks, e.g. marketing plans, legal documents, etc.

- www.sba.gov – a website with word templates to various tasks, e.g. marketing plans, legal documents, etc.

- www.nvca.org – standardized templates for venture financing.

- www.wsgr.com – an automated term sheet generator for venture capital fundraising.

- www.seriesseed.com – standardized templates for seed financing contracts, documents, etc.

- www.score.org – a website with word templates to various tasks, e.g. marketing plans, legal documents, etc.

- www.shakelaw.com – an app with a set of standardized contracts suited to you based on how you answer a set of intro questions. Also has features to help with online signing.

Forums for entrepreneurs and venture investors

- www.reddit.com – "Forum on everything". A social counterpart to Wikipedia.

Find jobs, employees, work space and funding

- www.angellist.com – a US website where startups can post job offers and seek funding.

- www.kickstarter.com – popular crowdfunding platform.

- www.indiegogo.com – crowdfunding platform.

- www.heydesk.com – find office space across the globe.

Relevant news sites on industries, technologies, entrepreneurship etc. and reading apps

- https://play.pocketcasts.com – an app for downloading podcasts for smartphones and tablets.

- www.amazon.com/kindle – integrated hardware/software system that can be used for downloading and reading e-books and other reading material.

- www.audiobooks.com – a website and app where you can find e-books, podcasts, blogs, etc. you can download.

- www.fastcompany.com – an online network for entrepreneurs with inspiring and useful articles.

- www.CBInsights.com – a website focusing on the venture capital market with tremendous analyses.

- www.flipboard.com – similar to feedly but different, haha.

- www.forentrepreneurs.com – an online network for entrepreneurs with inspiring and useful articles.

- www.futurity.org – aggregates university research within your personal field of interest.

- www.getabstract.com – gives 10 min abstracts of thousands of popular business books.

- www.audible.com – audiobooks that you e.g. can use for exercising, travelling, etc.

- www.fortune.com/tag/term-sheet – news on startups and the venture capital industry.

- www.feedly.com – a news feed aggregator that compiles news on subjects you request.

- www.medium.com – popular blogging platform.

- www.pitchbook.com – subscription-based database with information on unlisted companies, including venture capital investments/investment rounds.

- www.techcrunch.com – a leading news and blog website on entrepreneurship and venture capital.

- www.wikipedia.com – crowdsources online encyclopedia.

- www.youngupstarts.com – an online network for entrepreneurs with inspiring and useful articles.

- www.scholar.google.com – a part of Google's search engine: focusing on academic subjects, e.g. scientific papers, books, etc.

- www.webinarjam.com – find and share webinars.

- www.TED.com – the famous TEDTalks where talented speakers deliver presentations.

- www.hotjar.com – understand your customers better and optimize website.

- www.reddit.com – "Forum on everything". A social counterpart to Wikipedia.
- https://apolloapp.io – an app that can be used to screen reddit.
- www.google.com/alerts – a service that informs you when a given word or phrase is mentioned online - such as your company, product, competitor or yourself.
- https://trends.google.com/trend – a program showing recent trends in Google search. It thus shows what is popular in a given period.

Find investors and get funded

- www.seed-db.com – lists information on the world's most important accelerators.
- www.strictlyVC.com – platform with information on venture deals, blogs and tools for fundraising.
- www.gust.com – maps business angels and accelerators, and is a useful tool for entrepreneurs and venture capital investors.
- www.crunchbase.com – database covering investors, incubators, accelerators, venture capital firms and startups.
- www.thefunded.com – rating of ~7,000 venture capital firms and venture capital firm partners. Ratings provided by startups. Also, a discussion platform for funding.
- www.nvca.org – standardized templates for venture financing.
- www.wsgr.com – an automated term sheet generator for venture capital fundraising.
- www.seriesseed.com – standardized templates for seed financing contracts.

Become a professional board member

- www.nacdonline.com – created by the National Association of Corporate Directors: advisory on the board member role.

- www.pascalsview.com – helpful documents for startup board members. Created by The Working Group on Director Accountability and Board Effectiveness.

Develop business and marketing plans

- www.bplans.com – a website with word templates to various tasks, e.g. marketing plans, legal documents, etc.

- www.dynamicbusinessplan.com – provides tips and templates for writing a professional business plan.

- www.launchpadcentral.com – manage your business plan.

- www.entrepreneur.com – a website with word templates to various tasks, e.g. marketing plans, legal documents, etc.

- www.liveplan.com – a website with word templates to various tasks, e.g. marketing plans, legal documents, etc.

- www.sba.gov – a website with word templates to various tasks, e.g. marketing plans, legal documents, etc.

- www.seriesseed.com – standardized templates for seed financing contracts.

- www.score.org – a website with word templates to various tasks, e.g. marketing plans, legal documents, etc.

- https://enloop.com – a website that develops a business plan for you. You give the app some information about where you would like to be in five years. Then it will fill out a business plan for you who shows the way. It can be extremely valuable if you lack skills in, for example, economics. The app provides automatic, financial forecasts that can save you much time and money.

Develop social media strategies

- www.snapchat.com – some photo and video messaging platform primary used by the younger generations.

- https://sproutsocial.com – a program that helps you release content on several social media platforms at once.

- www.surveyswipe.com – an app where you can do mobile surveys.

- www.facebook.com – your marketing and communications platform.

- www.medium.com – popular blogging platform.

- www.twitter.com – popular social Media platform- best for short, factual opinions and especially commented links.

- www.Instagram.com – popular photo and video sharing platform.

- www.commun.it – tool to track Twitter followers.

- www.youtube.com – the world's largest video network. Create your own channel and upload videos.

- www.dlvr.it – a social media management tool that simplifies the online marketing efforts while making it less time consuming.

- www.vimeo.com – a leading platform for uploading and distributing video clips.

- www.slideshare.com – social media platform for sharing of PowerPoint, PDF slide presentations, etc.

- www.webinarjam.com – find and share webinars.

- www.typeform.com – create questionnaires and quizzes online.

- www.crowdio.com – 24/7 customer service chat for your business.

- www.agorapulse.com – a program that helps you publish content on multiple social media at once.

- https://buffer.com – a program that helps you publish content on multiple social media at once.

- www.canva.com – a tool to create illustrations for your blog posts, PowerPoint, etc.

- www.hootsuite.com – a program that helps you publish content on multiple social media at once.

- www.involver.com – a program that helps you publish content on multiple social media at once.

- www.zopim.com – a program that can integrate your platform, so you can chat with your clients. The program also comes with analysis of the number of visitors, etc.

- www.social-booster.com – a program that helps you publish content on multiple social media at once.

- www.socialclout.com – a program that helps you publish content on multiple social media at once.

- https://zencastr.com – a software application that allows you to record Skype or Hangouts audio conferences in high quality. Each participant's voice is recorded locally, after which the audio files are downloaded to Dropbox. Each audio file has a timestamp, so the whole conversation can be automatically reconstructed in high quality.

- www.zoom.us – an audio and video conference app.

- https://maitreapp.co – all-in-one reference market platform to launch your referrals, sweepstakes, raffles, ambassador programs, and pre-launch campaigns.

Marketing research

- www.illuminatecontent.com – marketing research platform.

- www.metricwire.com – marketing research platform.

- www.quicktapsurvey.com – marketing research platform.

- CompareApp – an app that lets you get user feedback.

- www.google.com/alerts – a service that informs you when a given word or phrase is mentioned online - such as your company, product, competitor or yourself.

- https://www.uservoice.com – an app where you can set up user-generated poles. Great for evaluating solutions to a problem.

- www.surveyswipe.com – an app where you can do mobile surveys.
- www.surveymonkey.com – an app (mobile and web-based) that can be used to generate surveys. The results of the surveys can be stored on your website and social media accounts.

Create and manage websites

- www.monitorbacklinks.com – great tool for the tech savvy entrepreneur: test the effectiveness of links on your website.
- www.squarespace.com – a website that can be used to create and control websites and blogs. See also WordPress.
- www.themeforest.net – affordable web designs.
- www.usertesting.com – a platform where you can get people to test a project, e.g. the user-friendliness of your website.
- www.uxtesting.io – test the user-friendliness of your app-based website.
- www.webflow.com – build your own website without having to code.
- www.wix.com – create a website in less than 10 min.
- www.wordpress.com – offers hosting and delivers standardized web design solutions. Wordpress makes it easy to create and run a website at an affordable price. See Squarespace.com for another example.
- www.google.com/analytics – a free website that offers detailed statistics and analytics for websites.
- https://usabilityhub.com – a crowdsourcing app where people can test the user-friendliness of your website.

Create press releases

- www.pressport.com – a software tool that can help you distribute press releases.
- https://presswire.com – a software tool that can help you distribute press releases.

Online marketing tools

- https://business.linkedin.com/sales-solutions/sales-navigator – an extension to Google Chrome that shows the LinkedIn profile for the person you are texting with by email. An easy tool to check if the email is connected to the person's LinkedIn profile.

- https://sumo.com – a program that lets you increase your e-mail subscriptions.

- https://usabilityhub.com – a crowdsourcing app where people can test the user-friendliness of your website.

- www.truegether.com – an online marketplace where you can sell products. Easy-to-use service.

- www.aweber.com – website and app that automates your e-mail marketing efforts.

- Boomerang – an extension for Google Chrome that you can use to schedule automated e-mails.

- www.canva.com – a tool to create illustrations for your blog posts, PowerPoint, etc.

- www.ecamm.com – a Mac software tool to record audio and video sessions on Skype or Facetime. Moreover, to do live recordings on YouTube, etc.

- www.mailchimp.com – a popular tool used to enhance your email marketing efforts.

- www.intercom.com – a tool that helps you communicate with clients. Ask for feedback, let clients ask questions, etc.

- www.nicereply.com – an app that can be used to get user feedback.

- https://adwords.google.com – a marketing program that you pay per lead / click you get when a person clicks on an ad on your website - the use of this also helps to move your page up in Google's ranking when searching for a topic.

- https://zencastr.com – a software application that allows you to record Skype or Hangouts audio conferences in high quality.

Each participant's voice is recorded locally, after which the audio files are downloaded to Dropbox. Each audio file has a timestamp, so the whole conversation can be automatically reconstructed in high quality.

- www.zoom.us – an audio and video conference app.
- https://yoast.com – a plug-in that you can use if you use WordPress. Yoast gives you a SEO score for all your sites and blog posts. Helps you improve your Google ranking.
- https://webengage.com – an app that administrates your sales funnel and dialogue with clients.
- www.surveymonkey.com – an app (mobile and web-based) that can be used to generate surveys. The results of the surveys can be stored on your website and social media accounts.
- www.surveyswipe.com – an app where you can do mobile surveys.
- https://maitreapp.co – all-in-one reference market platform to launch your referrals, sweepstakes, raffles, ambassador programs, and pre-launch campaigns.

Dashboard tools to monitor the business

- www.plecto.com – dashboard software.
- www.cluvio.com – dashboard software.
- http://try.wrike.com – dashboard software.
- www.geckoboard.com – dashboard software.
- https://agencyanalytics.com – dashboard software.
- https://funnel.io – integrates performance data into dashboard, spreadsheets, etc.

Easy-to-use web shop tools

- www.shopify.com – web shop as a service.
- www.woocommerce.com – web shop as a service.

- www.magento.com – web shop as a service.
- www.prestashop.com – web shop as a service.

General efficiency tools

- https://business.linkedin.com/sales-solutions/sales-navigator – an extension to Google Chrome that shows the LinkedIn profile for the person you are texting with by email. An easy tool to check if the email is connected to the person's LinkedIn profile.

- www.pandadoc.com – an app that lets you create a catalog of elements, e.g. text fragments and pictures that can be used for marketing, sales offer, contracts, presentations, etc. Here you can download different components into a single document with a single click.

- www.escrow.com – safe transactions where the payment is realized by delivery of product. Can be used when purchasing expensive web domains.

- www.dictation.io – a website for voice recognition that will save you time if you will dictate longer documents.

- www.wikijobs.com – tips and tricks on tests and interview techniques related to the hiring process.

- AdobeFill&Sign – an app to sign PDF documents from a smartphone or apple computer.

- www.camcard.com – a mobile app that can scan business cards.

- www.dropbox.com – secure file storage system. Share files.

- https://due.com – a website and app that helps you write invoices and other administrative payments.

- www.google.com/drive – secure file storage system. Share files.

- https://hangouts.google.com – an online communication tool that you can use to write, talk and do video conferences. Easy to use.

- www.glympse.com – an app that can be used to book meetings and afterwards send real-time location of you to a given person who can follow your location.

- iPassword – an app where you can store all your passwords, account numbers and other confidential information – securely.

- LastPass – a program that helps you remember all your passwords for different home pages, so you are not forced to do it yourself.

- Scanner Pro – an app that can be used to scan documents. Also allows you to upload to e.g. Dropbox or Google Drive.

GLOSSARY

Accelerator – a company that helps other companies with the start-up phase in return for receiving shares in those companies.

Accruing dividends – VCs can ask for accruing dividends. This means that the VC must have x% dividend before other shareholders receive any dividend.

Advisory board – an advisory committee or an expert panel. This provides non-binding, strategic advice in relation to management, business structure, etc.

Affiliate marketing – an alliance opportunity where, for example, you pay partners to lead potential customers to your website via theirs.

Aggregation strategy – a strategy that ignores segments and instead targets the whole market.

Agile business development – a way to find your product/market fit. This method is about making a demo, which is tested on customers and then modified – and then you repeat until the product is perfect. This process is called a customer discovery loop.

All-or-nothing – a strategy where, for example, you make an offer to which one can say yes or no, but if one says no, there is no way one can buy the product.

Angel investors – they invest in a company during the early stages. If those investors are professional, they are called super angels.

Angel round – venture investment made by angel investors.

Anti-dilution – a protection for a former investor in connection with new investment rounds. It is thus a protection for an investor against a down round.

Aperiodic discounting – a pricing strategy in which you make discounts at unpredictable times.

Application programming interface (API) – a software interface which allows a piece of software to integrate with another piece of software. When software from a company has an API, it provides other software developers with the ability to write software that works along with that.

Arbitrage – a business model where you buy something cheap somewhere and sell it at a higher price somewhere else. What makes it arbitrage as opposed to any other price gain is that you can see the two prices' simulations as you do the trade.

As-a-service model – a pricing strategy where you sell the access to the use of a product, for example by having monthly subscription terms.

Backdoor reference – backdoor is a term used in connection with references and recruitment. Backdoor references are those which a candidate has not provided themselves.

Back-of-the-envelope calculation – a rough calculation. Named because such a calculation typically will be written down on what is available next to you, such as the back of an envelope.

Backstop – in its original meaning, an object that is used as a barrier or support. In this book, it is used in connection with founders where the backstop is the one who has to inject capital into the company if there is more need.

Blockbuster model – when you make a huge hit, e.g. a movie, a piece of music or a computer game, and it is propagated and may even go viral.

Blue ocean strategies – innovative strategies that minimize competition.

Bond capital – a loan, which has to be repaid after an agreed time schedule.

Bootstrapping – a term used in the venture industry. It means that you manage to start a business with almost no capital or no capital at all. This may be done by (i) getting very quick sales, (ii) using very cheap labour, (iii) living from consultancy income.

Brand building – a business model in which branding is your core competence and the goal is that everyone will know your brand eventually.

Brand extensions – when big and strong brands sell limited use of rights of their brand to other companies.

Bridge – an investment round for companies which have already been through an investment round but want to wait before proceeding to the next round to achieve a higher valuation. In this case, you are making a bridge investment round.

Burn – an industry term for how much a start-up loses per month or per year.

Buy-back rights – the company or its shareholders' right to buy shares from another shareholder, typically from a co-founder or C-suite staff who are leaving the company.

Buy-out – a term usually used in context with equity funds that buy out existing shareholders.

Canned – a slang term used by journalists for a video or audio recording recorded for later distribution.

Cap table – a table showing the concrete asset allocation before and after a possible capital increase.

Carry – an expression of the profit or loss that is included if you have invested at a given interest rate and financed this with another interest rate. A trade where this figure is positive (i.e. the investment yields greater interest than financing) is called a carry trade.

Carve-out – when a company sells a minority of the shares in a newly established subsidiary.

Cash flow – the total amount of capital that is being transported out of and into a given company.

Category king – a company that has defined a new category in the market and become perceived as its leader.

Central aggregator – a business model where you gather other people's products or services in one integrated solution such as a media platform.

Chief financial officer (CFO) – a C-suite title. A CFO is the finance director.

Closer – a sales person who is particularly good at making sales closings.

Closing – the final stage of the sales process, which leads to the customer signing the agreement.

Cloud computing – a term covering software and services being delivered through the internet. Cloud computing is a common name for the use of SaaS (software as a service), PaaS (platform as a service) and IaaS (infrastructure as a service).

Comparables – a model for valuating a business. A business is being compared to a competitor, for example, or an otherwise similar business.

Complementary pricing strategy (loss leader pricing) – a strategy to subsidize the core product and instead earn money on spare parts, add-ons, refills, etc. The product on which one is consciously losing money is called a loss leader.

Consolidation play – a business model where you are merging companies in an industry. This is also sometimes called a roll-up.

Co-pricing – an alliance strategy where the end user ends up buying two or more companies' products in a single package and thereby obtains a discount.

Corporate earn-out – when a company does product development for another company. You have a deal with the other company that they can buy your company at a later stage and/or you have the right to sell them your shares.

Corporate finance house – a company that provides loans and other types of credit. One such corporate finance house can also help you with selling your business.

Crowdfunding – a way to raise capital from a large group people. This can be done by giving this group discounts on the first products that are made, etc.

Crowdsourcing – a contraction of 'crowd' and 'outsourcing'. Crowdsourcing is a method for outsourcing problems or tasks to a relevant network of people.

C-suite – a C-suite position is a job that starts with 'chief', such as chief technology officer or chief executive officer.

Customer development – a branch of agile business development, where you cooperate with your potential customers and develop the product for and to them. Here, you observe their reactions.

Customer discovery loop – a process that is used in conjunction with agile business development, where you first produce a demo, test it with customers, modify the product and repeat this with short intervals.

Customer life value – how much you earn on a customer, from the first to the last time the customer buys or pays for your product or service.

Customer relationship management (CRM) – a system that contains data about your customer relations, which is used to process and apply valuable knowledge of your customers.

Decoy effect – when you get people to buy more or more expensive products by adding more products or services to your assortment.

Detail specification – a document that illuminates the components and materials required, for the product to be made.

Differentiation strategy – a strategy in which you basically address many or all segments, but make sure to customize your marketing mix to each segment.

Diluted valuation – a valuation of a company's share price which takes into account that the number of stocks will grow due to issued stock options to employees, for example.

Discounted cash flows (DCF) – future cash flows are estimated and converted into a total present value, which is discounted (reduced) with a discount factor as compensation for the time to wait until the money is expected to arrive. A given income in the near future is thus attributed at greater value than an identical income in the distant future.

Disrupting – when a business through innovation of products and services disrupts an existing business model.

Dividend – the dividend payment on your shares in a company.

Dividend tax – the tax you pay on your dividend coming from shares.

Dominance strategy – how companies tackle production, marketing and service to achieve dominance in a market segment.

Down round – when investors, for example, buy shares in a company at a lower rate than what the company was valued at in the latest investment round.

Drag-along rights – if you, for example, own 50% of the shares in your company and receive a bid from anyone who wants to buy your business, you may force (pull) the other investors to complete the exit.

Due diligence (DD) – something that an investor is doing after a term sheet is signed. Here, they make a thorough analysis and inspection of your business.

Dumb money – refers to money taking form as an investment coming from, for example, family and friends.

Earned media – publicity you do not pay for. This is something that start-ups should focus on.

Ecommerce – for example, if you buy something from a website through the internet.

Employee stock ownership plans (ESOPs) – employees' rights but not duty to buy shares in the company. The rights are typically issued at fair value on the issue date.

Enterprise resource management software (ERM) – software that takes care of order issuing, inventory management, etc. You can combine your own ERM system with your distributor's ERM system to increase switching costs.

Escape clause – something to add to your contract before a capital injection from an investor. An escape clause allows you to leave the deal if the money has not been paid before an agreed date, for instance.

Escrow – for example, if you are supposed to receive an investment and the capital is deposited in a locked bank account which will be opened only when all the paperwork is completed, then you say that the money is in escrow.

Evangelizers – a term being used about consumers of a product, who believe that the product is so amazing that they are happy (and completely free) to recommend and speak highly about it to their acquaintances.

Exit value – the designation of the value of a business when it is sold. Exit value is usually used in connection with start-ups.

Factoring – a phenomenon where one financial company buys another company's receivables (outstanding bills). The financial company pays these bills minus a commission immediately and then takes over the task of collecting the receivables.

Fair value – the term for a rational and impartial valuation of, for example, a share. This is based on what a realistic market price would be for the product, service or asset.

Fair-weather friend – a person on whom you cannot count during tough times.

Fake door – a way to test your product before you really produce it. Fake door is especially used within the digital world where a company is to test a new website, for instance. It may give a fraction of users access to the new website without the users knowing and thereby the company can test it.

Family office – families who have a fortune of typically more than $300 million often get a company to manage the money separately.

First mover – the business that is the first to bring a product or service to a market. This can give the business a competitive advantage.

First-to-file – a legal system which is being used in all countries. It determines who has the right to patent an invention.

Franchise – a system for marketing of goods and/or services. The franchisor sells access to the franchisee who operates the business according to the franchisor's concept. McDonald's is an example of a company using franchise.

Front-door reference – a term used in relation to references and recruitment. Front-door references are those a candidate has provided themselves. The candidate, of course, expects that these references will leave a positive impression of them.

Full ratchet – a branch of anti-dilution, where former investors hedge themselves in the best possible way. If a full ratchet is included, the value of the investors' shares does not fall when a possible down round occurs.

Functionality specification – a document which specifies what a product should at least be able to do.

Green-shoe option – used in conjunction with a stock exchange listing. A green-shoe option allows banks to sell up to 15% more shares than the original figure, which is determined by the issuer, if the demand allows it.

Guerrilla marketing – a marketing strategy which is about creating great attention without using the money it would normally cost. This is done by creating surprises as a starting point.

Help desk – a resource whose purpose is to provide customer or end-user information about a company's product(s) and service(s).

Human resources (HR) – the people who deal with a company's labour. Today, HR departments typically are responsible for controlling everything to do with employees.

Incubator – a company or organization whose purpose is to support, guide and develop start-ups to make them viable. Incubators can help with counselling, financial support, office facilities, etc.

In-house – something will be done at the office and thus not outside of the company or the organization's four walls.

Initial public offering (IPO) – listing of a company on a public stock exchange.

In kind – the opposite of 'in cash'. In kind is a payment done with, for instance, furniture, agreements, patent rights, working hours, etc.

Intellectual property rights (IP) – includes inventions and designs.

Internal rate of return (IRR) – an expression of the average annual percentage profit of the actual invested funds in a capital fund or venture capital fund.

Internal venture – some companies choose to work as serial entrepreneurs via the creation of internal ventures.

Intrapreneur – a person or group who starts a new company or business within an existing company where they are employed.

Inversion – when a company buys a larger company to move to the headquarters of the larger company, for example.

Joint marketing organization – an alliance strategy in which companies cooperate to establish a joint sales organization, which will imply cost savings and greater impact.

Joint venture – a company form in which two or several companies (parties) form an economic collaboration to start a company together (a joint venture).

Key performance indicator (KPI) – metrics which are used to define the factors that are necessary for a company or organization to succeed.

Lead – a contact on, for example, a potential investor or customer for your business. Lead can also be used in conjunction with a call centre where there is a person you can call.

Lead investor – when several VC funds invest in a company, they select a lead investor who is acting as smart money on their common behalf.

Letter of intent (heads of agreement) – a non-binding paper that outlines one or more agreements between two or more parties.

Liquidation preference – something that most VCs will insist on getting as their capital first will be rewarded at a potential exit in some cases. This preference means that VCs have priority to their cut in connection with an exit.

Liquidity event – a sale, listing or other event of a start-up company, which enables its shareholders to convert their previously illiquid shares to cash.

Live due diligence – when an investor follows a start-up over a protracted period of time in order to sense how well it performs, keeps its promises and adapts to challenges.

Lock-up – an expression used in association with receiving capital from investors. A lock-up on stocks means that you cannot sell your shares for a number of years after the investment.

Long-tail strategy – a strategy to focus on multiple niche segments of a market.

M&A – short for 'mergers and acquisitions'. It is thus a merger of several companies.

Management buy-out (MBO) – when the company's management buys the company's shares.

Market penetration – refers to the companies which want to create growth for themselves using their current products in the market in which they are already located.

Market requirement document (MRD) – a document describing customer needs for one product or service.

Market segment – a subdivision of an economic market, which has a homogeneous structure.

Marketing alliance – an agreement made across companies where they join forces, for example to undertake cross-selling or joint marketing.

Max drawdown – the accumulated burn, until you start making money again.

Merging – when one business connects with another company to become a bigger unit.

Me-too start-ups – start-ups that base their business idea on doing like everyone else.

Mezzanine – a temporary funding element which characterizes both loan and equity. It happens as the last funding before an exit opportunity or profitability.

Micro-multinational – a small or medium-sized business, which operates globally.

Minimum viable product (MVP) – a product that has enough features to be useful. An MVP is typically used in connection with the further development of a product. Test clients receive an MVP, after which they provide feedback that can be used in the further development.

Mission statement – also known as an elevator pitch, it is a brief explanation of the company's goals. This explanation should be somewhere between 20 and 60 seconds.

Money-only – refers to investments where the investor has the expertise to advise you and is doing so.

Network orchestration – simply means that instead of you taking care of the production, you let someone else do it. This means that you focus on gathering the threads.

Niche dominance – a business model in which you are operating on a very limited market, but you almost own it.

Niche strategy – a strategy in which you select a single or a few segments and target your efforts towards them.

No shop/no talk agreement – agreement made during a corporate acquisition process where the selling party agrees to keep the talks confidential and not to shop the deal elsewhere.

Non-disclosure agreement (NDA) – a legal agreement between two or more parties that must share confidential material which must not be disclosed to third parties.

Non-participating preferred – used in conjunction with liquidation preferences, means that if a business is sold at an exit value that is lower than the original valuation, other shareholders will not get any of the exit value.

Non-solicit agreement – prohibits a company from hiring any of your employees for a fixed period of time. Often used in connection with trade-sale negotiations.

Off-the-shelf – standardized articles that are not individually customized to the customer.

One-night stand – a way to test your product before you actually produce it. When using a one-night stand method you deliver the full service without investing in all the necessary infrastructure to sustain it. An example of this can be a pop-up store.

Options/warrants – share subscription rights. This means that you can buy a share at a specific price until a certain expiration date.

Original equipment manufacturer agreements (OEM agreements) – an alliance strategy where manufacturers sell another company's products under their own name and brand (private label).

Outsider entrepreneurs – entrepreneurs coming from outside the relevant business area. It is rather the rule than the exception that it is outsider entrepreneurs who enter a market and revolutionize it.

Outsourcing – when a company chooses to buy goods/services which it would otherwise have produced/delivered itself, from a subcontractor. The rationale to do this can be to achieve (i) better quality by using a specialist, (ii) a lower price or (iii) a higher return on invested capital.

Paid media – the opposite of earned media, i.e. publicity that you pay for, for example through ads on Facebook or similar.

Part closing – getting the customer to agree to buy if you fulfil certain conditions.

Peers – a model for valuating a business. The company is compared to its 'peers'. The peers model is therefore quite similar to the comparable model.

Penetration pricing – a pricing strategy in which a company in the beginning has a very low price on its product or service to enter the market.

Performance and development review – conversation which, among other things, can be used to tell employees when they are performing well and when they are not.

Pinocchio – a 'non-living product' which is used to test the idea of a potentially correct product.

Pitch deck – a brief presentation of a company to potential funding partners, typically made in PowerPoint.

Poison pill – contract clause that causes costs or loss of investor rights if specific events take place.

Post-money – an expression of how much a business is worth after receiving an investment.

Premature scaling – when you move on too rapidly and too early, so your business cannot follow the growth.

Pre-money – an expression of how much a business is worth before receiving an investment.

Pre-seed round – venture investment before a product is available.

Press kit – background information, images or similar, which can typically be downloaded by the press from the company's website.

Price batch – a pricing strategy where you get discounts on purchases of multiple products or services.

Priming – a concept within the psychological world. Priming is the phenomenon being used when you automatically find something more fun if you make a happy grimace while hearing/reading/seeing it.

Private equity – capital funds, which normally inject capital but at the same time buy existing shareholders' shares so the capital fund has the majority of shares.

Product/market fit – refers to being in a healthy market with a product that can satisfy that market.

Profit multiplier – a business model in which you reuse the same product in many different contexts – for example, a movie running in the cinema, which will later be on DVD, made into toys, etc.

Profit pool – the total profit that is in one industry/sector.

Pundits – experts who offer opinions in mass media.

Quiet period – commences before an IPO roadshow. It is a period when the company may not comment on anything which in some way can affect the demand for its shares.

Recruiter – (or recruitment consultant) is employed to recruit people to a company.

Red herring – a disclosure document. A red herring is a comprehensive and detailed documentation with descriptions of the business, which is made prior to external funding or listing such as in an IPO.

Red ocean strategies – strategies that due to lack of innovation lead to fierce competition.

Roadshow – a kind of presentation of the company where you travel around the country and present for analysts and potential investors. Such a roadshow is used in conjunction with an exit.

Sale and lease-back – when selling assets that have no intellectual property rights (IP). For example, if a company owns office properties or production properties but sells them to a pension fund, after which it creates one long-term lease.

Scaling – an expression which is most often used within the entrepreneurship industry. It is mainly used in conjunction with growth entrepreneurs who make their business multiply (grow quickly).

Search engine marketing (SEM) – a form of internet marketing where you promote your website by improving its visibility on Google SERPs (search engine result pages), for instance. This happens through paid marketing.

Search engine optimization (SEO) – a method/tool to promote your location on various search engines. This is a free form of marketing.

Second market discounting – a pricing strategy where you sell the same product under two different names and for two different prices. Thus you can target multiple segments with the same product.

Seed round – venture investment where there is a rudimentary product but no documentation of the business model working commercially as yet.

Series A round – the first major financing round for a company where the capital comes from venture capital companies.

Served available market (SAM) – a marketing term for the potential customers that can be expected to buy the product.

Share options – a financial instrument, whose value depends on a variety of factors, for example time horizon and share price.

Shareholders' agreement (SHA) – a legal agreement between the shareholders of a company, most commonly used in start-ups.

Shotgun clause – an agreement between, for example, two founders, where the first can offer to buy the other's shares at a given price, which the first founder chooses. Once such an offer has been made, however, the other has an automatic pre-emptive right to buy the first one's shares for the same price. Typically, the other has 20–40 days to either buy or sell.

Shouting employee – an outgoing person who glorifies themselves but who also often seeks a promotion beyond what their talent justifies. They are often not terribly loyal.

Skimming pricing – a pricing strategy, where you start out taking a high price for a product and then reduce the price.

Skunk works – a company lets some of its employees work with projects that they believe are fascinating, in a way where it is not aligned with the daily routines in the company.

The result is a job that is reminiscent of the work you see in a start-up.

Smart money – refers to investments where the investor has the expertise to advise you and is doing so.

Social media management software (SMMS) – programs that help you optimize your performance on social media. For example, programs that help you publish an article on multiple social networks simultaneously.

Software development kit (SDK) – contains instructions that enable third parties to create software that will work with your own software.

Solo dealer discount – a pricing strategy in which you give a vendor a discount if that supplier promises not to use other competing products.

Solutions provider – a business model where you focus on the individual customer and their individual needs.

Spinoff – when you take a part of the overall business and make it into an independent business.

Split releases – a method to test alternative versions of a product or service. For example, you can give half of your customer group access to a new update while the other half uses a previous version.

Stand-alone solution – a product which is typically quite new in an emerging market where it has a relatively basic functionality. In the later growth market, a number of variants and applications to the product will typically be added.

Storyteller – a type of person who is really good at opening a sales process.

Sweat equity – a person who works as an unpaid consultant in a start-up in return for shares in the business.

Switching costs – the costs associated with changing supplier. Switching costs are used most often in connection with penetration barriers, describing how difficult it is to penetrate a new market.

SWOT analysis – a simple procedure for assessing a company's position in a market. SWOT stands for strengths, weaknesses, opportunities and threats.

System integrator – used in connection with value-added resellers where it denotes complex solutions within, for example, IT.

System sales – used for more technical sales, where you split the technical team from the commercial team.

Tag-along rights – rights for investors. It is assumed that if a shareholder chooses to sell their shares, then some or all shareholders are entitled to sell their shares to the same buyer and at the same price.

Take-back clause – clause in a shareholders' agreement or employment agreement stating that the company or other shareholders can buy the employee's shares on their resignation.

Target market – a market which you would like to enter with your business.

Term sheet – used about procurement of capital. Basically, a term sheet is a shortened and simplified version of the shareholders' agreement.

Ticket size – indicates how much an investor usually invests in a single project.

Total addressable market (TAM) – an expression used by marketers for the market universe. TAM is the theoretical possible customer base.

Trade sale – when you are selling a business or parts of a business to another company, typically within the same industry.

Unbalanced scaling – when accelerating parts of a business before all parts are ready.

Unicorn exits – start-up companies being traded to more than $1 billion.

US GaaP – an American set of accounting principles, which a company may choose to follow. GaaP stands for 'generally accepted accounting principles'.

User stories – a sentence or two describing a customer's activities with the product. User stories are used in conjunction with agile business development.

Value proposition – a marketing term that denotes an innovation, service or feature, whose goal is to make a business or product attractive to customers.

Value-added reseller – an alliance strategy where a distributor adds value to your product.

Venture capital fund – capital invested in start-up companies. A venture capital fund makes such investments on behalf of its investors, who typically are predominantly pension funds.

Venture debt – loans designed for start-ups, since start-ups usually cannot borrow money from a bank. Typically, venture debt is combined with warrants that give the lender the right to buy shares in the company if it goes well.

Vesting – to 'vest' means that you gradually get your options over a period. The typical period is four years. If you leave the company after two years, for example, you will vest only half of your options.

Viral coefficients – a factor that is typically used regarding video clips or other social media productions which are so good that people share them with their friends, who share them with their friends, etc. If a viral coefficient is 1, it means that each person shares the video with one other person.

Whispering employee – an employee or talent who is relatively quiet and self-extinguishing, yet is proficient and loyal.

White label – also private label. This is when a distributor sells your product and at the same time is allowed to make a version of the same product under its own brand, which the distributor then earns more on.

White papers – factual analysis of market needs where you also describe how the same product fits in as a solution for the market.

Whitespace – a space where there is a problem (for example, if there is something that annoys you and/or your friends) and where there is no solution yet.

Wholesale – sales of large consignments to retailers.

Working capital optimization – you streamline your working capital and thereby avoid having to raise new capital instead.

ENDNOTES

Chapter 1

1   Hurst, E.G. and Pugsley, B.W. (2010). *Non-Pecuniary Benefits of Small Business Ownership*, University of Chicago.

2   Gage, D. (2012). The Venture Capital Secret: 3 out of 4 Start-Ups Fail, *The Wall Street Journal*, 20 September.

3   D'este, P. (2008). Gaining from Interacting with University: Multiple Methods for Nurturing Absorptive Capacity, *DRUID*.

4   Gompers, P.A., Kovner, A., Lerner, J. and Scharfstein, D.S. (2006). Skill vs. Luck in Entrepreneurship and Venture Capital: Evidence from Serial Entrepreneurs, *SSRN*.

5   Statistic Brain (2016). Startup Business Failure Rate by Industry, available at: http://www .statisticbrain.com/startup-failure-by-industry/

6   Golla, S., Holi, M., Johann, T., Klandt, H. and Kraft, L. (2008). The Development of Venture-Capital-Backed and Independent Companies: An Empirical Study Among Germany's Internet and E-Commerce Start-Ups, *New Technology-Based Firms in the New Millennium* 6.

7   Business ideas that are completely new, and therefore in the beginning have minimal competition, are called blue-ocean strategies. The opposite is red-ocean strategies, where there is competition.

8   Wikipedia (2016). Stanford Marshmallow Experiment, available at: www.en.wikipedia.org/ w/index.php?title=Stanford_marshmallow_ experiment&oldid=733813191

9   OPP (2017). MBTI Type and Entrepreneurship, available at: http://people.cpp.com/rs/788-YSM-155/images/Type%20and% 20entrepreneurship%20survey%20report% 20v3b%20FINAL%20-%20CPP.pdf

10   Freeman, M.A., Johnson, S.L., Staudenmeier, P.J. and Zisser, M.R. (2015). Are Entrepreneurs Touched with Fire?, available at: www.michaelafreemanmd.com/ Research.html

11   Mart, G. and Street, R. (2008). *Who: The A Method for Hiring*, Ballantine Books.

12   Duckworth, A. (2016). *Grit: The Power of Passion and Perseverance*, Scribner.

13   Shane, S. and Stuart, T. (2002). Organizational Endowments and the Performance of University Start-ups, *Management Science* 48, no. 1, pp. 154–170.

14   Howe, J. (2006). The Rise of Crowdsourcing, available at: http://www.wired.com/2006/06/ crowds

15   Hard Work Pays, dailymail.co.uk, 13 April 2004.

16   Moskowitz, T.J. and Vissing-Jorgensen, A. (2002). The Returns to Entrepreneurial Investment: A Private Equity Premium Puzzle?, *American Economic Review* 92, no. 4, pp. 745–778.

17   Hamilton, B.H. (2000). Does Entrepreneurship Pay? An Empirical Analysis of the Returns to Self-Employment, *Journal of Political Economy* 108, no. 3, pp. 604–631.

18   Christensen, C.M. and Bower, J.L. (1996). Customer Power, Strategic Investment, and the Failure of Leading Firms, *Strategic Management Journal* 17, no. 3, pp. 197–218.

19   Elfebein, D.W., Hamilton, B.H. and Zenger, T.R. (2009). *Entrepreneurial Spawning of Scientists and Engineers: Stars, Slugs and Small Firms*, Washington University in Saint Louis.

20   Gimeno, J., Folta, T.B., Cooper, A.C. and Woo, C.Y. (1997). Survival of the Fittest? Entrepreneurial Human Capital and the Persistence of Underperforming Firms, *Administrative Science Quarterly* 42, no. 4, pp. 750–783.

21   The Startup Compass Inc. (2015). Global Startup Ecosystem Ranking, available at: https://startup-ecosystem.compass.co/ser2015/

22   Azoulay, P., Jones, B.F., Kim, J.D. and Miranda, J. (2018). Age and High-Growth Entrepreneurship, MIT and NBER, 23 March.

23   Wasserman, N. (2013). *The Founder's Dilemmas: Anticipating and Avoiding the Pitfalls That Can Sink a Startup*, Princeton University Press.

24   Elfebein, D.W., Hamilton, B.H. and Zenger, T.R. (2009). *Entrepreneurial Spawning of Scientists and Engineers: Stars, Slugs and Small Firms*, Washington University in Saint Louis.

25   Chen, J., Reilly, R. and Lynn, G. (2005). The Impact of Speed-to-Market on New Product Success: The Moderating Effects of Uncertainty, *IEEE Transactions on Engineering Management* 52, no. 2, pp. 199–213.

Chapter 2

1   www.theringer.com/2017/3/1/16040820/5-hour-energy-manoj-bhargava-philanthropy-92e639077f6f

2   McCormack, M.H. (1986). *What They Don't Teach You at Harvard Business School*, Bantam Books.

3   Hollingworth, C. (2013). Put a pencil in your mouth – the power of priming, available at http://www.marketingsociety.com/the-library/put-pencilyour-mouth-power-priming

4   Hampton, K., Goulet, L.S., Marlow, C., et al. (2012). Why most Facebook users get more than they give, PewResearchCenter, available at: www.pewinternet.org/2012/02/03/why-most-facebook-users-get-more-than-they-give/

Chapter 3

1   Gallo, C. (2015). *Talk Like TED: The 9 Public-Speaking Secrets of the World's Top Minds*, St Martin's Press.

2   https://coschedule.com/blog/how-often-to-post-on-social-media/

Chapter 4

1   Trelles-Tvede, S. (2016). What I Traded 1350 Vodka Red Bulls in for, TEDxKEA, available at: www.youtube.com/watch?v=8QndiGDebeE

Chapter 5

1   Stevens, G.A. and Burley, J. (1997). 3000 Raw Ideas Equals 1 Commercial Success!, *Research Technology Management* 40, no. 3.

2   Jobs, S. (1996). Wired, February, available at: www.wired.com/1996/02/jobs-2/

3   Christensen, C. (1997). *The Innovator's Dilemma: When New Technologies Cause Great Firms to Fail*, Harvard Business Review Press.

Chapter 7

1   Florida, R. and King, K.M. (2016). *Rise of the Global Startup City*, Martin Prosperity Institute.

2   Ibid.

3   Gompers, P. and Lerner, J. (2006). *The Venture Capital Cycle*, MIT Press.

4   Florida, R. (2002). *The Rise of the Creative Class. And How It's Transforming Work, Leisure and Everyday Life*, Basic Books.

5   Tax Foundation (2012). Capital Gains Rate By Country, 2011 (OECD), available at: www.taxfoundation.org/article/capital-gains-rate-country-2011-oecd

6   The Startup Compass Inc. (2015). Global Startup Ecosystem Ranking, available at: https://startup-ecosystem.compass.co/ser2015/

7   Ibid.

8   Ibid.

9   Creandum (2015). Nordic Tech Is on Fire – Almost 10% of Global BUSD Exits over Past 10 Years, available at: https://medium.com/creandum-family/nordic-tech-is-on-fire-almost-10-ofglobal-busd-exits-over-past-10-years-e52baf4de61#.davu5br1m

10   Cochrane, J.H. (2005). The Risk and Return of Venture Capital, NBER Working Paper No. 8066.

11   Cambridge Associates (2017). U.S. Venture Capital Index and Selected Benchmark Statistics.

12   Harris, R.S., et al. (2014). Private Equity Performance: What Do We Know?, *Journal of Finance* 69, issue 5, 1851–1882.

13   Acevedo, M.F. (2016). Building Momentum in Venture Capital across Europe, available at: www.kfw.de/PDF/Download-Center/Konzernthemen/Research/PDF-Dokumente-Studien-und-Materialien/Building-Momentum-in-Venture-Capital-across-Europe.pdf

14   Ibid.

15   Invest Europe (2016). 2015 European Private Equity Activity.

16   Ibid.

17   Simply stated, IRR stands for internal rate of return and is the average profit to the investors of the money invested, bearing in mind that the money invested varies a lot over the investment period. A more complete definition is: The IRR is the interim net return earned by investors (limited partners) in the fund from inception to a stated date. It is calculated as an annualized effective compounded rate of return using cash flows given to and drawn from investors, together with the quarter-end valuation of the fund's unliquidated holdings or residual value as a terminal cash flow to investors. Pooled IRR is an IRR obtained by aggregating all funds in a sample into a pool as if they were a single fund.

18   All funds' IRR exceed any sub-category because it is based on overall top quartile rather than sub-sector top quartile.

19   Thomson Reuters and EVCA (2014). 2013 Pan-European Private Equity Performance Benchmarks Study.

20   Hege, U., Palomino, F., et al. (2008). Venture Capital Performance: The Disparity Between Europe and the United States, available at: https://mpra.ub.uni-muenchen.de/39551/1/MPRA_paper_39551.pdf

21   Creandum (2015). Creandum Nordic Exit Analysis 2015.

Chapter 8

1   Named after Max Marmer, who started the Startup Genome project and who also founded Compass.

2   Morris, G. (2012). Average Venture Capital Deal Sizes Globally in 2012 – December 2012, available at: http://www.preqin.com/blog/0/6044/vc-deals-2012.9,12

3   fundable.com. Startup Funding Infographic, available at: http://www.fundable.com/learn/resources infographics/startup-funding -infographic

4   Swisher, K. (2010). Series Seed Documents – With an Assist From Andreessen Horowitz – To Help Entrepreneurs with Legal Hairballs, available at: allthingsd.com

5   Wasserman, N. (2013). *The Founder's Dilemmas: Anticipating and Avoiding the Pitfalls That Can Sink a Startup*, Princeton University Press.

6   Ibid.

7   Wiltbank, R. and Boeker, W. (2007). Returns to Angel Investors in Groups, available at: https://papers.ssrn.com/sol3/papers.cfm?abstract_id=1028592

8   https://angelresourceinstitute.org/research/report.php?report=101&name=2016%2520Angel%2520Returns%2520Study

9   Wasserman, N. (2013). *The Founder's Dilemmas: Anticipating and Avoiding the Pitfalls That Can Sink a Startup*, Princeton University Press.

10   The Startup Compass Inc. (2015). Global Startup Ecosystem Ranking, available at: https://startup-ecosystem.compass.co/ser2015/

11   Wasserman, N. (2013). *The Founder's Dilemmas: Anticipating and Avoiding the Pitfalls That Can Sink a Startup*, Princeton University Press.

12   https://github.com/ethereum/wiki/blob/master/drafts/%5Benglish%5D-old-ethereum-whitepaper.md

13   https://coinjournal.net/vitalik-buterin-90-icos-will-fail/

14   Mikey, T. (2016) One-third of U.S. Startups That Raised a Series A in 2015 Went Through an Accelerator, *PitchBook*, 5 February.

15   Cowan, D. (2014). In Ramsinghani, M., *The Business of Venture Capital*, John Wiley & Sons.

16   The Startup Compass Inc. (2015). Global Startup Ecosystem Ranking, available at: https://startup-ecosystem.compass.co/ser2015/

17   Wasserman, N. (2013). *The Founder's Dilemmas: Anticipating and Avoiding the Pitfalls That Can Sink a Startup*, Princeton University Press.

18   Ramada, A.l., Peterson, D. and Lochhead, C., et al. (2016). *Play Bigger*, HarperCollins.

19   The Startup Compass Inc. (2015). Global Startup Ecosystem Ranking, available at: https://startup-ecosystem.compass.co/ser2015/

20   Wasserman, N. (2013). *The Founder's Dilemmas: Anticipating and Avoiding the Pitfalls That Can Sink a Startup*, Princeton University Press.

21   Thomson Reuters and EVCA (2014). 2013 Pan-European Private Equity Performance Benchmarks Study.

Chapter 9

1   DocSend. What We Learned from 200 Startups Who Raised $360M, available at: http://www.docsend.com/view/p8jxsqr

2   Miller, C.C. (2013). Google Ventures Stresses Science of Deal, Not Art of the Deal, *New York Times*, 23 June.

3   The Danish Growth Fund (2016). What Can We Learn from 15 Years of Venture Investments?, available at: www.vf.dk/

4   DocSend. What We Learned from 200 Startups Who Raised $360M, available at: http://www.docsend.com/view/p8jxsqr

5   World Economic Forum (2017). A computer was asked to predict which start-ups would be successful. The results were astonishing, available at: www.weforum.org/agenda/2017/07/computer-ai-machine-learning-predict-the-success-of-startups/

6   Huet, E. (2017). These Are the 50 Most Promising Startups You've Never Heard Of, Bloomberg, March 9, available at: www.bloomberg.com/graphics/2017-fifty-best-startups/

7   Davis, A. (2017). Venture-Capital Firms Use Big Data to Seek Out the Next Big Thing, *The Wall Street Journal*, 24 April.

8   Balachandra, L. and Corbett, A. (working paper). Calm, Cool and Competent: The Impact of an Entrepreneur's Displayed Emotions on Investor Decisions; Balachandra, L. (working paper). Pitching Trust: Investors Value Character Over Competency; Balachandra, L.

(forthcoming). Don't Pitch Like a Girl! How Gender Stereotypes Influence Investor Decisions, *Entrepreneurship Theory and Practice.*

9   Pentland, S. and Olguín, D. (2010). Defend Your Research: We Can Measure the Power of Charisma, available at: https://hbr.org/2010/01/defend-your-research-we-can-measure-the-power-of-charisma

10   Payne, B. (2007). Valuation of Pre-revenue Companies: The Venture Capital Method, available at: entrepreneurship.org, 1 July. See also Fund, S. (2015). *The Angel Investor Market in 2015: A Buyer's Market*, Center for Venture Research.

11   Ramsinghani, M. (2014). *The Business of Venture Capital*, John Wiley & Sons.

12   Kawasaki, G. (2006). The Top Ten Lies of Entrepreneurs, available at: www.guykawasaki .com/the_top_ten_lie_1-3/

13   Blank, S. (2011). Tune In, Turn On, Drop Out – The Startup Genome Project, available at: http://www.steveblank.com/2011/05/29/tune-in-turn-ondrop-out-the-startup-genome-project/

Chapter 10

1   Miller, C.C. (2013). Google Ventures Stresses Science of Deal, Not Art of the Deal, *New York Times*, 23 June.

2   Gorman, M. and Sahlman, W.A. (1989). What Do Venture Capitalists Do?, *Journal of Business Venturing* 4, no. 4, pp. 231–248.

3   Wasserman, N. (2013). *The Founder's Dilemmas: Anticipating and Avoiding the Pitfalls That Can Sink a Startup*, Princeton University Press.

4   Marmer, M., Herrmann, B.L., Dogrultan, E., et al. (2012). *Startup Genome Report – A New Framework for Understanding Why Startups Succeed*, Startup Genome.

5   Amit, R., MacCrimmon, K.R., Zietsma, C., et al. (2000). Does Money Matter?: Wealth Attainment as the Motive for Initiating Growth-Oriented Technology Ventures, *Journal of Business Venturing* 16, issue 2, pp. 119–143.

6   Wadhwa, V., Aggarwal, R., Holly, K., et al. (2009). *The Anatomy of an Entrepreneur: Family Background and Motivation*, Ewing Marion Kauffman Foundation.

7   Davidsson, P. and Honig, B. (2003). The Role of Social and Human Capital Among Nascent Entrepreneurs, *Journal of Business Venturing* 18, issue 3, pp. 301–331.

8   The Startup Compass Inc. (2015). Global Startup Ecosystem Ranking, available at: https://startup-ecosystem.compass.co/ser2015/

9   Wasserman, N. (2013). *The Founder's Dilemmas: Anticipating and Avoiding the Pitfalls That Can Sink a Startup*, Princeton University Press.

10   Ibid.

11   Marmer, M., Herrmann, B.L., Dogrultan, E., et al. (2012). *Startup Genome Report – A New Framework for Understanding Why Startups Succeed*, Startup Genome.

12   Gompers, P.A., et al. (2006). Skill vs. Luck in Entrepreneurship and Venture Capital: Evidence from Serial Entrepreneurs, NBER Working Paper No. 12592.

13   Wasserman, N. (2013). *The Founder's Dilemmas: Anticipating and Avoiding the Pitfalls That Can Sink a Startup*, Princeton University Press.

14   Ibid.

15   Ibid.

16   Ibid.

17   Marmer, M., Herrmann, B.L., Dogrultan, E. and Berman, R. (2012). *Startup Genome Report – A New Framework for Understanding Why Startups Succeed*, Startup Genome.

Chapter 11

1   www.inc.com/jeff-bussgang/scaling-a-business-is-hard.html

2   Wasserman, N. (2013). *The Founder's Dilemmas: Anticipating and Avoiding the Pitfalls That Can Sink a Startup*, Princeton University Press.

3   The Startup Compass Inc. (2015). Global Startup Ecosystem Ranking, available at: https://startup-ecosystem.compass.co/ser2015/

4   OECD. (2006). Tax Policy Study No. 11: The Taxation of Employee Stock Options.

5   Kaplan, S. et al. (2009). Should Investors Bet on the Jockey or the Horse? Evidence from the Evolution of Firms from Early Business Plans to Public Companies, *The Journal of Finance* LXIV, no. 1 February.

6   Wasserman, N. (2013). *The Founder's Dilemmas: Anticipating and Avoiding the Pitfalls That Can Sink a Startup*, Princeton University Press.

7   Ibid.

8   https://twitter.com/richardbranson/status/449220072176107520?lang=en

9   Oncken, W.Jr. and Wass, D.L. (1999). Management Time – Who's Got the Monkey?, *Harvard Business Review*, November.

10 Horowitz, B. (2014). *The Hard Thing About Hard Things*, HarperCollins.

Chapter 12

1   Ellis, S. (2009). The Startup Pyramid, available at: www.startup-marketing.com/the-startup-pyramid

2   Marmer, M., Herrmann, B.L., Dogrultan, E. and Berman, R. (2012). *Startup Genome Report – A New Framework for Understanding Why Startups Succeed*, Startup Genome.

3   Ibid.

4   Poppendieck, M. and Poppendieck, T. (2003). *Lean Software Development – An Agile Toolkit*, Addison-Wesley Professional.

5   Cohen, D. (2010). Small Asks First, available at: http://www.davidgcohen.com/2010/10/28/smallasks-first/

6   National Geographic (2013). The Decoy Effect, available at: www.youtube.com/watch?v=33aaQdtD20k

7   Iyengar, S.S. and Lepper, M. (2000). When Choice Is Demotivating – Can One Desire Too Much of a Good Thing?, *Journal of Personality and Social Psychology* 79, no. 6, pp. 995–1006.

8   Bygrave, W.D., et al. (2007) Pre-Startup Formal Business Plans and Post-Startup Performance: A Study of 116 New Ventures, *Venture Capital Journal* 9, no. 4, pp. 1–20, October.

9   Startup Genome (2011). Startup Genome Report 1, available at: https://startupgenome.com/

10 Blank, S. and Dorf, B. (2012). *The Startup Owner's Manual*, K&S Ranch Publishing.

Chapter 13

1   www.marketingmag.com.au/news-c/ibms-ceo-on-data-the-death-of-segmentation-and-the-18-month-deadline

2   Ramadan, A., et al. (2016). *Play Bigger*, HarperCollins.

3   www.apple.com/newsroom/2010/01/27Apple-Launches-iPad

Chapter 14

1   Marmer, M., Herrmann, B.L., Dogrultan, E. and Berman, R. (2012). *Startup Genome Report – A New Framework for Understanding Why Startups Succeed*, Startup Genome.

2   Moore, G.E. (2014). *Crossing the Chasm*, HarperCollins.

Chapter 15

1   Gerken, L.C. (2014). *The Little Book of Venture Capital Investing*, John Wiley & Sons.

Chapter 17

1   Specifically, we recommend that you start with one of the following three books: Swensen, D.F. (2005). *Unconventional Success: A Fundamental Approach to Personal Investment*, Free Press; Siegel, J.J. (2002). *Stocks for the Long Run: The Definitive Guide to Financial Market Returns and Long-Term Investment Strategies*, McGraw-Hill; Kaplan, P.D. (2011). *Frontiers of Modern Asset Allocation*, John Wiley & Sons.

ABOUT THE AUTHORS

Lars Tvede, serial entrepreneur and venture capitalist, was born in Denmark but lives in Zug, Switzerland. As a youngster, he completed two simultaneous studies at the Royal Veterinary and Agricultural University and Copenhagen Business School while co-founding two companies. He later spent a great deal of his career in the financial sector as well as being a private investor and currency trader. In parallel, he has founded several high-tech companies that have won numerous international awards for entrepreneurship and technology, including the Wall Street Journal Europe Innovation Award, the Red Herring Global 100 Award, the Bulli Award and the IMD Swiss Start-up Award.

He has written 15 acclaimed books about stock trading, general economics, crisis theory, market analysis, creativity, information technology and the future, which to date have been published in more than 50 editions and in 11 different languages. In *Guru Guide to Marketing*, he is listed as one of the world's leading thinkers in marketing strategy.

In 2016, Lars co-founded Nordic Eye, a venture capital company which in its first full year generated 203% IRR and returned more than the original commitments to its investors in the form of a distribution (dividend).

Mads Faurholt-Jorgensen is a serial entrepreneur and best-selling author. He has started over 20 companies across technology, financial services, marketing, HR, and education, with thousands of employees, and investors such as Goldman Sachs, Alibaba, Peter Thiel and the World Bank.

Prior to starting his current company, Nova Founders Capital, Mads was Global Partner and Managing Director of the German internet giant, Rocket Internet; Head of Asia at Groupon (the world's fastest growing company,), and Management Consultant at McKinsey & Company.

Mads received his bachelor from Copenhagen Business School and his MBA from the Massachusetts Institute of Technology.

For further *Entrepreneur* content, please visit www.tvede-faurholt.com.

INDEX